Building a Language-Focused
Curriculum for the Preschool Classroom

Volume I:

A Foundation for Lifelong Communication

Building a Language-Focused Curriculum for the Preschool Classroom

Volume I:
A Foundation for Lifelong Communication

edited by

Mabel L. Rice, Ph.D.
University Distinguished Professor
Department of Speech-Language-Hearing
University of Kansas, Lawrence

and

Kim A. Wilcox, Ph.D.
Chair
Department of Speech-Language-Hearing
University of Kansas, Lawrence

·P·A·U·L·H·
BROOKES
PUBLISHING C♀

Baltimore · London · Toronto · Sydney

Paul H. Brookes Publishing Co.
Post Office Box 10624
Baltimore, Maryland 21285-0624

Typeset by Brushwood Graphics, Inc., Baltimore, Maryland.
Manufactured in the United States of America by
BookCrafters, Chelsea, Michigan.

Building a Language-Focused Curriculum for the Preschool Classroom is a two-volume set:
    Volume I: *A Foundation for Lifelong Learning*
    Volume II: *A Planning Guide*
To order Volume II, contact Paul H. Brookes Publishing Co., Post Office Box 10624, Baltimore, Maryland 21285-0624 (1-800-638-3775).

This book is printed on recycled paper.

Library of Congress Cataloging-in-Publication Data

Building a language-focused curriculum for the preschool classroom / edited by Mabel L. Rice and Kim A. Wilcox.
    p.   cm.
    Includes bibliographical references and index.
    Contents: v. I. A foundation for lifelong communication.
    ISBN 1-55766-177-4 (v. 1)
    1. Language arts (Preschool). 2. Language experience approach in education. 3. Education, Preschool—Curricula. I. Rice, Mabel. L. II. Wilcox, Kim A.
LB1140.5.L3B85   1995
372.6—dc20   94-49085
                                                              CIP

British Library Cataloguing-in-Publication data are available from the British Library.

Contents

About the Editors

Mabel L. Rice, Ph.D., University Distinguished Professor, Department of Speech-Language-Hearing, University of Kansas, 1082 Robert Dole Human Development Center, Lawrence, Kansas 66045

Dr. Rice received her doctoral degree from the University of Kansas, where she is University Distinguished Professor of Speech-Language-Hearing and Director of the Child Language Doctoral Program and the Merrill Advanced Studies Center. She has held Visiting Scientist appointments at the Center for Cognitive Science at the Massachusetts Institute of Technology (MIT) and the Harvard Graduate School of Education. She has extensive research and clinical experience with children with specific language impairment (SLI). Early in her career she worked as a speech-language pathologist in public schools. In collaboration with Kim A. Wilcox, she established the demonstration Language Acquisition Preschool (LAP) at the University of Kansas. Her current research addresses several aspects of the condition of SLI: social and academic consequences, morphology, lexical learning, and preschool language intervention. Her publications include the edited volumes *The Teachability of Language* and *Toward a Genetics of Language*, as well as numerous journal articles and invited chapters.

Kim A. Wilcox, Ph.D., Chair, Department of Speech-Language-Hearing, University of Kansas, 3031 Robert Dole Human Development Center, Lawrence, Kansas 66045

Dr. Wilcox is Professor and Chair of the Department of Speech-Language-Hearing at the University of Kansas and Director of the department's Native American Training Program. He received his bachelor of arts degree from Michigan State University and both his master's and his doctoral degrees from Purdue University. Much of Dr. Wilcox's research has focused on the acoustic form of the speech of people with communication disorders. Presently, he is examining the speech of children with delayed phonological skills. Dr. Wilcox is also an accomplished instructor, having received several awards for teaching excellence.

Contributors

Betty H. Bunce, Ph.D.
Director
Language Acquisition Preschool
Adjunct Assistant Professor
Department of Speech-Language-Hearing
3031 Robert Dole Human Development
  Center
University of Kansas
Lawrence, Kansas 66045

Janet Ellsworth, M.S., CCC-SLP
Director of Special Education
Jenks Public Schools
Administration Building
205 East B Street
Jenks, Oklahoma 74037

Julia Eyer, Ph.D., CCC-SLP
Research Associate
Department of Audiology and Speech
  Sciences
Heavilon Hall
Purdue University
West Lafayette, Indiana 47907

Pamela A. Hadley, Ph.D., CCC-SLP
Assistant Professor
Department of Speech and Hearing Science
Arizona State University
Box 870102
Tempe, Arizona 85287

Sherrill R. Morris, M.A., CCC-SLP
Doctoral Candidate
Department of Speech-Language-Hearing
3031 Robert Dole Human Development
  Center
University of Kansas
Lawrence, Kansas 66045

Susie Ray, M.A., CCC-SLP
Speech-Language Pathologist
Early Education Center
303 East Bigger Street
Post Office Box 399
Hutchinson, Kansas 67504

C. Melanie Schuele, M.A., CCC-SLP
Visiting Instructor
Department of Communication Sciences
Case Western Reserve University
11206 Euclid Avenue
Cleveland, Ohio 44106

Julie F. Sergeant, M.S.Ed.
Project Coordinator
School-Linked Community Services Grant
USD #497
Diagnostic Center
936 New York
Lawrence, Kansas 66044

Terri Torres, M.A., CCC-SLP
Speech-Language Pathologist
Early Education Center
303 East Bigger Street
Post Office Box 399
Hutchinson, Kansas 67504

Ruth V. Watkins, Ph.D., CCC-SLP
Assistant Professor
University of Illinois
Department of Speech and Hearing Sciences
901 South Sixth Street
Champaign, Illinois 61820

Preface

The establishment and evaluation of a new language intervention model for preschool children is, in our experience, a rather effortful enterprise. At the beginning it has some of the feel of the old Mickey Rooney and Judy Garland movies, in which someone says, "Let's have a play!" This is followed by an inevitable sequence of unforeseen challenges, pratfalls, changes of cast, and other borderline disasters until, ultimately, all is resolved, the show goes on, and it seems to be a solid performance with a long run.

In the case of the Language Acquisition Preschool (LAP), whose story is the topic of this volume, this comparison has some striking truth to it. We won't burden the reader with the challenges and pratfalls, and the ways we resolved them, but any seasoned practitioner would know to expect them.

Where this comparison between the movies and our story does not quite apply is with regard to the children and families who were the participants in this performance. Whatever agonies of implementation and evaluation were encountered, they were mostly at the level of the professionals working their way through a new approach to language intervention. The saving grace throughout the process was the participation of the children and their families. The children have shown us much about the best way to proceed, and when we have listened and understood what we saw, we have moved forward. Frequently, the parents have served as guides in this endeavor. Perhaps the most powerful feature of a naturalistic approach to language intervention is that it is possible for children to guide the process, and thereby avoid the worst applications of adult logic and intuition.

In this volume, the topics are introduced by scenes or vignettes drawn from activities involving the children or their parents as the primary participants. It is our hope that these scenes can highlight some of the main themes of this exposition. Unfortunately, however, not all of the reality of interactions with children and their parents can be translated into print. To the extent that this volume captures the children's guidance, readers will find meaningful direction in their own interactions with families and children.

This volume describes the operating principles and basic implementation strategies associated with a language-focused preschool curriculum. Although the book is designed as a resource for those working with young children, a detailed description of specific classroom activities is beyond its scope. Speech-language pathologists, early childhood educators, and others looking for specific implementation suggestions are directed to the second volume in this set, *Building a Language-Focused Curriculum for the Preschool Classroom, Volume II: A Planning Guide*, written by Betty Bunce, Director of the Language Acquisition Preschool at the University of Kansas. In that work, Dr. Bunce explains how one utilizes the principles outlined in developing classroom activities that are both language focused and developmentally appropriate. Volume II also provides more than 100 classroom-tested activity ideas.

The cast for implementation of the language-focused curriculum (LFC) has included many people. The key players are noted in the authorship of the chapters of this volume. In a very real sense, the program, like a play, has been a team event. In addition to the authors listed here, we wish to acknowledge the participation of others. Early on, we were fortunate to have sage advice and counsel provided by Lily Wong Fillmore of the University of California at Berkeley and Judith Johnston of the University of British Columbia. We wish to thank them especially for their patient insistence that a theme-based curriculum was the preferred approach. Events have, of course, validated their wisdom. Also important were the two first occupants of the family services coordinator position, Georgia Liebhaber and Vicki Turbiville.

Initial funding for the Language Acquisition Preschool was provided by a grant funded by the U.S. Department of Education, Handicapped Children's Early Education Program, Grant #G008630279, with Mabel L. Rice and Kim A. Wilcox as Principal Investigators. Subsequent funding for much of the research reported here was provided by Grant #HO24U80001 from the U.S. Department of Education, with Mabel L. Rice and Marion O'Brien as Principal Investigators. Further support was available from research trainees funded by U.S. Department of Education Grant #HO29D90046, with Mabel L. Rice as Principal Investigator.

We are very proud of the fact that this demonstration program has come to be a local service option that is simultaneously integrated into the clinical preparation activities of the University of Kansas. Implementation of LAP preceded the federal legislation that targeted services for children ages 3–5 years (i.e., PL 99-457, the Education of the Handicapped Act Amendments of 1986, and PL 102-119, the Individuals with Disabilities Education Act Amendments of 1991). Thus, the program anticipated service delivery systems that were to come. There were few precedents for working out the details of full incorporation into the local service delivery system. Such a collaborative arrangement of university-based training and research with local service delivery requires vision and foresight, and much good sense and good will, on the part of all participants. We are indebted to Ron Schmidt, Special Services Coordinator, and Don Herbel, Director of Special Education, at USD 497, our local school system, for their support of the preschool. We are also grateful to Jane Wegner, Director of the Schiefelbusch Speech-Language-Hearing Clinic at the University of Kansas, for the many ways in which she facilitates the training mission of the preschool.

Many student speech-language pathologists and students of early childhood education have received practicum experiences in the LAP classroom. In addition, practitioners from near and far have come to receive inservice in the classroom. Virtually every one of these people has brought questions and comments that have sharpened our sense of understanding of the LFC and the concentrated normative model of language facilitation. In a similar way, the audiences at our symposia and workshops sponsored by professional organizations have contributed to the materials presented in this volume. We have not always had the answers, but we have tried to listen to and understand the questions.

Most of all, we are indebted to the parents who have entrusted their children to our care and to the children who have participated in the LFC. Virtually every day brings new interactions and a myriad of little occasions in which there is reason to rejoice in a child's new word, newfound willingness to initiate a conversation with another child, or increased use of some pesky grammatical marker. It has been a privilege and a pleasure to be a part of this endeavor.

REFERENCES

Bunce, B. (1995). *Building a language-focused curriculum for the preschool classroom. Vol. II: A planning guide.* Baltimore: Paul H. Brookes Publishing Co.

Education of the Handicapped Act Amendments of 1986, PL 99-457. (October 8, 1986). Title 20, U.S.C. 1400 et seq: *U.S. Statutes at Large, 100,* 1145–1177.

Individuals with Disabilities Education Act Amendments of 1991, PL 102-119. (October 7, 1991). Title 20, U.S.C. 1400 et seq: *U.S. Statutes at Large, 105,* 587–608.

Building a Language-Focused
Curriculum for the Preschool Classroom

Volume I:

A Foundation for
Lifelong Communication

~1~

Creating a Language-Focused Curriculum for Preschool Children

Mabel L. Rice

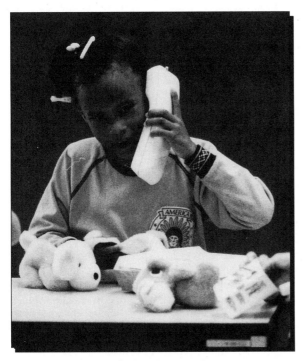

The furniture in the preschool classroom has been moved aside to make way for the rows of chairs that are now filled with the families of the children. This is the end-of-the-semester performance, a special event when the children perform. Afterward, there will be a potluck luncheon, with food prepared at home and brought to share with classmates and teachers. The food is appealing, but the real attraction is the children. When the audience arrived, they slipped into chairs as close to the front as possible so they could see their child, and their children could easily see them and the pride and encouragement that beams from their faces during the performance. Many brothers and sisters are present as well and they, too, want to be sure to have a good view.

The restless and self-conscious rustle of waiting stops as the row of little children files into the front of the room, sandwiched between a teacher in front and a teacher at the rear, who gently guide the children to their designated places in front of the row of chairs along the stage. A little boy veers a bit out of line as he greets his little brother who toddled from the front of the audience to be near him. The parents' cameras and videocameras click and whir to capture their child's entrance. Some children walk with confidence and poise, others adopt a shy posture, and a few just openly stare back at the audience. At 3–5 years old, these youngsters have yet to learn about public posturing. They are charmingly themselves, without artifice or guile. They are also, for the most part, all dressed up. Although the staff and parents are dressed casually, obvious care was given to how the children were dressed. Some of the children are wearing funny hats or odd-looking capes, which, as the audience learns later, are really pretend animal horns and the costumes of Good Guys or Bad Guys, for the skits to follow. The ethnic diversity evident in the group is worthy of a United Nations classroom, with children from China, Korea, Yugoslavia, Colombia, and India mingled with white and African American children. What seems most striking is their common demeanor, the ways in which they are all children, and the ways in which all of their families exhibit pride in their very existence.

The program begins with an introduction by the teacher. Next, the children warm up with a song, "The Eensy-Weensy Spider Went Up the Water Spout," and they all move their arms and hands to pantomime the words. Some children sing in big voices, some in small voices, some just mouth the words, and some just stand and watch. All options seem to be equally suitable, depending on the child. Then the program moves to the hard part. The children enact one of their favorite stories, *Are You My Mother?* Each child has a part in the play. Each child gets to say something, although for some of the children the spoken part is minimal, consisting of a single word, such as "No," or making an animal noise, such as "Mooo." The important thing is that for that brief moment, the center of the stage and the center of the audience's attention is on that child. Parents beam through the moment, even if the child's voice is too small to be heard clearly. The execution is not as important as the occasion. The program is wrapped up with another song, and then the children's favorite thing, the LAP cheer, "Give me an L!, L! Give me an A!, A! Give me a P!, P! What does that spell? LAP! What? Say it a little louder. LAP! Yeah!" The children yell out the LAP cheer, and then move to join their families who give hugs and compliments for their performance.

The staff in the back of the room never tire of these performances, although they are a regular feature of the Language Acquisition Preschool (LAP). In many ways, they capture much of the motivation for LAP. The occasion highlights the ways in which children have common interests and needs, although the children actually vary in a fundamental way. Although it is not discernible to most of the audience, some of the children have impairments in language aptitude, so that they are quite delayed in their mastery of the communication skills that serve as the social glue for interactions with peers, adults, and family members. The language limitations of the international children and their families are obvious in that they are learning English as a second language. Some of the international children are relatively comfortable with English after some time in LAP, whereas others are obvious beginners. The language limitations are less obvious for the local children whose language learning is effortful. Of all the children, it is the children who are having difficulty learning English as their first language who are quite likely to end their careers as public speakers when they leave LAP to begin kindergarten. In the future, even in elementary school, the opportunities will go to children with proven verbal ability. In a society that places a premium on verbal competency and high achievement as criteria for public performance, children who are unintelligible, or who are awkward in their sentence formulations and word choices, are seldom chosen to perform. In fact, children's verbal capabilities upon school entry affect many aspects of their subsequent academic experiences.

The opening vignette begins our story of the Language Acquisition Preschool with an end-of-the-semester performance, a performance in which all of the children participate, as do the families and the staff. What is striking in this scene is that it is a very "normal" activity for a preschool classroom; public performances, especially those intended for appreciative parents, are not out of the ordinary for young children. What is somewhat less usual about LAP's performance is the mixture of students and the fact that all children participate. Even in preschool settings there is a tendency to select the children with the best verbal skills for the speaking parts. What is quite unusual about LAP is the rationale that underlies this scene, the previous experiences that set the stage for the event, and the ways in which the children, parents, and staff come to interact together in ways that enhance children's speech and language abilities.

This chapter presents the reasons that the Language Acquisition Preschool was established and describes the participants—the staff who have developed and carried out the language-focused curriculum (LFC) of the preschool classroom and the children who have experienced it. The reason for LAP's existence begins with recognition of the importance of preschool experiences in preparing young children for school entry, and the ways in which language acquisition is an important precursor for academic preparation. That topic is addressed below. A brief description of how the Language Acquisition Preschool came to be established and its primary objectives are then outlined. This chapter also contains descriptions of the children who have been enrolled in the preschool and the professional staff who have carried out the preschool's objectives. Finally, the chapter concludes with a preview of the subsequent chapters.

EARLY INTERVENTION: PREPARATION FOR SCHOOL

For All Children

Children's readiness for school is a matter of national concern. In 1991, President George Bush focused attention on preschoolers when he announced his six goals for U.S. schools. The first goal was that by the year 2000, all children will come to school "ready to learn." This goal was immediately endorsed by politicians, educators, and other citizens. Its worthiness was appreciated and carried forward by the Clinton administration, which entered office in 1994. PL 103-227, the Goals 2000 Education America Act of 1994, has as its first goal that children will be ready to learn upon school entry. It is widely recognized that in order for children to succeed in school, they must have the appropriate language, social, and cognitive skills to serve as a foundation for the opportunities and challenges of the school setting. Across the United States, states and communities are developing blueprints for action, mobilizing efforts to prepare children for school entry.

In what ways are children currently not ready to go to school? A timely report answers that question. In the 1980s, the Carnegie Foundation for the Advancement of Teaching launched a study in which, among other things, it conducted a survey of more than 7,000 kindergarten teachers. When teachers were asked what problem *most* restricted school readiness, the majority of teachers responded, "deficiency in language." This problem was named more frequently than emotional maturity, general knowledge, and social confidence (Boyer, 1991).

Language as a Key to Learning

The teachers' concerns reflect the fact that language is a key to learning. This is so for several reasons, which are summarized in Table 1. One of these reasons is that a child who does not understand what the teacher says is unable to follow instructions. This child will be vulnerable when the kindergarten teacher says, for example, "All of you who put your things away neatly and quickly can line up by the door." He or she may not understand the embedded clause, "who put your things away neatly and quickly." Instead of putting away his or her things, the youngster may immediately go to the door. In this case, the teacher may perceive the child as misbehaving instead of misunderstanding.

A second reason is that much of classroom teaching is conducted by verbal description and direction. If children cannot follow this information, they will be unable to encode it correctly and store it in memory for later application to new learning.

A third reason is that youngsters with language impairments have limited resources for demonstrating their knowledge and explaining their reasoning. For example, if their vocabularies are limited they will be less able to participate in naming activities or in describing their experiences.

A fourth reason that language is so important for school entry is that language skills are strongly related to subsequent reading skills (Snow & Tabors, 1993). Children who have strong language skills are at a marked advantage for the transition to literacy, which in turn serves as a central tool in formal instruction.

A fifth reason is that language is vitally important for communicating the expected rules for classroom behavior. If children do not understand the rules for talking in the classroom, they may speak out of turn, speak too loudly, interrupt other children, or "talk back" to the teacher. These behaviors, in turn, may be regarded as socially inappropriate. In addition, these children may be unable to explain why they seem to disregard the rules of conduct.

Finally, a sixth reason is that language ability is central to the ability to establish friendships with other children. The development of social relationships with other children is an important achievement of the early childhood period. Children who are unable to establish friendships with their peers have a poorer prognosis for successful educational experiences (Parker & Asher, 1987).

Table 1.   Why language is important for children in classrooms

1. Children may not understand the verbal instructions given by adults.
2. Much of classroom teaching is conducted by verbal description and direction.
3. Children with language impairments have limited resources for demonstrating knowledge and explaining their reasoning.
4. Language skills serve as a precursor to the development of literacy skills.
5. Language is vitally important for communicating the rules for classroom behavior.
6. Language ability is central to the ability to establish friendships with other children.

Problems with Language Readiness

There are numerous ways in which children ca[n]
guage readiness. Some children whose languag[e]
garten may have limited school-related vocabula[ry]
or unusual conversational patterns; however, the[y]
these expected competencies readily on their [own]
children may show a delay in language acquisiti[on]
below the expectations for their age. It is not al[ways obv]ious to which
group an individual youngster may belong. These distinctions require
careful individualized assessment by a trained speech-language pathologist. Preschool children identified as having speech or language disorders
are eligible for special services, which are mandated under the auspices
of Part B of PL 101-476, the Individuals with Disabilities Education Act
(IDEA). Unfortunately, speech-language pathology services are not widespread. In a survey conducted by Wolery et al. (1994), 45% of Head Start
programs, 51% of public school prekindergarten programs, 17% of public
school kindergartens, and 92% of community programs reported that
they did *not* employ a speech-language pathologist, even on a part-time
basis. Inclusive programs were more likely than noninclusive programs
to employ speech-language pathologists.

For Children with Language Impairments

The language impairments of children can occur in combination with
other disabilities, or exist as a sole source of impairment (cf. Rice &
Schuele, 1994). Other disabilities likely to have language impairment as
a concomitant condition are hearing disability, mental retardation, and
socioemotional disorders. In addition, a sizeable number of children
seem to have language impairments despite otherwise typical developmental milestones. These children can be difficult to identify. They can
blend with a group of preschool children and yet have significant problems with language acquisition. These children are the major focus of
the LAP curriculum; they are described in further detail below.

For some time it has been recognized that language impairments are
a prevalent type of disorder in the preschool years. Of the preschool children who received special education services in 1986 (the most recent
year for which categorical data are available at the national level), 69%
were categorized as having language impairments (Office of Special Education Programs, 1988). This would include children whose language impairments are secondary to other disorders, as well as those for whom
the language impairment is primary.

There is clear reason, then, to believe that early language acquisition is a crucial area of school readiness across the range of children's aptitudes. Readiness concerns apply to children who are capable of learning
but not attuned to the language demands of the traditional classroom
setting, as well as to children struggling to acquire language skills. Although there is widespread recognition that children need to develop language skills during the preschool years, language skills are often overlooked as a specific part of a child's preschool experiences. In fact, some

of the leading early childhood curriculum books do not even mention language development as a specific developmental goal (e.g., Bank Street Curriculum [Mitchell & David, 1992]), or, if language development is mentioned, it is treated as a matter of cognitive or social development. Our perspective is that the area of language warrants special emphasis, which need not be at the expense of the other traditional curricular goals and can be interwoven into many aspects of the curriculum. This special emphasis will be beneficial to all preschool children, but especially so for children with language limitations.

THE NEED FOR A LANGUAGE-FOCUSED CURRICULUM

Our intent in establishing the Language Acquisition Preschool was to provide a language-focused curriculum (LFC) that pervaded all aspects of a preschool classroom in a way that integrated language enhancement activities into the general activities designed to prepare children socially and cognitively for the transition to kindergarten. This classroom, we believed, could facilitate language acquisition for children whose language competencies were unfolding according to normative expectations, and for children whose language milestones were lagging behind or who were learning English as a second language.

Some related developments were available to guide us in this design. One was the growing recognition of the value of naturalistic contexts for language learning and intervention. This is evident, for example, in the activity-based curriculum developed by Bricker (1993). This curriculum is designed for children from birth to 3 years of age, a time during which language emerges from simple play activities. Its focus on simple acts of communication, first words, and simple sentences places it at a developmental level earlier than that of preschool classrooms, which typically include children ages 3–5 years whose language skills are beyond that level. From a language intervention perspective, beginning in the late 1980s there has been increased awareness of the value of language intervention in naturalistic settings (cf. Norris & Hoffman, 1990; Weitzman, 1992). The available writings offer general characterizations of desirable settings for language intervention although the particulars are not well specified. Such language intervention programs are often implemented with a group of children with language impairments, without other children in the group.

What we set out to do with LAP was more particular. Our criteria are summarized in Table 2. We wanted to highlight that *all* preschool children can benefit from activities to enhance their language acquisition, insofar as children with better verbal skills are better prepared for school entry. We believed that attempts to enhance language acquisition require adherence to the principles of children's language development and must be consistent with how children use language in their spontaneous utterances. We preferred a classroom curriculum that would adhere to many of the time-honored practices for the preparation of children for school entry. In particular, we wished to provide instruction within the context of developmentally appropriate practice in early

Table 2.   Criteria for a language-focused curriculum for language intervention

1. The curriculum should be designed for *all* preschool children to benefit from activities to en-
    hance their language acquisition, insofar as children with better verbal skills are better pre-
    pared for school entry.
2. The curriculum should adhere to the principles of children's language acquisition.
3. Many of the time-honored practices for the preparation of children for school entry should
    be followed, along with developmentally appropriate practice with regard to children's cogni-
    tive and social development.
4. Care should be taken to ensure that children with speech and language impairments are
    educated in a classroom with their typically developing peers in the least restrictive environ-
    ment (LRE).
5. Programming staff should ensure that children with language intervention needs are not
    separated from the group in ways that highlight their limitations; therefore, children should
    not be identified for individual therapy sessions outside the room.
6. Parental involvement should be recognized as an important component of any efforts to de-
    velop children's language, social, and cognitive skills.

childhood curricula, in which the instruction was appropriate for levels
of preschoolers' cognitive, social, and motivational functioning (see
Richarz, 1993, for discussion).

We wanted to ensure that children with speech and language impairments were educated in a classroom with their typically developing
peers. This is stipulated by IDEA in the requirement that services be provided in a least restrictive environment (LRE). We wanted to ensure that
the children with language intervention needs were not separated from
the group in ways that highlighted their limitations; therefore, children
were neither identified for individual therapy sessions nor removed from
the group for instruction. Finally, we recognized that parental involvement is an important component of any efforts to develop children's language, social, and cognitive skills.

A program that met these criteria would constitute a language-
focused curriculum. Because there was reason to believe that an LFC
would be an effective approach to early childhood intervention and none
was available, we set out to develop and evaluate such a program.

ESTABLISHMENT AND MAINTENANCE OF
THE LANGUAGE ACQUISITION PRESCHOOL

The Language Acquisition Preschool was established in 1985, with funding as a 3-year demonstration program provided by what was then the
Handicapped Children's Early Education Program of the Department of
Education (Award #G008630279). LAP subsequently received financial
support from the University of Kansas and the Kansas Early Childhood
Research Institute (OSEP Award #HO24U80001). From the outset, LAP
has been affiliated with the University of Kansas and has served three
major objectives: 1) to provide services to young children, 2) to be a training site for the development of practitioners in speech-language pathology and early childhood intervention, and 3) to facilitate research. In this
volume, we highlight the first and third objectives. Initially, LAP was designed as a service delivery system with feasibility for local school systems. As of 1994, LAP is incorporated into the local community's service

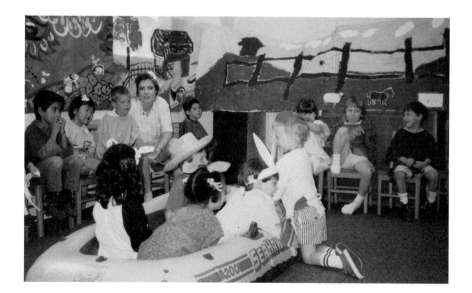

delivery options for children with speech and language impairments. LAP's LFC (see Table 2) has also been implemented elsewhere (as described in the final chapter of this volume). We regard this transition from the university to the local school system and replicated implementations elsewhere as important indicators of the ecological validity of the LFC and of LAP. In short, the LFC is a viable clinical service delivery model with documented program effectiveness (see Chapters 9 and 10).

THE CHILDREN ENROLLED IN LAP

The LAP classroom meets on a half-day basis, 4 days a week. One class meets in the morning, another in the afternoon. The maximum enrollment is 21 children in each class. The children are evenly distributed across three groups: 1) children with speech-language impairments; 2) children who are learning English as a second language; and 3) children who are developing within the range of normative expectations for speech and language, cognitive, and social development. In the classroom, there is variation according to ethnic identity and parental social class. Children may enter the class at any time, although we prefer to enroll the children with speech and language impairments as close to age 3 as possible. Because these children are enrolled when they are identified as needing intervention, some have been enrolled as late as during the summer prior to their entry into kindergarten that fall.

It is important to note that fully a third of the children in each class are typically developing. This mixture of children is crucial, in that it provides, at any one time, many children who are possible conversational partners who can illustrate the targeted patterns of speech and language, and do so in the context of ongoing play activities. This means that there are children in the classroom for the language-learning children to identify with and emulate. We believe that this mixture constitutes the best example of LRE for language acquisition and intervention.

The children targeted for enrollment in LAP are youngsters who meet conventional clinical criteria for diagnosis with speech and/or language impairment. This group neither represents the entire caseload of speech-language pathologists, nor encompasses all children with clinically significant speech and language problems. The LAP classroom does not include children with significant intellectual impairments, hearing loss, and sociobehavioral problems. The selection of this group allowed us to test the LFC with a sample of children who, although far from homogeneous, are less diverse than a group including children who have associated impairments. An additional reason for these enrollment specifications was that it was possible to study program outcomes as a function of speech-language limitations, relatively independent of cognitive, social, or severe perceptual limitations. Almost all of the available literature about similar intervention programs is concerned with children with multiple disabilities, and in those cases it is not possible to determine which of the findings are attributable primarily to communication impairments and which are attributable to other factors. Finally, it was possible for us to have a set of selective criteria because, in our community, appropriate alternative preschool placements are available. Thus, a decision not to enroll a child in LAP did not present us with the ethical problem of denying needed clinical services to children.

As the LAP program has matured, it has been adapted in other settings. Some implementations are described in Chapter 12 of this volume. In the other settings, a broader definition of eligible children has been used with less stringent exclusionary criteria. Thus, it seems that the LFC framework is applicable beyond the group of children with whom it was developed, and who are described in detail here.

Children with Specific Language Impairment

The criteria that we have followed for enrollment of children in LAP are such that all of the youngsters with specific language impairment (SLI) would qualify for educational services in the public schools of our state. A discussion of the nature of their speech and language impairments is provided in Chapters 2 and 5. The criteria for enrollment include inclusionary as well as exclusionary considerations; they are as follows:

1. All of the children are between 3 and 5 years of age.
2. All of the children demonstrate levels of intellectual ability within or above the normal range, as measured by the Kaufman Assessment Battery for Children (Kaufman & Kaufman, 1983).
3. None of the children demonstrate clinically significant difficulties with social or emotional development.
4. None of the children demonstrate a physical or visual impairment.
5. All of the children pass a hearing screening for typical levels of acuity.
6. All of the children demonstrate clinically significant difficulties in speech and/or language development.

Children are identified as having SLI if they meet at least two of the following criteria:

1. A clinically significant impairment in receptive vocabulary, as evidenced by a score 1 or more standard deviations below the mean for their age on the Peabody Picture Vocabulary Test–Revised (PPVT–R) (Dunn & Dunn, 1981)
2. A clinically significant impairment in language skills, as evidenced by a score 1 or more standard deviations below the mean for their age on the receptive and/or expressive portion of the Reynell Developmental Language Scales–U.S. Edition (Reynell & Gruber, 1990)
3. A clinically significant deficit in expected sentence length, as evidenced by a mean length of utterance (MLU) below the predicted range for their chronological age (Miller, 1981)
4. A clinically significant deficit in grammatical development, as evidenced by nonmastery of at least two age-appropriate grammatical morphemes (de Villiers & de Villiers, 1973)
5. A clinically significant deficit in speech skills, as evidenced by a low percentile score on the Goldman-Fristoe Test of Articulation (GFTA) (Goldman & Fristoe, 1986), and limited intelligibility of spontaneous speech

Children Learning English as a Second Language

There is another group of children who have communication limitations and who offer many parallels to the children with SLI, but who do not have SLI. These are children learning English as a second language (ESL). These youngsters are appearing in the public schools in ever-increasing numbers as a consequence of the flood of immigrants to the United States during the 1980s. A current estimate is that, nationally, there are 3.3 million children with limited English proficiency (Hakuta, 1993).

Educators have struggled with how to implement language-appropriate instructional programs. Although few generalizations can be drawn, one that is noncontroversial is that second language teaching is most effective in the early stages of language acquisition (cf. Chapter 6; Tabors & Snow, in press). Furthermore, if children learning English as a second language can be well on their way to mastery of English by kindergarten, they will be better prepared for school entry. Introduction of English to non-native speakers in preschool programs is a desirable way to develop new language skills in a naturalistic and meaningful context (Tabors & Snow, in press). Thus, there is a need for effective preschool language facilitation for children learning English as a second language, as well as children with SLI, if all children are to be "ready to learn" when they begin kindergarten.

The children learning English as a second language were included in the LAP classroom as a way of evaluating the effectiveness of the LFC for these children and the children with SLI. Children for whom English is a second language also were thought to add positively to the program in two ways. First is that they would add to the cultural diversity. The children's home countries and home languages were diverse and literally represented a worldwide distribution. Second, their language diversity would help establish a metalinguistic awareness of the forms of language, and the fact that there is a certain arbitrariness about language.

One must speak English, not Japanese, in order to be understood in the classroom. One must be intelligible, and one must use words in the expected ways. Thus, there could be a naturalness in the focus on linguistic forms and repetition of targeted structures if some of the children in the classroom were obviously learning a new language.

The children learning English as a second language who were selected for enrollment in LAP met the following criteria:

1. Ages 3–5 years
2. Native language other than English
3. Recent arrival in the United States, with little or no previous exposure to the English language or American culture
4. Scores within the normal range of performance on the Kaufman Assessment Battery for Children (Kaufman & Kaufman, 1983) (To allow for some cultural acclimation prior to testing, the test is administered during the second semester of enrollment.)

Typically Developing Children

Approximately one third of the children who attend LAP are native speakers of English and are exhibiting typical patterns of language development; these children are drawn from the community. They meet the first five criteria specified above for children with SLI. It is important to note that there is a balance of children, such that fully one third of the children in the classroom are developing language in a typical fashion. We have also, whenever possible, included children from ethnic minorities within the group of typically developing children.

LAP'S PROFESSIONAL STAFF

LAP's core professional staff consist of a classroom teacher and a full-time classroom aide. The teacher for the period of time reported in this volume is dually certified in early childhood education and in speech-language pathology. If such a dually certified teacher is not available, it would be possible, with some minor modification, to implement the LFC with a collaborative arrangement of an early childhood educator and a speech-language pathologist. An additional staff member is the family services coordinator, who is responsible for the liaison between the children's caregivers and the classroom (see Chapter 8). For much of the history of LAP, there have been two co-directors who have been responsible for the funding and the research aspects of the program.

OVERVIEW OF THIS VOLUME

The chapters in this volume describe the language-focused curriculum that was developed during the initial phases of implementation of the Language Acquisition Preschool and report what has been learned during the years of its implementation. The book provides a rationale for the approach used, describes the guiding principles of the LFC and how it is implemented, reports its use with children and families, and analyzes its effectiveness in enhancing children's speech and language skills. Included are findings from the classroom that reveal the ways in which young children's language competency interacts with their social development, and what happens to the children as they leave the program and enter school.

The development of the LFC was based on what is known about children's language acquisition and language impairment; this information is summarized in Chapter 2. In Chapter 3, a concentrated normative model (CNM) of the technology of language intervention, which characterizes the framework underlying the language focus of the curriculum, is described. The ways in which the CNM influences the LFC are laid out in operational guidelines for the design of a classroom-based intervention program. The specific techniques for implementation of the LFC are then described in detail in Chapters 4, 5, and 6. In Chapter 7, findings are reported about the ways in which verbal interactions and social relationships among preschoolers are influenced by their language competencies. Chapter 8 describes the parent component of the LFC. The speech and language outcomes at the immediate conclusion of children's participation in LAP are described in Chapters 9 and 10. Long-term outcomes, when children are in elementary school, are described in Chapter 11. Finally, in Chapter 12 are descriptions of clinical settings in which the LFC has been replicated outside of the LAP classroom. As a whole, these chapters constitute a report of what happens to children when they are enrolled in LAP, the subsequent changes in their speech and language performance, and the long-term outcomes of their preschool experiences.

REFERENCES

Boyer, E.L. (1991). *Ready to learn: A mandate for the nation.* Princeton, NJ: Carnegie Foundation for the Advancement of Teaching.

Bricker, D. (Ed.). (1993). *Assessment, evaluation, and programming system (AEPS) for infants and children. Vol. 1: AEPS measurement for birth to three years.* Baltimore: Paul H. Brookes Publishing Co.

de Villiers, J.G., & de Villiers, P.A. (1973). A cross-sectional study of the acquisition of grammatical morphemes. *Journal of Psycholinguistic Research, 2,* 267–278.

Dunn, L.M., & Dunn, L.M. (1981). *Peabody Picture Vocabulary Test–Revised.* Circle Pines, MN: American Guidance Service.

Goals 2000 Education America Act of 1994, PL 103-227. (March, 1994). Title 20, U.S.C. 5801 et seq: *U.S. Statutes at Large, 108,* 125–280.

Goldman, R., & Fristoe, M. (1986). *The Goldman-Fristoe Test of Articulation.* Circle Pines, MN: American Guidance Service.

Hakuta, K. (1993). *A blueprint for the second generation: Federal education programs for limited English-proficient students.* Stanford, CA: Report of the Stanford Working Group.

Individuals with Disabilities Education Act (IDEA)—Part B—Assistance to States for the Education of Children with Disabilities Program and Preschool Grants for Children with Disabilities; Final Rule. 34 CFR Parts 300–301, September 29, 1992.

Kaufman, A.S., & Kaufman, N.L. (1983). *Kaufman Assessment Battery for Children.* Circle Pines, MN: American Guidance Service.

Miller, J.F. (1981). *Assessing language production in children: Experimental procedures.* Needham Heights: Allyn & Bacon.

Mitchell, A., & David, J. (1992). *Explorations with young children: A curriculum guide from the Bank Street College of Education.* Mt. Rainier, MD: Gryphon House.

Norris, J.A., & Hoffman, P.R. (1990). Language intervention within naturalistic environments. *Language, Speech, and Hearing Services in Schools, 21,* 72–84.

Office of Special Education Programs. (1988). *Tenth annual report to Congress.* Washington, DC: U.S. Government Printing Office.

Parker, J.G., & Asher, S.R. (1987). Peer relations and later adjustment: Are low-accepted children "at risk"? *Psychological Bulletin, 102,* 357–389.

Reynell, J.K., & Gruber, C.P. (1990). *Reynell Developmental Language Scales–U.S. Edition.* Los Angeles, CA: Western Psychological Services.

Rice, M.L., & Schuele, C.M. (1994). The speech and language impaired child. In E. Meyen & T. Skrtic (Eds.), *Exceptional children and youth* (4th ed., pp. 339–374). Denver: Love Publishing.

Richarz, S. (1993). Innovations in early childhood education: Models that support the integration of children of varied developmental levels. In C.A. Peck, S.L. Odom, & D.D. Bricker (Eds.), *Integrating young children with disabilities into community programs: Ecological perspectives on research and implementation* (pp. 83–107). Baltimore: Paul H. Brookes Publishing Co.

Snow, C.E., & Tabors, P.O. (1993). Language skills that relate to literacy development. In B. Spodek & O.N. Saracho (Eds.), *Language and literacy in early childhood education* (Yearbook in Early Childhood Education) (Vol. 4, pp. 1–20). New York: Teachers College Press.

Tabors, P.O., & Snow, C.E. (in press). English as a second language in preschool programs. In F. Genesee (Ed.), *Reading, writing, and schooling in English as a second language.* New York: Cambridge University Press.

Weitzman, E. (1992). *Learning language and loving it.* Toronto, Ontario, Canada: Hanen Centre Publication.

Wolery, M., Venn, M.L., Schroeder, C., Holcombe, A., Huffman, K., Martin, C.G., Brookfield, J., & Fleming, L.A. (1994). A survey of the extent to which speech-language pathologists are employed in preschool programs. *Language, Speech, and Hearing Services in the Schools, 25,* 2–8.

~2~

Language Acquisition and Language Impairment

Mabel L. Rice

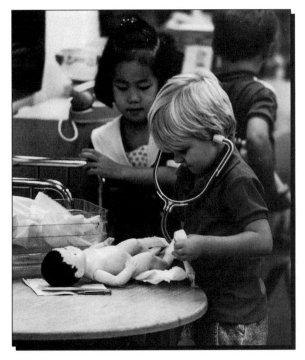

This chapter provides an overview of current models of children's language acquisition and a brief description of the condition of specific language impairment (SLI). The intent is to highlight the competing accounts of the everyday accomplishments of youngsters, who, with apparent ease, readily join the world of language users. At the same time, there are children who seem to have all of the necessary requirements in place for language acquisition, but who nevertheless do not readily make the transition into language. Explanations for the condition of delayed language emergence are related to explanations of typical language acquisition.

One way to think of this is to imagine language acquisition as a train in which the cars are coupled together in a certain way, a train that follows a track and adheres to certain principles of gravity, acceleration, rate, and motion. For most children, the train leaves the station at some time between 12 and 24 months of age, and picks up momentum during the preschool years. For children with language impairments, the train is slow in leaving the station, and some of the cars are particularly slow, as if coupled with a bungee cord that allows them to drag behind the others.

It is essential that interventionists who work with young children come to understand what is known about children's language acquisition and why such acquisition may be slow to appear; in effect, early interventionists need to understand how the train is configured and the principles that guide its momentum. Adult intuitions are often quite erroneous with regard to how language emerges, so it is unsound to proceed on the basis of assumptions alone.

The caveat to be offered here is that the following discussion is intended only to highlight some of the main findings and issues in the study of children's language acquisition. It does not constitute a comprehensive review of the topic. Readers are encouraged to follow the trail of references for further information.

LANGUAGE ACQUISITION

There is no agreed-upon, conventional account of children's language acquisition. Instead, there are two opposing points of view, with associated differences in scientific methods. Central to the differences is the way in which language is regarded. For this discussion, the two positions will be referred to as *developmental* and *linguistic.* Their key differences are summarized in Table 1.

The Developmental View of Language Acquisition

One group of theorists believes that language is a part of children's general cognitive abilities, governed by the same learning mechanisms that apply to other developmental domains, such as social development. This *developmental view* emphasizes the social and cognitive dimensions of children's language acquisition, the ways in which early language seems to emerge in the context of interactions with other language users, the motivating power of the desire to communicate with others, the richness of the conceptual underpinnings of children's word acquisition, and the subtleties of social insights reflected in discourse abilities (Gleason, 1993). These theorists emphasize the meanings and uses of language. Within this perspective, a child is regarded as an active, self-directed learner, capable of constructing rules for words and language structures and rules for the use of language in social settings. The emphasis is on contextualized language—that is, language embedded in interactions carried out in social contexts, such as preschool classrooms, mother–child interactions, and interactions with playmates. This framework is evident in the new generation of early childhood curricular materials, such as in Bricker (1993) and Weitzman (1992).

Table 1.   Developmental versus linguistic views of language acquisition

Developmental	Linguistic
Language as cognitive/social ability	Distinct, innate language abilities
Emphasis on meanings and uses	Emphasis on specific, formal grammatical aspects
Active, self-directed learner working largely in an *inductive* mode	Active, self-directed learner working largely in a *deductive* mode
Descriptive studies	Theoretically motivated studies
Analysis of linguistic environment of the child; description of adult talk	Analysis of probability of adult feedback for targeted structures
Sociocultural contexts	Linguistic universals
Language is acquired, not taught	Language is acquired, not taught

Studies within the developmental framework provide detailed descriptions of the language competencies of children of differing ages, such that we now know a great deal about the forms and uses of children's language, especially from infancy through the preschool years (cf. Gleason, 1993). Also of interest are fine-grained analyses of the linguistic environment that a child encounters, including descriptions of mothers' talk to babies and young children and teachers' talk to students. Sociocultural attitudes are also regarded as important, with studies of cross-cultural differences in attitudes about children's language abilities and performance and ways of talking with children (Crago & Cole, 1991; Heath, 1989). The developmental perspective, then, has provided valuable documentation of children's language abilities across levels of development; identified intricate linkages of social, cognitive, and linguistic development; and described ways in which the language environments of children can differ as a function of sociocultural contexts.

An important conclusion from the developmental language studies is that language is not "taught." Instead, children "acquire" language as a consequence of their ability to interpret their surroundings and make sense of linguistic forms, and their need to communicate with others. At an early age, children "construct" their linguistic systems. They are not bound to literal imitations of what they hear. (In fact, they make principled errors unlike what they hear, based on their own rule systems—errors such as "goed" for "went," and creative uses such as "you're combing me baldheaded.") Furthermore, they do not require explicit praise and reinforcement for their early linguistic efforts. Instead, language acquisition seems to serve as its own reinforcer; the increasingly effective attempts to communicate, or the cognitive benefits intrinsic to the linguistic system, seem to inspire youngsters to stay focused on the process. In any event, for most children linguistic competencies appear to emerge without conscious effort on their part, as a natural outcome of their explorations of their world, as they play with toys and interact with siblings, playmates, and parents.

Although the exact role of adult input is a matter of scientific dispute, there is general agreement that the adults do not "teach" language in a conventional sense of "I say–you say." Instead, children are able to pick up on subtle adjustments in adult talk, whether it is directed at the children or overheard as adults converse. In fact, there are distinct differences across cultures in the amount of language that parents regard as appropriate for children and the styles of adult talk to children; nevertheless, children acquire their native language, so it is difficult to infer some universal "right way" to talk with children (Crago & Cole, 1991; Heath, 1989). At the same time, there is some evidence that there may be counterproductive approaches. Highly directive adults, those who insist that youngsters "talk right," who drill children on words and sentences or issue many commands, are more likely, despite their good intentions, to delay rather than enhance children's language development (Cross, 1984). Children seem to recoil from attempts to force their language performance, perhaps because it introduces a self-consciousness that is incompatible with the underlying acquisition mechanisms.

The Linguistic View of Language Acquisition

The alternative point of view, the *linguistic* perspective, emphasizes the ultimate outcomes, the full linguistic system that children must achieve (Atkinson, 1992; Goodluck, 1991; Jackendoff, 1994; Pinker, 1994). Whereas much of the developmental literature has focused on the meanings of children's utterances and the social contexts in which they encounter and use their language, the linguistic approach is motivated by a theory of language structure, the formal grammatical mechanisms that are not always apparent in the utterances themselves (particularly in the incomplete and underspecified utterances of children). There are, of course, competing models of grammatical structure. The most widely known model builder is Noam Chomsky (cf. Chomsky, 1980), whose evolving formal models have captured the imaginations of many scholars.

The linguistic approach differs from the developmental perspective in several fundamental ways. First, language is differentiated from social and cognitive representational systems. Language is thought to be represented in the mind in distinctive ways. Second, the language faculty is regarded as an innate capacity, intrinsically incorporated into human brain structures. Third, it is thought that there is a *universal grammar*, composed of a fundamental set of linguistic procedures and structures that generate the surface forms of differing languages. Fourth, children's language acquisition is viewed as a problem of adjusting or tuning their innately provided universal grammar to match the grammar of their native language. They do this by picking up on various distinctive properties of their native language as they hear it spoken by others. Fifth, the level of relevant language description is very specific. Whereas developmental studies often measure language accomplishments in a broad sense, such as performance on a standardized, omnibus test, or descriptions such as the number of utterances, the length of utterances, or the kinds of words used, linguistic analyses typically focus on particular grammatical structures or relations.

As an example of a linguistic focus, consider the way in which verbal agreement is marked in standard English and what children must attend to in order to acquire this knowledge. It is grammatical to say "I go," "you go," "they go,"and "he goes." The final -s in "goes" is characterized as the need to mark "agreement" between subject and verb in the case of third-person singular subjects, such as "he" in "he goes" or "dog" in "the dog runs." Agreement is a formal property of many languages, in which "formal" implies no clear semantic correlates. One cannot find an instance of "agreement" in the world; in the examples given, it marks a relationship between the linguistic categories of subject and verb. So, children cannot rely on their appreciation of meanings or social insights to solve this problem. Part of the problem is that they must learn, for English, to mark only the third-person singular subjects. Thus, they cannot assume the -s goes on verbs that appear with "I," "you," or "they." Adults seem unlikely to point out this restriction to them, insofar as most adults do not notice it, but nevertheless adults follow the convention in their own utterances. Yet children are surprisingly adept in working this out. By 5 years of age, they use -s for the contexts in which it is required and avoid its use in the contexts in which it is not required.

Although third-person singular agreement may appear to be a specialized grammatical insight, in current linguistic theory agreement marking (which is much more dominant in non-English languages) is thought to be part of a grammatical package that includes marking for past tense and for case (e.g., he/him, she/her differentiations). Thus, what may appear to be a small piece of grammar may instead be part of a larger package of interrelated parts of the linguistic structures (cf. Haegeman, 1991; Pollock, 1989; Radford, 1990). The point is that a specific piece of the grammar, such as verbal agreement, can reveal the challenges a child faces in acquiring language (where at least some of the important components do not have ready semantic or social correlates), and the underlying interconnectedness of grammar.

In the linguistic account, children's rapid language acquisition is to be expected because it is supported by innate acquisition mechanisms. Further predictions are: 1) language abilities may be at least partially dissociated from social and cognitive abilities; 2) language aptitude may run in families, as a consequence of inherited linguistic mechanisms; and 3) in general, environmental input plays a minimal role in children's ability to acquire language. In other words, language acquisition is not dependent on an enriched linguistic input in which adult language users carefully "explain" language by means of clear examples of what is "right" and explicit feedback when a child is "wrong" (cf. Pinker, 1994).

A Composite View of Language Acquisition?

There would seem to be obvious advantages of a comprehensive account of children's language acquisition, one that successfully integrated the developmental and linguistic perspectives. Intuitively, the three dimensions of social, cognitive, and linguistic knowledge are operative as children acquire the multiple aspects of language, as they learn new words, carry on conversations, and formulate conventionally constructed sentences. Clearly, each of these perspectives has important insights into the acquisition process and offers arguments and evidence that must be explained adequately. Yet a synthesis or amalgamation does not appear to be on the horizon. The technical issues involved, the differences in methodologies, and the various pressures of the sociology of science conspire to keep the two competing models apart.

The reason to introduce the two perspectives here is that a full explanation of why some children have problems acquiring language, and how to lay out an effective intervention program, requires an appreciation of each of these perspectives. Therefore, practitioners have the dubious task of arriving at some sort of workable composite of the two perspectives, a composite perhaps more feasible at the applied level than at the technical, scientific levels.

SPEECH AND LANGUAGE IMPAIRMENTS

Although the large majority of children acquire language without apparent difficulty, this is not the case for all children. It has been estimated that 5%–10% of otherwise typically developing children have specific difficulties in mastering their native language (cf. Rice & Schuele, 1994; Tomblin, in press). "Communication disorders" is the diagnostic descriptor for this condition (American Psychiatric Press, 1994), in which there are observed "impairments" of speech and language.

In order to discuss the notion of impairments, it is necessary to distinguish between "speech" and "language." For the sake of expository convenience, the two notions are often combined in the umbrella term, "language." However, language consists of the following components:

1. Minimal units of meaning, known as morphemes, which come in two forms: free and bound (The free forms are words. The bound forms are affixes, which must attach to words and express meanings, such as plural and tense marking.)
2. Semantics, the ways in which meaning is represented in language, which generally involves word meanings and the ways in which words are organized according to meanings
3. Syntax, the ways in which words are organized into phrases and sentences
4. The sound system, the ways in which sounds are combined to create morphemes (Phonology is the study of how the sound system is represented in the grammar of a language.)

To return to the distinction between speech and language, roughly speaking, speech is what you hear on the telephone; language is the underlying system of mental representation that can formulate a message that can be communicated by talking, writing, or signing. Language has morphological, semantic, syntactic, and phonological dimensions.

It is conventional in the clinical field of speech-language pathology to differentiate between speech impairments and language impairments. The former refer to problems pronouncing sounds, which can be due to problems in recognizing that the sounds of language are organized into families of sounds (a problem of mental representation), or as a result of problems of motor control (a problem of being unable to move the muscles of speech production in an appropriate manner). In actual practice, it is often difficult to distinguish between these two levels of speech, but there are conceptual advantages to the distinction. Children with significant speech problems often have limited intelligibility. "Language impairments" generally refers to problems in understanding or using morphemes, words, or sentences, or in using these components in a manner appropriate to the conversational context.

Speech and/or language impairments can be a primary area of developmental disability, or secondary to other limitations. Children with intellectual impairments, hearing impairment, or severe sociobehavioral problems often have associated speech and language difficulties. The

children of interest here are those for whom speech and language impairments are their primary area of disability. Because their impairment is specific to language, they are conventionally referred to as children with *specific language impairment* (SLI). (When referring to SLI, "language" is used in the umbrella sense, encompassing "speech" as well.) (For an overview of the literature on SLI, see Watkins and Rice, 1994.)

It is possible for speech and language acquisition to be clinically dissociated, with a significant problem in one dimension and not the other. At the level of surface symptoms, there are children with speech problems only, and children with language problems who at the same time have clearly articulated speech, and children for whom aspects of both dimensions are problematic. Approximately half of children with SLI fall into the last category, although definitive statistics are not yet available (Shriberg, Kwiatkowski, Best, Hengst, & Terselic-Weber, 1986).

Clinically, youngsters with SLI are operationally defined as those whose developmental speech and language milestones are far behind age expectations, but whose cognitive abilities are within typical (or border-line typical) limits, whose hearing is not significantly impaired, and whose social development does not indicate clinically significant aberrations. This is often determined by performance on standardized tests and typically supplemented by informal observations and descriptions of spontaneous language.

Typical clinical profiles for these children demonstrate a delay in attainment of their major speech and language developmental milestones, relative to their same-age peers. First words and sentences are typically delayed in emergence. A rough clinical diagnostic sign for the condition of SLI is fewer than 50 words in the expressive vocabulary of a 24-month-old child. During the preschool years, relative to their same-age peers, children with SLI may have limited intelligibility, reduced sentence length, limited vocabulary, and particular problems with grammatical morphemes, such as third-person singular agreement, tense marking, and case errors. Such children may have problems in understanding language as well as producing it, or with production only. It used to be assumed that these children eventually "outgrew" their difficulties, but recent findings suggest that is probably not the case. Instead, their problems are likely to persist and take a somewhat different form as they move into more advanced language levels (e.g., Aram, Ekelman, & Nation, 1984; Bishop & Edmundson, 1987; Paul & Alforde, 1993; Thal, Tobias, & Morrison, 1991). As they move through elementary school, children with SLI often encounter difficulties making the transition into literacy and may be identified as having dyslexia. Individuals with SLI are less likely than their peers without SLI to attend or complete college (Parlour, 1990).

Social Consequences of Atypical Speech and Language Development

Recent findings in our laboratory suggest that children with SLI may experience some social consequences of their limited speech and language ability. Preschool youngsters with SLI are not fully incorporated into the conversational interactions with their peers, even though they are active play partners (Rice, 1993) (see Chapter 7). These youngsters are also less popular among their peers. When their classmates are asked to nominate who they like to play with, the children with SLI are more likely to fall into the "not liked" category than the "liked" category (Gertner, Rice, & Hadley, 1994). Finally, adults (including teachers) may confuse symptoms of language impairment with symptoms of limited intellectual ability or socioeconomic status. On the basis of listening to speech samples from children with SLI and typically developing children, adult judges rated the intelligence, social development, and leadership aptitude lower for the children with SLI, along with lower estimates of parental intelligence and socioeconomic status. This is particularly troublesome, given that SLI is a condition that crosses levels of parental intelligence, income, and professional status (Rice, Hadley, & Alexander, 1993).

Theories About Etiology of SLI

There is no known etiology of SLI, although a number of causes have been proposed and there is a lively literature debating the possibilities. One possible factor, though, has generally been eliminated. Within the range of typical adult–child interactions, it is generally believed that a youngster's speech and language impairments are not attributable to some form of negligent or "bad talking" on the part of parents. Current theories tend to postulate an inherent child limitation instead of faulty environmental input, at least within the typical range of input. In cases of severe neglect, language acquisition is vulnerable (cf. Culp et al., 1991).

One possibility is that SLI is an inherited condition. There are several reasons to believe that this might be the case. Tomblin (in press) summarized the available literature showing that the risk for SLI increases with the extent to which there is common genetic material. He reported that the risk rate for SLI in the population at large is .05. The risk for a first-degree family member is .21; if the first-degree family member is of the same sex, the risk is .28. The risk for same sex dyzygotic (i.e., fraternal) twins is .33; for monozygotic (i.e., identical) twins, the risk is .71. There is, then, evidence that risk is related to genetic factors.

Another suggestion of an inherited condition comes from the fact that many children with SLI have problems with the formal properties of language, especially morphology, such as tense and agreement markings. Such linguistic limitations may correspond to individual variations in innate linguistic capacities. Although such observations are highly suggestive of a particular problem with linguistic structures, that possibility has yet to be confirmed. What is needed is careful documentation of the surface symptomology of SLI, and how that is or is not linked to genetic mechanisms; such documentation is not available. A major challenge is that individuals with SLI change their grammar as they age, such that the early problems with tense and agreement markings are not as obvious at later stages of development. Furthermore, the symptomology is relatively complex, typically involving vocabulary development, as well as morphology, and, possibly, other dimensions as well (cf. Rice, in press, for a discussion of the issues involved in the search for a genetic basis of language acquisition and language impairment).

It has been argued that children's difficulty with language acquisition is attributable to underlying difficulties with the processing of incoming linguistic information. This difficulty could be part of an inherited vulnerability for language acquisition. Competing accounts focus on different aspects of processing demands. Candidate areas of difficulty include memory for speech sounds, or detection and interpretation of the small unstressed parts of grammar, such as the bound morphology or small function words (e.g., "in" and "a") (Gathercole & Baddeley, 1990a, 1990b; Leonard, 1989; Tallal & Stark, 1981). In the scientific literature investigating possible processing problems, the outcomes are mixed and inconclusive. There is evidence of certain processing vulnerabilities, but it is difficult to know if the observed differences provide sufficient explanation for the observed linguistic limitations.

At another level, the vocabulary limitations of children with SLI have been linked to difficulties with word retrieval and mechanisms for storage in long-term memory. Preschool children with SLI also have documented limitations, relative to their peers, in the ability to form a quick interpretation of a new word, an ability that is very robust in typically developing children. Thus, children with SLI tend to lag behind their peers in the accumulation of words that they understand (cf. Ellis-Weismer, 1994; Rice, Oetting, Marquis, Bode, & Pae, 1994). Finally, it has been argued that children with SLI may have subtle deficiencies in their mental representational abilities, although these deficiencies are not sufficient to limit their performance on standardized nonverbal intelligence tests (cf. Johnston, 1994).

It is apparent, then, that there is no single etiological factor identified as the cause of the SLI condition. Although this area of scientific inquiry is relatively new and not yet widespread, the available findings suggest that it is quite likely that SLI is not a single, specific disorder, at least at the level of surface symptomology. Instead, there are multiple ways in which speech and language can be impaired. There has long been a clinical conviction that individuals diagnosed with SLI can be sorted into subgroups on the basis of clinical profiles. These attempts have generally been inconclusive as well, except at the most general levels (e.g., "speech" versus "language," or "good understanding but limited expressive skills"). One of the difficulties, then, in determining an etiology is to arrive at a useful way of describing the nature of the speech and language impairments. Sufficient information does not yet exist to allow the clear differentiation of subgroups of individuals with SLI. If distinct problems can be discerned, it would be possible to determine if different etiological factors contribute more heavily to one type of problem than to another.

Although identification of causal factors will help our understanding of SLI and may provide some comfort to the families of individuals with the condition, we need not wait for such information to become available in order to plan effective intervention. The issue of how to enhance speech and language development is not fully dependent on identification of causal mechanisms. For example, if it is conclusively demonstrated that SLI is an inherited condition, there will still be the need to design environmental conditions that maximize the operative acquisition mechanisms. Although children with SLI may have specific problems related to language acquisition, they also have considerable learning resources that must be actualized for them to acquire language. What is needed, then, is a means of intervention that builds on the many resources that children bring to the language acquisition task and highlights language in a way that is likely to activate their language-learning mechanisms. To return to the train metaphor, it is not necessary to build the entire train and the principles that control its movement, but it is necessary to give the train a boost in leaving the station, to work on the coupling in order to keep the cars in alignment, and to maintain momentum as the train heads down the track.

REFERENCES

American Psychiatric Press. (1994). *Diagnostic and statistical manual of mental disorders* (4th ed). Washington, DC: Author.

Aram, D.M., Ekelman, B.L., & Nation, J.E. (1984). Preschoolers with language disorders: Ten years later. *Journal of Speech and Hearing Research, 27,* 232–244.

Atkinson, M. (1992). *Children's syntax: An introduction to principles and parameters theory.* Cambridge, MA: Basil Blackwell.

Bishop, D.D.U., & Edmundson, A. (1987). Language-impaired 4-year-olds: Distinguishing transient from persistent impairment. *Journal of Speech and Hearing Research, 52,* 156–174.

Bricker, D. (1993). *Assessment, evaluation, and programming system (AEPS) for infants and children. Vol. 1: AEPS measurement for birth to three years.* Baltimore: Paul H. Brookes Publishing Co.

Chomsky, N. (1980). *Rules and representations.* New York: Columbia University Press.

Crago, M.B., & Cole, E. (1991). Using ethnography to bring children's communicative cultural worlds into focus. In T. Gallagher (Ed.), *Pragmatics of language: Clinical practice issues.* San Diego, CA: Singular Publishing Group.

Cross, T.G. (1984). Habilitating the language-impaired child: Ideas from studies of parent–child interaction. *Topics in Language Disorders, 4,* 1–14.

Culp, R.E., Watkins, R.V., Lawrence, H., Letts, D., Kelly, D.J., & Rice, M.L. (1991). Maltreated children's language and speech development: Abused, neglected, and abused and neglected. *First Language, 11,* 377–389.

Ellis-Weismer, S. (1994). *Factors influencing novel word learning and linguistic processing in children with specific language impairment.* Presentation at the 15th Annual Symposium on Research in Child Language Disorders, Madison, WI.

Gathercole, S.E., & Baddeley, A.D. (1990a). Phonological memory deficits in language disordered children: Is there a causal connection? *Journal of Memory and Language, 29,* 336–360.

Gathercole, S.E., & Baddeley, A.D. (1990b). The role of phonological memory in vocabulary acquisition: A study of young children learning new names. *British Journal of Psychology, 81,* 439–454.

Gertner, B.L., Rice, M.L., & Hadley, P.A. (1994). The influence of communicative competence on peer preferences in a preschool classroom. *Journal of Speech and Hearing Research, 37,* 913–923.

Gleason, J.B. (Ed.). (1993). *The development of language.* Columbus, OH: Charles E. Merrill.

Goodluck, H. (1991). *Language acquisition: A linguistic introduction.* Cambridge, MA: Basil Blackwell.

Haegeman, L. (1991). *Introduction to government and binding theory.* Oxford, England: Basil Blackwell.

Heath, S.B. (1989). The learner as cultural member. In M.L. Rice & R.L. Schiefelbusch (Eds.), *The teachability of language* (pp. 333–350). Baltimore: Paul H. Brookes Publishing Co.

Jackendoff, R. (1994). *Patterns in the mind: Language and human nature.* New York: Basic Books.

Johnston, J.R. (1994). Cognitive abilities of children with language impairment. In R.V. Watkins & M.L. Rice (Eds.), *Communication and language intervention series: Vol. 4. Specific language impairments in children* (pp. 107–121). Baltimore: Paul H. Brookes Publishing Co.

Leonard, L.B. (1989). Language learnability and specific language impairment in children. *Applied Psycholinguistics, 10,* 179–202.

Parlour, S.F. (1990). *Familial risk for articulation disorder: A 28-year follow-up.* Unpublished doctoral dissertation, University of Minnesota, Minneapolis.

Paul, R., & Alforde, S. (1993). Grammatical morpheme acquisition in 4-year-olds with normal, impaired, and late-developing language. *Journal of Speech and Hearing Research, 36,* 1271–1275.

Pinker, S. (1994). *The language instinct: How the mind creates language.* New York: William Morrow and Company.

Pollock, J. (1989). Verb movement, universal grammar, and the structure of IP. *Linguistic Inquiry, 20,* 365–424.

Radford, A. (1990). *Syntactic theory and the acquisition of English syntax: The nature of early child grammars of English.* Oxford, England: Basil Blackwell.

Rice, M.L. (1993). "Don't talk to him; He's weird." A social consequences account of language and social interactions. In A.P. Kaiser & D.B. Gray (Eds.), *Communication and language intervention series: Vol. 2. Enhancing children's communication: Research foundations for intervention* (pp. 139–158). Baltimore: Paul H. Brookes Publishing Co.

Rice, M.L. (Ed.). (in press). *Toward a genetics of language.* Hillsdale, NJ: Lawrence Erlbaum Associates.

Rice, M.L., Hadley, P.A., & Alexander, A.L. (1993). Social biases toward children with speech and language impairments: A correlative causal model of language limitations. *Applied Psycholinguistics, 14,* 445–471.

Rice, M.L., Oetting, J.B., Marquis, J., Bode, J., & Pae, S. (1994). Frequency of input effects on word comprehension of children with specific language impairment. *Journal of Speech and Hearing Research, 37,* 106–122.

Rice, M.L., & Schuele, C.M. (1994). The speech and language impaired child. In E. Meyen & T. Skrtic (Eds.), *Exceptional children and youth* (4th ed., pp. 339–374). Denver: Love Publishing.

Shriberg, L., Kwiatkowski, J., Best, S., Hengst, J., & Terselic-Weber, B. (1986). Characteristics of children with phonological disorders of unknown origin. *Journal of Speech and Hearing Research, 51,* 140–161.

Tallal, P., & Stark, R. (1981). Speech acoustic-cue discrimination abilities of normally developing and language impaired children. *Journal of the Acoustical Society of America, 69,* 568–574.

Thal, D., Tobias, S., & Morrison, D. (1991). Language gesture in late talkers: A one-year follow-up. *Journal of Speech and Hearing Disorders, 48,* 18–24.

Tomblin, J.B. (in press). Genetic and environmental contributions to the risk for specific language impairment. In M.L. Rice (Ed.), *Toward a genetics of language.* Hillsdale, NJ: Lawrence Erlbaum Associates.

Watkins, R.V., & Rice, M.L. (Eds.). (1994). *Communication and language intervention series: Vol. 4. Specific language impairments in children.* Baltimore: Paul H. Brookes Publishing Co.

Weitzman, E. (1992). *Learning language and loving it.* Toronto, Ontario, Canada: Hanen Centre Publication.

~3~

The Rationale and Operating Principles for a Language-Focused Curriculum for Preschool Children

Mabel L. Rice

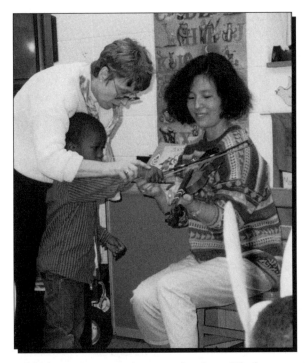

The need for a language-focused curriculum (LFC) was established in Chapter 1 of this book. We wished to establish a setting for language intervention that was appropriate for preschool children, adhered to the principles of children's language acquisition, followed developmentally appropriate practice with regard to children's social and cognitive development, ensured that children with specific language impairment (SLI) were educated in a least restrictive environment (LRE) and were not singled out for special treatment, and recognized that parents are important participants in the intervention endeavor.

As we worked to create this setting, the greatest challenge came in specifying the details. The literature pointed in the direction of establishing an environment that was likely to *activate* children's language acquisition, rather than *train* language one skill at a time. It was also the case that the ordinary preschool classroom was unlikely to be effective for the children with SLI. So, there needed to be particular techniques and principles introduced into the classroom curriculum that served to focus on language acquisition. It was necessary to develop a model of language intervention that accommodated these goals.

CONCENTRATED NORMATIVE MODEL OF LANGUAGE INTERVENTION

The model that guides the language-focused curriculum is called a concentrated normative model (CNM), which is summarized in Table 1. The normative focus of the CNM is addressed here first, followed by a discussion of its concentrated features. The *normative* aspects of this model reflect a commitment to an approach that emphasizes the commonalities across children and the strong potential of young children's developmental momentum. This has several effects. One is that language intervention is conducted in a naturalistic early childhood classroom setting, much like other preschool classrooms. The second is that the methodology draws heavily on existing normative models of language acquisition. The descriptive information in the normative literature about children's language acquisition provides essential markers for expected linguistic and communicative milestones. Furthermore, the normative literature illuminates underlying mental mechanisms and processes instrumental to language acquisition and suggests ways in which a child's interactions with other speakers can influence and facilitate language acquisition. Third, in keeping with the normative emphasis on the importance of a child's home as a context for language use, participation of families in the language intervention program is vigorously encouraged. Fourth, it is recognized that although language acquisition is intimately associated with a child's emerging social and cognitive competencies, it is at the same time a distinctive domain of aptitude. Furthermore, this domain may need special attention for a significant proportion of young children, if they are to meet the normative expectations for participation in kindergarten.

The *concentrated* aspects of the CNM recognize the distinctiveness of language as a developmental domain and the need to provide two

Table 1.   Concentrated normative model of language intervention

Concentrated aspects	Normative aspects
Concentrates on language in the classroom	Emphasizes commonalities across children and strong potential of the developmental momentum
Generally emphasizes the centrality of language in the curriculum	Allows for intervention in the classroom
Uses special techniques to draw children's attention to targeted linguistic forms	Is consistent with normative models of language acquisition
Provides planned redundancy	Emphasizes the participation of families
	Recognizes that language is a distinctive domain of development
	Recognizes that language teaching requires special emphasis

forms of concentrated emphasis on that domain. One is the recognition that *language and communication skills permeate most of an early childhood curriculum*. Although there is widespread recognition that children need to develop language skills during the preschool years, it is also the case that language skills are often overlooked as a specific part of a child's preschool experiences. Our perspective is that the area of language warrants special emphasis, which need not be at the expense of the other traditional curricular goals, and can be interwoven into many aspects of the curriculum. This special emphasis will be beneficial to all preschool children, but especially so for children with language limitations.

The second sense of concentration is the *need to highlight specific language skills* in order for children to notice the differences between linguistic forms, as well as the functional uses and outcomes of communication. This highlighting can come in several ways. One is the use of special techniques for drawing a child's attention to targeted forms as the teacher uses them or as the child produces them, such as focusing on key contrasts in linguistic forms, repeating what the child says, moving a new word to the end of the sentence, or pronouncing a word in an emphatic, or highly stressed, way. The other way is to provide planned redundancy, so a youngster can hear past tense markings or new vocabulary items, over and over again in interesting ways. Thus, a concentration on language, its role throughout the early education curriculum, and the need to highlight specific instances, especially for some children, is a natural complement to the normative focus, in order to maximize a youngster's developmental momentum. At the same time, these techniques of concentrating on language provide a language-enriched environment that is qualitatively, as well as quantitatively, different from the language input that a child is likely to experience outside of the classroom.

The concentrated normative model aligns well with current educational policy initiatives (cf. Chapter 1). This chapter provides some background information for implementation of the CNM in preschools, and then moves into some of the particular features of the Language Acquisition Preschool (LAP) classroom. The initial section highlights current developments in early intervention and the importance of language acquisition as a developmental achievement of the preschool years. Next are sections that describe children's language acquisition and the condition of specific language impairment. These are followed by a description of the children enrolled in LAP. The chapter concludes with the principles that guide the implementation of the CNM in the LAP classroom.

ENHANCING LANGUAGE ACQUISITION

The best source of information about naturalistic interactive techniques for the enhancement of language acquisition is the literature describing the ways in which caregivers speak to their children. There is a bit of a paradox here, in that such techniques may not be *necessary* for activating the language acquisition process for most children. At least the current conclusion is that, for most children, there is no "correct" or "necessary" way for adults to adjust their speech to them, beyond the requirement of talking with them in the course of everyday events. At the same time, it is also the case that certain features of language input can enhance language acquisition. Although such ways of adjusting talk to children are usually not *necessary*, they can *facilitate* the rate of language acquisition. These features of language input, then, can serve as the basis for the development of specific interactive techniques for language instruction.

In the development of the LFC, we were guided by reports of features of parental input that are thought to promote children's language development. Among them are the following:

- Child-centered talk (i.e., talk about what the child is doing)
- Semantically contingent talk (i.e., talk that repeats content in the child's utterances)
- Talk embedded in familiar interactive routines or scripts, such as book reading (Butler, 1984; Lieven, 1984)

We enlarged upon these techniques considerably and developed new ones (e.g., focused contrasts) in order to highlight specific linguistic distinctions. These techniques are described in detail in Chapter 4.

We were further struck by the similarity in what was reported as effective for typically developing children and what was advocated for children learning English as a second language (cf. Tabors, 1987). Accounts of second language learning emphasized that language proficiency is best developed in supportive contexts that supply cues necessary for comprehension. Thus, optimal talk to children who are learning English is that which is understandable, interesting, and/or relevant, and provided in sufficient quantity. A "here and now" orientation is helpful, as is the use of contextual information. Other helpful techniques are adults' modification of interactions by means of devices such as self- and other-repetition, confirmation and comprehension checks, and clarification requests. All of these techniques have been advocated as good practice for intervention with children who have language impairments.

There was reason, then, to expect that the development of a language-facilitating classroom setting that would be of benefit to children with SLI would benefit children learning English as a second language as well, and vice versa. Furthermore, our intuitions were that these youngsters could bring complementary characteristics to the classroom. The second-language competence of the children learning English as a second language would help draw attention to the arbitrary conventions of language, which would help children with SLI in their ability to focus on language as a system of communication. Conversely, the children with SLI would have better English skills than the non–English-speaking children, although less complex than typically developing children, so the children with SLI could serve as useful language models. Furthermore, the simplified input appropriate for each of these groups and concern about comprehension processes would be suitable for both groups.

Thus, our consideration of the children to be enrolled in the classroom was guided by our consideration of the normative language acquisition literature, and our development of the concentrated normative model of language intervention. This led to the mix of children in the classroom described in Chapter 1.

LANGUAGE INTERVENTION

The language-focused curriculum (LFC) and the associated CNM led to a departure from conventional language intervention techniques. Conventional approaches emphasize carefully constructed language drills and speech practice sessions conducted by an adult with an individual child (or sometimes with a small group of children with SLI). In response to the emergence of a focus on pragmatics in the normative literature appearing in the 1970s and 1980s, there has been heightened recognition of the need to incorporate social uses of language in clinical settings, but this is often done in individual therapy sessions, in which an adult and child "pretend" to enact play sessions or conversations.

The effectiveness of the traditional methods, particularly with young children, receives a mixed report (cf. Fey, 1986; Leonard, 1981). On the one hand, it is possible to establish new skills in the therapy settings. Children learn how to label things, how to put plural affixes on nouns or tense markers on verbs, or how to pronounce selected words. On the other hand, often there is very little carryover of the newly trained skills to the actual conversations the child has outside the therapy room, with peers or adults of the "real world" (Hart & Rogers-Warren, 1978). The challenge, then, is to develop instructional methods that are meaningful for a child and are likely to be of immediate use in real-world conversational settings.

Our approach was to bring the setting to the child, instead of asking a child to imagine relevant contexts. Intrinsic to the setting are other children, who serve as playmates, conversational partners, models for language use, and sources of feedback on the effectiveness of communication.

Such inspiration is apparent in other models now available. For example, there is exploration of a whole language approach to preschool intervention (cf. Norris & Hoffman, 1990, 1993) and there are curricular materials that emphasize a social/cognitive approach in the classroom setting (cf. Bricker, 1993, for younger children; Weitzman, 1992, for preschool-age children). What is special about the LFC as formulated here is the adherence to the CNM, with an emphasis on the LRE requirements of IDEA, and the need to specify individualized education programs (IEPs) for each child. Also, what is noteworthy here is that the LFC was implemented and evaluated in a real classroom setting. Thus, in this volume the description of the LFC is accompanied by formal evaluation of the short- and long-term effectiveness of the LFC, documentation of the social interactions of children in the classroom, and description of replications of the LFC in settings beyond the LAP classroom.

To summarize, there are multiple advantages of a classroom-based language intervention program (see Table 2): 1) the program can be carried out in a way that is congruent with a concentrated normative approach; 2) such an approach is consistent with an LRE service model; 3) this approach is naturally attuned to a child's interests and social motivations for the use of language; 4) such programming allows for a meaningful, high-focused language curriculum, with naturalistic opportunities for redundancy, repetition, and practice; 5) it affords an opportunity for rich social interactions and the use of language in socially useful ways; and 6) this approach eliminates the need for an extra level of instruction to establish generalization. Language teaching contexts are embedded in real-world interactions.

The Language Acquisition Preschool serves as one possible instantiation of an LFC. There will surely be others to follow, which is a welcome state of affairs. What is needed are intervention settings suitable for particular children, in particular communities, with particular configurations of staff talents and resources. Variations in implementation are likely. A few such examples are provided in Chapter 11.

OPERATIONAL GUIDELINES FOR THE CONCENTRATED NORMATIVE MODEL

Implementation of the CNM was guided by a set of principles drawn from the normative language acquisition literature, from what is known about preschool children with speech and language impairments and effective language therapy, and from what is understood about recommended practices for early childhood intervention. These principles are presented here as a way of highlighting some of the main themes that will be elaborated upon in the chapters that follow. These principles can be summarized as follows (cf. Table 3).

Language Intervention Is Best Provided in a Meaningful Social Context

The most effective way to provide language intervention is by finding a meaningful social context. By "meaningful social context" we mean that the children use their language skills to interact with children and adults in a naturalistic manner, where the conversational intent and communicative needs and discourse outcomes are real. The children use their verbal skills to understand what the teachers say, to request assistance or make comments, to squabble over toys, and to role play in the dramatic play center. This means that when they successfully negotiate posses-

Table 2.   Advantages of a classroom-based language intervention program, utilizing a language-focused curriculum

1.   Can be carried out in a way that is congruent with the concentrated normative model (CNM)
2.   Is consistent with a least restrictive environment (LRE) for intervention
3.   Is naturally attuned to a child's interests and social motivations for the use of language
4.   Allows for a meaningful, language-focused curriculum with naturalistic opportunities for redundancy, repetition, and practice
5.   Affords opportunities for rich social interactions and socially useful language
6.   Eliminates the need for an extra level of training to establish generalization into spontaneous language use

Table 3.   Operational guidelines for the concentrated normative model

1. Language intervention is best provided in a meaningful social context.
2. Language facilitation occurs throughout the entire curriculum.
3. The language curriculum is rooted in content themes.
4. Language intervention begins with the child.
5. Verbal interaction is encouraged.
6. Passive language learning and overt responses are encouraged.
7. Children's utterances are accorded functional value.
8. Valuable teaching occasions can arise in child-to-child interactions.
9. Parents are valuable partners in language intervention programming.
10. Routine parent evaluations are an integral part of the program.

sion of a favorite toy, they have achieved a real payoff as a consequence of effective use of speech and language. Conversely, if their speech and language impairments limit their social effectiveness, they develop alternative strategies, as they are moving toward greater competencies. There is no need to simulate conversational interactions or to assume some sort of a difficulty gradient. The children are able to guide their own participation in meaningful social situations.

Language Facilitation Occurs Throughout the Entire Curriculum

There is no special "language time" in a classroom following the CNM. The opportunities to learn how to communicate are not artificially carved into 30-minute blocks. Instead, opportunities to model appropriate language forms, and to encourage youngsters to use new words or linguistic structures or sounds, are woven into the flow of ongoing events. These opportunities involve the use of specialized language interaction techniques, as reported in Chapter 4.

The Language Curriculum Is Rooted in Content Themes

The use of content themes is a standard way to organize an early education curriculum that lends itself nicely to a language-focused program. The designation of a theme allows for a common topic of reference, use of key vocabulary items, and the opportunity to provide planned redundancy in content over a few days' time. Children thrive in a certain amount of familiarity of routines and planned activities. When they know what the theme is, they can communicate about that topic, can plan for the next day's activities, and can develop more abstract cognitive representations of the given content area. Language, then, is embedded in the concepts and notions relevant to a particular theme, where meanings and words can become aligned.

Language Intervention Begins with the Child

A child's attempt to communicate starts with something of interest to the child, in a context with functional value for that child, as a means to communicate an idea, need, or want, or to respond to a conversational partner, to keep alive the linkages of interpersonal connectedness that can be achieved by successful communication. The best language intervention occurs when the adult interactions can be woven seamlessly into the child's discourse in a way that draws attention to targeted linguistic forms, without becoming obtrusive, making the child self-conscious, or demeaning the child's self-esteem.

These are the same features of successful interaction with adults. So, perhaps this principle can be rephrased as "language intervention begins with a person." The difference is that children's agendas are sufficiently different from adults', so that it often requires a bit of retraining for adults to learn to think again along the same lines as children.

The implementation of such a principle also follows some standard adult conventions for interaction. If the child determines the topic of conversation, it is a good sign that the topic is of interest. The adult, then, can try to follow up on the child's topics. Just as overt correction in public places is demeaning to an adult, children also seem to be put off by correction of their attempts to communicate when they are in the midst of an interaction. Another way in which there is similarity between children and adults is that children will be more likely to converse with adults who are good listeners, who wait until it is their turn to speak (thereby honoring the rules of a good conversation), and who regard a child's attempt to communicate as meaningful and socially valid.

Such an approach assumes that children can construct new pieces of their linguistic system if they are allowed the opportunities, and if there are appropriate redundancies and ways of highlighting the parts of the grammar, sound system, or vocabulary that are just within reach. This seems to be the case for children with SLI, children learning English as a second language, and typically developing children.

Verbal Interaction Is Encouraged

The most fundamental technique for developing language skills is to increase the opportunities for use. As children practice their newly developing skills, they have occasion to improve their accuracy and to reap the intrinsic benefits of successful conversational interactions. They can tell the teacher what happened at home last night, successfully negotiate for a toy or a turn at a game, or take a turn playing the role of the cashier at the fast food restaurant. Achieving this objective is clearly related to the principle that language intervention begins with the child. It is hard to imagine a successful language intervention preschool in which the children are sitting quietly while the teacher does all the talking.

Passive Language Learning and Overt Responses Are Encouraged

Complementary to the principle of encouraging verbal interaction is that sometimes children, especially children with SLI and children learning English as a second language, seem to need opportunities just to observe, to watch and listen as conversations flow around them. If there is sufficient redundancy and routine in settings to allow them to infer meanings and thereby align meanings with linguistic forms, they can begin to build their language comprehension in this way. Just as adult second language learners can benefit from observational opportunities, a time to "soak up" language, so can youngsters.

In adults' eagerness to teach children, they often behave as if the way to ensure learning is to ensure an immediate response. In the most inappropriate forms, this can begin to look like the old-fashioned "I say–you say" drills. Anyone who has experienced these knows that they have limited value as a way to teach language. Such relentless insistence on immediate responses is not only tiring to the learner, but it also lacks conversational validity. It violates the assumption of meaningful interaction and of valid conversational intent. Because almost all children do follow the impulse of their intentions to communicate, they will do so when they are ready and appropriate occasions are presented.

Children's Utterances Are Accorded Functional Value

If children's utterances are treated as meaningful attempts to communicate, they are more likely to achieve that status. Although this principle is embedded in the previous comments, it merits explicit mention. This principle is especially important with regard to children who have SLI or who are learning English as a second language. The initial utterances of these children in a classroom setting may have a tentative quality or limited intelligibility. Thus, it is especially important that adults recognize these early attempts and accord them a social value by responding to their content rather than their form.

Valuable Teaching Occasions Can Arise in Child-to-Child Interactions

Children's interactions with each other are meaningful contexts for emerging communication skills. It is one thing for a teacher to regard a youngster's comments as having communicative value. It is something of a much higher value when a child can initiate a conversation with a peer and have a successful exchange of comments, or, better yet, a successful negotiation about a play activity.

The development of peer interaction skills requires practice, opportunities to try them out. At the same time, preschool children have a deserved reputation for being blunt about their preferences for peer partners, and in the real world give-and-take of play interactions they can ignore or reject each other's advances. A certain amount of this rejection seems to be the stuff of childhood play interactions, and children seem to accept it readily.

However, if children with SLI and children learning English as a second language become overly dependent on teachers, they will lose out on opportunities to try out their skills. Therefore, it is important that teachers recognize occasions when peer interactions can be encouraged, albeit in a naturalistic manner.

This principle can be illustrated by comparison to a basketball team. In order to play on a basketball team, an individual must learn how and when to pass the ball to other members of the team. This learning takes place in the context of interactions among the team members. It is not enough to practice one-on-one with the coach, or to pass only to the coach when the team is practicing. In the course of learning how to pass in the middle of a game, sometimes the ball will be dropped or the pass will be stolen, but it is nevertheless crucial for a novice player to have experience in attempting to pass. In the same way, for children to learn how to carry out interactions with their peers, they must have the opportunities to practice the techniques with the other members of their social team.

Parents Are Valuable Partners in Language Intervention Programming

The essential contributions of families and home settings have been recognized in federal legislative guidelines for special education services. IDEA stipulates that services for infants and toddlers (up to 3 years of age) must include the development of individualized family service plans (IFSPs). The IFSP is to be determined in collaboration with family representatives. Thus, family members are recognized as integral parts of the service delivery and implementation system.

In a similar fashion, parents are included in programming for school-age children with disabling conditions. (School-age is defined as 3–21 years of age.) In LAP, as in other service settings, parents are represented in the planning of the required individualized education program (IEP) that guides the development of program goals and activities for each child.

The point to be made here is that, for maximal effectiveness, parental participation should permeate all aspects of intervention planning.

In short, the better informed the parents are and the more opportunities for them to provide feedback about their child, the more likely that there will be a synchrony between a child's home environment and that of the classroom. The goal is to make it as easy as possible for a child to move from the verbal interactive contexts of the classroom to that of the home and back. Redundancy and repetition of key concepts, linguistic frames, targeted word meanings, and key sounds or special words are desirable ways to maximize the establishment of internalized rules and representations that are likely to generalize across settings. This can only be achieved by close cooperation between the home and the school.

Routine Parent Evaluations Are an Integral Part of the Program

Parents do the evaluating in a CNM-based program; they are not the recipients of evaluation. There are multiple ways in which parental feedback can be sought, and LAP incorporates some of these possibilities. This form of consumer satisfaction information allows for a validity check on the curriculum, which is essential to programming based on the principles of meaningfulness, relevance to immediate communication needs, and children's needs.

FORMULATION OF INTERVENTION GOALS

Although the LFC and related CNM have what may be characterized as a holistic approach to language intervention, neither denies the value of identifying individual components of communicative competence that can be targeted as intervention goals for an individual child. Just as linguists have found it useful to partition language into components, so interventionists can focus on certain aspects of a child's communicative system in order to identify targeted goals for intervention. This is in contrast to certain interpretations of a whole language approach that argue for a nondivisible approach to language (cf. Norris & Hoffman, 1993). The CNM assumes that, with the goal of enhanced competency, certain language skills can be identified, targeted for special emphasis, and then monitored for change. It is also quite likely that change in targeted components of language also brings change in other aspects. Thus, there is likely to be a spreading effect, in that any partitioning of language is a somewhat artificial exercise, given that the components of language are intricately associated with each other. The value of targeted, discrete goals is that they allow for a shared sense among the interventionists as to the linguistic forms and functions to emphasize and contrast for an individual child. Such shared goals are essential for the coordination of efforts of the adults in the classroom and the collaboration with parents or other caregivers outside the classroom.

In summary, the language-focused curriculum advocated here is based on a concentrated normative model of language intervention and follows a set of operational guidelines for implementation in a language-focused curriculum. The specific techniques and curricular materials are described in Chapters 4, 5, and 6. The parent component is described in Chapter 8.

REFERENCES

Bricker, D. (1993). *Assessment, evaluation, and programming system (AEPS) for infants and children. Vol. 1: AEPS measurement for birth to three years.* Baltimore: Paul H. Brookes Publishing Co.

Butler, K.G. (Ed.). (1984). Language development and disorders in the social context. *Topics in Language Disorders, 4.*

Fey, M.E. (1986). *Language intervention with young children.* Needham Heights, MA: Allyn & Bacon.

Hart, B., & Rogers-Warren, A. (1978). A milieu approach to teaching language. In R.L. Schiefelbusch (Ed.), *Language intervention strategies* (pp. 193–235). Baltimore: University Park Press.

Individuals with Disabilities Education Act of 1990 (IDEA) PL 101-476. (October 30, 1990). Title 20, U.S.C. 1400 et seq: *U.S. Statutes at Large, 104,* 1103–1151.

Leonard, L.B. (1981). Facilitating linguistic skills in children with specific language impairment. *Applied Psycholinguistics, 2,* 89–118.

Lieven, E.U.M. (1984). Interaction style and children's language learning. *Topics in Language Disorders, 4,* 15–23.

Norris, J.A., & Hoffman, P.R. (1990). Language intervention within naturalistic environments. *Language, Speech, and Hearing Services in Schools, 21,* 72–84.

Norris, J.A., & Hoffman, P.R. (1993). *Whole language intervention for school-aged children.* San Diego: Singular Publishing Group.

Tabors, P.O. (1987). *The development of communicative competence by second language learners in a nursery school classroom: An ethnolinguistic study.* Unpublished doctoral dissertation, Harvard University, Cambridge, MA.

Weitzman, E. (1992). *Learning language and loving it.* Toronto, Ontario, Canada: Hanen Centre Publication.

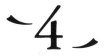

4

Language Intervention in a Preschool Classroom
Implementing a Language-Focused Curriculum

Betty H. Bunce and Ruth V. Watkins

It is Fitness Center Day in dramatic play and one child is jumping on a mini-trampoline as several children watch. A speech-language pathologist describes what is happening. "Look, Jennifer is *jumping*. She *is jumping* high." As the child jumps off to let another have a turn, the clinician remarks, "Jennifer *jumped* off. She *jumped* a long time on the trampoline." With these brief remarks, the clinician is providing focused contrasts for Jim, a child who is waiting for a turn. One of Jim's therapy goals is to increase his knowledge and use of past tense. The past tense is easily contrasted with the present in this short interchange. The clinician describes the appropriate action in a naturalistic manner with no pressure on Jim to comment.

The "fitness center" also has a stationary bike (a tricycle mounted so that only the front wheel can turn), barbells made out of giant Tinker Toys, mats, and a bench step. The "owner" has a counter with a sign-up sheet and towels. Emily waits for a turn on the stationary bike, but each time it is free another child climbs on. Finally, Emily approaches the teacher, points, and says "Mine." The teacher suggests to Emily that she ask the child on the bike for a turn. In redirecting Emily to the other child, the teacher provides the words for the child to use, "Say 'my turn, please.'" Emily approaches Jhad and repeats, "Turn, please." Jhad, having heard the exchange between the teacher and Emily as well as hearing Emily's own request, relinquishes the bike. In this way, the use of redirects by the teacher can provide the assistance that children with specific language impairment (SLI) need in order to make their newly acquired language forms useful in the everyday world of preschool.

In the quiet area, a child is standing looking at the chalkboard. This child loves to write the alphabet on his parent's computer but is more hesitant to write at school. The clinician asks if he wants to draw on the chalkboard. He responds, "otay." The teacher hands him a piece of chalk and then says, "Billy, you say 'otay,' but I say 'okay'" as she makes a T and then a K. Billy watches and tries to say the /k/ sound. With prompting to keep his tongue down and back, Billy is able to approximate the /k/ sound. Before this incident, Billy had heard the /k/ modeled (and contrasted) many times, but he had rejected attempts to get him to produce the sound. As the adult walks away, Billy keeps practicing his new sound to himself. The next day, he comes in and tells the teacher that he has a new cat, using the correct /k/ sound instead of /t/. His mother reports that he has spent the evening labeling things to find out if they begin with the /t/ or with the /k/ sound. Within 2 weeks, Billy is correctly using the /k/ sound in most contexts. Billy's knowledge of the alphabet provided the clinician a way to present the necessary focused contrast for him to understand what needed to be changed. Initial therapy for Billy had included many models of correct productions and periodic checks to see if Billy could produce /k/. These periodic probes allowed the clinician to monitor Billy's productions, while preventing opportunities for practicing incorrect productions. The probes also allowed the clinician to take advantage of a "teachable" moment when Billy was ready to make changes.

A clinician is sitting at the art table with three children who are making gingerbread men out of pieces of construction paper. The goals for Paul, one of the children, are to increase appropriate use of regular past tense and to improve initial /s/ production. The clinician models correct production of past tense by noting that the children have pasted on the eyes, glued on the buttons, or pounded the paper to make it stick. The forms are easily contrasted with the present tense (e.g., Mary pounds the paper) as the children construct their project. Paul turns to the clinician and says, "Wook, fanta ka." The clinician does not completely understand and asks, "What?" The child repeats. The clinician still does not understand but responds, "I see." Knowing that Paul often uses an /f/ for /s/, the clinician continues to ponder what the child could mean. Several of the children are putting hats on their gingerbread men. Paul again holds his up and says, "Fanta ta." This time the clinician realizes that with a red hat the gingerbread man has become Santa Claus, and she is able to respond, "What a good Santa Claus. I like Santa." She is able to continue to highlight correct production of /s/ by asking the other children to "See Paul's Santa." Two or more goals can often be addressed in the same activity, a possibility that is sometimes planned and sometimes played out as the opportunity arises.

These vignettes provide glimpses into a classroom where language intervention is embedded in the common classroom activities. The vignettes, respectively, illustrate several key strategies in classroom intervention: 1) the use of focused contrast in naturally occurring interactions, 2) intervention in different kinds of activities, and 3) the interweaving of multiple goals in one activity. The purpose of this chapter is to describe in greater detail how to implement a language-focused curriculum (LFC), which involves the use of a concentrated normative model (CNM) of language intervention. To do this, an overview of classroom intervention is first presented. Then specific facilitation techniques are defined and examples of the techniques provided. Next, the roles and responsibilities of the adults in the classroom are outlined. Some of these responsibilities include being a language facilitator, providing assessments, and monitoring child progress. Finally, the curriculum supporting the intervention is described in detail and goals for a typical child are presented.

INTERVENTION IN THE CLASSROOM

Critical features of classroom intervention include the classroom setting, the curriculum, and the interactive techniques. The structure and organization of the classroom and the theme-based curriculum provide a *context* conducive to language intervention. The adults' *verbal interactions* with the children in this context provide the actual intervention. As emphasized in Chapter 1, the context and verbal interactions are two complementary and inseparable components of the concentrated normative model of language intervention in the classroom setting.

Developing appropriate classroom-based intervention depends on careful consideration of children's social and cognitive needs and abilities, along with recognition of the considerable variation in individual children's linguistic aptitude. An operating assumption is that linguistic competency can be selectively limited so that children who share many social and cognitive interests and aptitudes can have extreme differences in language competencies. The overarching goal of intervention is to bring *all* children to age-appropriate language competencies. This intervention philosophy is in keeping with the idea that children are active learners who construct their interpretation of the world of objects (cf. Piaget, 1974), and the social interactions of people (cf. Vygotsky, 1978). Such a social/cognitive constructionist view is evident in early childhood curricular materials (e.g., the High Scope model described by Hohmann, Banet, and Weikart, 1979). What is provided here, in addition, is an emphasis on language and the ways in which language and communication permeate a child's preschool experiences. In a general way, the approach is similar to whole language approaches, in that language use is embedded in the context of everyday classroom events. Yet, in the specific ways in which the curriculum is implemented, there is a focus on particular aspects of linguistic forms and uses. As the opening vignettes indicate, the intent is to draw the child's attention to targeted linguistic forms and the use of those forms to carry out conversations and discourse.

Also recognized in this approach is an awareness of the ways in which social and language abilities influence each other. As described in Chapter 7, children with limited language ability are vulnerable for the development of appropriate peer relationships (Gertner, 1993; Rice, Sell, & Hadley, 1990). It may be difficult for them to negotiate for a favorite toy or for turns. Children with competent verbal skills can attempt to get a desired object by saying, "I'll give you this truck if you let me have that car." Children with limited language, however, may have to resort to simpler means, such as saying "mine" or grabbing the car. The former strategy is more likely to be effective than the latter. It also may be difficult for children with language impairments to provide verbal explanations or excuses in order to defend themselves. This is problematic because a child may, at times, be accused of actions not intended or of actions not performed. Not being able to explain one's actions can be particularly harmful to peer relationships. Resorting to grabbing a pencil, instead of saying, "I need the pencil for just a minute" may cause the child with a language impairment to be less liked or actively avoided by peers.

Finally, the language-focused curriculum model is part of a trend to move language intervention from exclusively one-to-one adult-directed settings into more interactive contexts (Constable, 1987; Duchan, 1986; Dudley-Marling & Searle, 1988; Fey, 1986; Johnston, 1985; Miller, 1989; N.W. Nelson, 1989; Norris & Hoffman, 1990; Rice, 1986). The program described in this volume, the Language Acquisition Preschool (LAP), serves as a field-tested example of how this type of intervention programming can be achieved. In this program the natural communicative interactions are the building blocks for the majority of the language intervention events and activities.

GENERAL LANGUAGE FACILITATION STRATEGIES: DESCRIPTION AND RATIONALE

The guiding principles of LAP are delineated in Table 1. The following general language facilitation strategies outline the implementation of these guidelines.

1. *Provide opportunities for language use and interaction,* which addresses the first nine guidelines. The LFC is designed to provide different kinds of interesting activities that will entice the children to participate. Some examples include dramatic play activities, art activities, block or puzzle play, outdoor playtime, storytime, music time, and so forth. Also, parents are sometimes invited to participate in an activity with the children. The different activities require different levels of communicative competence, but all children can participate. Communication is important and errors in form are expected. Sometimes the production errors indicate progress and are evidence of rule learning. Children with specific language impairment have many opportunities to hear language produced, to interact with others verbally and nonverbally, and to

Table 1. Operational guidelines for the concentrated normative model

  1. Language intervention is best provided in a meaningful social context.
  2. Language facilitation occurs throughout the entire curriculum.
  3. The language curriculum is rooted in content themes.
  4. Language intervention begins with the child.
  5. Verbal interaction is encouraged.
  6. Passive language learning and overt responses are encouraged.
  7. Children's utterances are accorded functional value.
  8. Valuable teaching occasions can arise in child-to-child interactions.
  9. Parents are valuable partners in language intervention programming.
  10. Routine parent evaluations are an integral part of the program.

observe interactions. The children are encouraged to participate but are not required to do so.

2. *Include familiar classroom routines to support language learning*, which addresses Guidelines 1, 2, 4, 5, and 7. The use of familiar classroom routines helps the children acquire knowledge of what is expected of them and what words or phrases will give them access to various interactions. For example, the children quickly learn what is expected when their name card is held up during roll call, what their duties are when they are helper-for-the-day, and what questions to ask during sharing or snacktime.

3. *Use dramatic play activities to build world knowledge and accompanying language*, which addresses Guidelines 1, 3, 4, 5, 6, 7, and 8. Dramatic play activities are introduced by describing and role playing various aspects of the activity. Although a variety of possible verbal scripts are modeled to emphasize new vocabulary, there are no memorized scripts. Possible uses for different props are also demonstrated. Children are then encouraged to role play the activity, interacting with each other and negotiating for favorite roles and/or props.

4. *Encourage social interaction among children*, which addresses Guidelines 1, 5, 7, and 8. Many activities are not adult directed in order to provide the children with the space and freedom needed to interact with each other. Adults often redirect a child's request to other children, providing a verbal model if necessary. Social interaction provides linguistic input that is comprehensible to the learner. By observing and interacting with the other children, children with specific language impairment can figure out the meaning of words, sentences, and concepts and can model their own productions after those of others.

5. *Provide ongoing information to parents regarding daily activities and intervention needs*, which addresses Guidelines 1, 5, 8, 9, and 10. A weekly newsletter is given to the parents at the beginning of each week to inform them of upcoming activities. Parents can then query their children about specific, rather than general, school happenings; that is, parents can ask their children about whether they enjoyed playing rodeo, doctor, or airplane pilot, rather than asking them, "What did you do in school today?" which too often elicits, "Nothing" as a response. Generalization of new forms and structures from school to home is aided by talking about school activities. Communication regarding a child's needs and progress is maintained by means of face-to-face conferences and notes to and from parents and the speech-language pathologist or teachers.

Techniques of Linguistic Input

Although a variety of intervention techniques that can be used in the classroom have already been illustrated, the nature of focused linguistic input warrants further elaboration. Some of these intervention techniques are derived from research in caregiver–child interactions and the influence of certain adult language characteristics on children's linguistic development (e.g., Hoff-Ginsberg, 1986; Hoff-Ginsberg & Shatz, 1982; Snow, 1984). Several features of caregiver language have consistently been shown to influence child language acquisition positively. One such feature is semantic contingency; mothers who use a high number of semantically related responses to their children's utterances tend to raise children who develop linguistic skills at a faster rate than children whose mothers do not reply in a semantically contingent manner (Cross, 1984; Lieven, 1984; Nelson, Denninger, Bonvillian, Kaplan, & Baker, 1984). This technique may be particularly effective for enhancing a child's vocabulary development. Another positive feature of maternal input is acknowledgment of child utterances. Mothers who are positively responsive to their children's linguistic attempts tend to have children with accelerated language development (Cross, 1984; Snow, Midkiff-Borunda, Small, & Proctor, 1984). Positive responses surely contribute to a child's motivation to talk and participate in verbal interactions. Finally, mothers who talk more tend to have children who talk more (Cross, 1984; Hoff-Ginsberg, 1991). Conversely, some ways of interacting with children are associated with slower rates of language acquisition. Heavy use of commands and direct questions may not facilitate linguistic development (Lieven, 1984).

The extent to which techniques that have a positive influence on language development are *necessary* for language acquisition for typically developing children is disputable, at best. As noted in Chapter 3, a causal direction has not been clearly established. It is also important to note that most aspects of verbal interaction are also highly culture-specific. So, for example, encouraging mothers to be less directive with their children may be highly inappropriate in some groups. What are important for the purposes of intervention are the ways to maximize environmental support for language acquisition. There is little doubt that adult acknowledgment of child utterances, positive encouragement, provision of semantically contingent responses, and frequent talking with children can each, and collectively, be regarded as potentially helpful techniques.

In order to maximize their effectiveness, these caregiver interactive techniques have been extended and fine-tuned in the classroom setting, in ways intended to target key linguistic structures (see Table 2). Stimulation strategies involving focused contrasts, modeling, recasting, and redirects (see below) provide ways for the adult to make semantically contingent comments and be responsive to the child's communication attempts. In addition, individual interactions with children who have language impairments are sometimes "engineered," or steered toward a

Table 2. Techniques of linguistic input in the classroom

1. Provide many opportunities for language use.
2. Use focused contrasts.
3. Model appropriate sounds, structures, and functions.
4. Provide event casts (ongoing descriptions of actions).
5. Use open questions.
6. Expand child's utterances.
7. Recast child's utterances.
8. Provide redirects and prompted initiations.
9. Use scripted play activities.

particular goal. These interactions are contrived in a manner likely to involve certain sounds, words, and language features. More frequently, however, interactions are child directed, and the adult use of language-promoting strategies occurs in response to child activities and interests. Similar intervention strategies can be applied in planned and incidental language-learning occasions.

Providing Opportunities for Language Use

A basic strategy for enhancing linguistic skills in the classroom is to provide opportunities for language use and interaction. A primary goal of the LAP classroom is to provide rich and interesting activities that stimulate language, with materials and events worth talking about, to receptive conversational partners, both peer and adult. Furthermore, teachers must arrange the conversational environment in a manner that provides opportunities for language use. A language-facilitating preschool classroom requires teachers and aides who are comfortable being quiet; if adults in the classroom constantly fill up the language "space," there is little incentive or opportunity for children to participate in verbal interchange. Quiet moments in a classroom are not negative. On the contrary, they provide time for reflection and they encourage child initiations.

By arranging materials and personnel in a manner such that all of the children's needs are not automatically met, the environment can provide language opportunities. This may mean having markers available at the art table without any paper or failing to put cups out in advance for snacktime. In brief, the idea is to provide opportunities for children to learn and practice requesting materials or assistance when they need it (a technique first described in detail in the milieu approach [Hart & Rogers-Warren, 1978]). In addition, rearranging minor elements in the daily routine can also act as a language-stimulating event. If calendar time is part of the daily circle routine, occasionally leaving it off the agenda can produce comments and questions such as "What day is today?" and "Is it Tuesday?" This type of question provides child-initiated opportunities for discussions that do not typically occur if the same schedule is maintained consistently.

Providing language opportunities through a rich and stimulating environment and allowing language use are central to all other strategies for linguistic enhancement. However, provision of a stimulating environment is not enough. Other strategies are needed in order to focus children's attention on linguistic forms and uses, per se. These strategies or techniques include focused contrasts, modeling, event casting, open questions, expansions, recasts, redirects and prompted initiations, and scripted play.

Focused Contrasts

Focused contrasts highlight contrastive differences in speech sounds, lexical items, and/or syntactic structures. This technique works at two levels. The first level is one of corrective feedback in which negative evidence is provided to the child (e.g., /t/ versus /k/ example in the opening vignettes). Focused contrasts make explicit the error versus the correct form in a manner that allows the child to recognize the differences. The procedure can be a brief focusing of attention on the crucial features in an interaction or it can involve several interchanges. The second level involves modeled contrasts in adult talk. These contrasts are embedded in the ongoing descriptions. For example, if the plural marker /s/ is the target, both the singular form and the plural form would be used. For example, a child might be playing with cars. The clinician could request one car, and then ask for two other cars. Gestures indicating what was desired would accompany the verbal requests. During play, the adult would continue to contrast the forms. The focused contrasts highlight for the child features that are relevant or crucial to the distinction to be made. To some extent, other strategies such as modeling, event casting, expansions, recasts, and scripted play are ways to provide focused contrasts to help the child attend to the crucial features of the target linguistic form. These two levels, corrective feedback and modeled contrasts, may be especially well suited to advancing the language skills of children with speech and language impairments and children learning English as their second language.

Modeling

One frequently used language facilitation strategy is modeling, or giving the child a model of the target sounds, words, or forms. These models often contain structures that the child does not yet produce. The child is offered the opportunity to repeat or respond to the model but is not required to do so. Most of the time the model is incorporated in a naturally occurring interaction, although extra emphasis or stress may be placed on a particular feature to highlight it. The models usually take the form of a statement or comment.

Event Casting

Event casts provide an ongoing description of an activity and are similar to the voice-over descriptions of athletic events provided by sports broadcasters. Teachers and other adults frequently use event casts (cf. Heath, 1986) as a means of language enrichment. Event casts can be used by adults during relatively teacher-directed times of the day; for example, in a group pudding-making activity, the teacher might narrate the event with "I'm opening the package, and now I'm pouring the mix into the bowl. Now, it's time for the milk. I'll put the milk in. What should I do now? Okay, stir it. I'll get out all the lumps." Furthermore, an adult can use event casts during play with children who are quiet, hesitant, or shy in the classroom setting. Describing a child's play actions or one's own activities can promote the child's language production.

Event casts serve two facilitative functions. First, event casts provide a sort of language "bath," insofar as they can accompany and describe ongoing activities. This language bath allows children to hear language pertinent to ongoing events. Second, event casts can be used to encourage children to use oral problem-solving strategies by modeling their use. As the classroom teacher solves a bridge-building problem, she can narrate her activities, "I wonder if this block will fit. No, it's too big.

Oh, maybe if I turn it around. Yes, now it fits." This oral problem-solving model can assist children in learning to use such a strategy in working through their own daily challenges.

A cautionary note should be added here regarding the use of event casts. Although event casts are useful in describing ongoing activities, constant or highly frequent use of this intervention strategy would result in an adult-dominated classroom language environment. Thus, event casts are best used sparingly, during moments in the classroom day when descriptions of events or activities are desired. The descriptions can provide a means for children to connect events and language and may be particularly helpful in modeling problem-solving strategies.

Open Questions

Open questions are questions that have a variety of possible answers. Examples of open questions include "What do you think will happen next?", "Why do think that happened?", and "What do you think we should do next?" Open questions contrast with "test," or closed, questions. Test questions usually demand a specific answer often consisting of one- or two-word utterances. Examples of test questions include "What color is this?" and "What is this?" Test questions involve pressure to respond and to respond "correctly." Test questions are appropriate for testing the child's knowledge, but are not necessarily a good way to facilitate language acquisition. Because open questions are real questions in which the adult does not necessarily know the answer, there is less pressure to provide a specific response. If a child draws a picture and then shows it to the adult, more language may be generated by the child if the adult says, "Can you tell me about your picture?" than if the adult says, "What's that?"

Expansions

Expansions occur when the adult repeats a child's utterance, filling in the missing features. For example, if a child omitted a verb ending, as in the phrase "He ride bus," the adult could respond by saying "Yes, he rides the bus." Expansions serve two purposes. First, the adult affirms that the child has communicated effectively; and second, the adult provides a model for achieving more adult-like forms.

Recasts

A recast is a conversational adjustment through which basic semantic information is retained while syntactic structure is altered (Baker & Nelson, 1984). Children's utterances can be recasted by maintaining meaning but changing the grammatical form. For example, the utterance "He walks home now" could be recast as, "You're right. He is walking home." Thus, a recast: 1) is temporally adjacent to the child's original utterance, 2) maintains the basic meaning of the child's utterance, and 3) changes one or more elements of the original utterance. Recasts are believed to promote linguistic development because they maintain the child's original ideas or meaning and present them in grammatically altered sentences. Thus, the child's attention may be drawn to the new forms or words expressed. Recasts show alternative ways to form sentences without disrupting communication. Recasting is a natural response that does not appear artificial or contrived, and does not disrupt conversational interactions with young children. Furthermore, recasting can be both tailored to a specific child's goals or provided in a more general manner to promote linguistic abilities.

A second way recasts can be incorporated into the language of the classroom occurs when teachers and classroom personnel recast their own utterances. This technique is particularly useful in teacher-directed moments of the classroom day. The teacher simply provides pairs of original and recast sentences in his or her language (e.g., "Today is Tuesday. It's Tuesday." or "Mike's drinking his juice. He's drinking apple juice."). These sentence pairs can aid children in recognizing relations between varied syntactic forms expressing the same meanings and/or can highlight new words and their meanings. In addition, teachers can occasionally incorporate this technique into reading or talking about the text of stories (e.g., "The monster is catching the boys. He's catching them.").

Redirects and Prompted Initiations

Two intervention techniques used in the LFC to encourage children's interactions with each other are redirects and prompted initiations. A redirect occurs when the child approaches an adult and makes a request that could be made to another child. For example, children waiting for a turn on a swing might approach an adult and say "My turn on the swing." In this situation, the adult would typically redirect the child's initiation by suggesting that the child talk with the individual on the swing. In some cases, additional assistance could be provided in the form of a model, such as "Tell Jill, 'it's my turn.'" An alternative situation is that involving a prompted initiation in which the child does not make the initial request to the adult. Instead, the adult initially suggests or prompts the child to approach another child in order to play or request an item. These redirecting and prompting techniques can assist children with language-impairments to learn to initiate interactions and effect change directly instead of relying on an adult as the mediator. In this way, interactions among children are promoted.

Scripted Play

Scripted play is a valuable intervention procedure because it provides opportunities for verbal communication within a meaningful context. A script (Constable, 1986; Nelson, 1981, 1986) is a representation of an event, an ordered sequence of actions organized around a goal, and includes actors, actions, and props. For example, most people have a script for eating at a restaurant, including the sequence of events of ordering, eating, and paying, and involving customers, waiters or waitresses, and a cashier. Scripts do allow variations, but generally center around the same goal. There are both similarities and differences in eating at a fast food restaurant and in having dinner at an expensive restaurant.

The notion of scripts as event representations is used throughout the classroom day in LAP. Familiar daily routines, such as arrival time, circle time, and snacktime, develop into scripted event representations for young children. This familiarity acts as a basis upon which language experiences can be built. Children know that they will eat during snacktime; this stimulates discussion of what the daily snack is, who brought it, how it was prepared, and other possible variations on the general snack theme.

In addition to a general use of scripts as structure for the daily LAP routine, scripts are inherent to the LAP curriculum center time. More specifically, each day in LAP, a particular dramatic play activity is available for children to select. Dramatic play activities involve using scripts for such things as everyday events (e.g., grocery shopping, gardening, cooking, cleaning), special events (e.g., vacation, camping, fishing), and occupations (e.g., mechanic, veterinarian, electrician). This list provides only a small sample of possible dramatic play activities (cf. the second volume in this series, *Building a Language-Focused Curriculum for the Preschool Classroom, Volume II: A Planning Guide* [Bunce, 1995]).

Enhancement of World Knowledge and Language   Scripted dramatic play activities are designed to enhance the children's world knowledge and the language that accompanies it. Typically, preschool children require some background, introduction, and priming for the dramatic play script of the day. This is generally provided by a discussion or demonstration prior to the actual activity—roles are introduced, the use of props is demonstrated, and the basic goal(s) are discussed. Children will frequently contribute their existing knowledge of the script during such discussion. The comments "Our cat was sick" and "He got a shot" were heard during the introduction to a visit to the veterinarian play script. After even an initial introduction to a new script, children begin to build a skeletal event representation for a particular activity and carry out a dramatic play script with limited adult direction and/or intervention.

Stimulation of Language Exchanges   From the perspective of language intervention, scripted dramatic play activities serve a variety of functions. First, and perhaps foremost, they stimulate language exchanges, particularly exchanges among children. As children assume roles in dramatic play interactions—as customers or cashiers, veterinarians or pet owners—they practice verbal negotiation skills as they exchange essential props. One of the children with typically developing language skills might request the cash register with utterances like "My turn for the register" or "Can I have a turn now, please?" Children with language impairments may begin by making no verbal requests at all, then advance to primitive requests such as "Gimme that," and ultimately arrive at more sophisticated polite forms like "Can I use that, please?" Hearing the verbal negotiations of typically developing children and practicing with the normal models provides an optimal learning ground for children with language impairments. An occasional adult model or recast is typically all that is needed to set the wheels of dramatic play negotiations in motion.

Facilitation of Social Interactive Skills   In a more general sense, dramatic play activities are central to the facilitation of social interactive skills. Of all times during the LAP day, the dramatic play activity is built on interaction and is difficult, if not impossible, to carry out without conversational exchange. By nature, dramatic play activities encourage children to initiate conversations with peers and adults and to respond to peer and adult initiations. The familiar, repetitive structure of dramatic play activity scripts enhances the likelihood of interactive success for children with language impairments. After hearing a teacher or peer act as waiter, saying repeatedly "Do you want more coffee?", the child with a language impairment can take the waiter role and initiate with "More coffee?" In this way, the roles and structure of dramatic play scripts assist the social interactive skills of children with language impairments.

Scripted dramatic play activities constitute a key language intervention strategy used in the concentrated normative model of classroom intervention. It is here that opportunities for verbal communication about both familiar and unfamiliar objects and events take place. It is here that a child can practice social interactive skills, particularly child–child interactions. These activities capitalize on the interactions of children with special needs with their typically developing peers. Also, it is here that the child can practice language form as well as function and use. There are many opportunities for the adult to provide focused linguistic input about events and objects of interest to the child during scripted play activities.

In summary, strategies for facilitating language learning within the classroom setting hinge on providing an environment where many opportunities for natural language use and interaction occur. There must be opportunities for both child–child and adult–child talk. There must be a balance between activities that provide new information and concepts requiring new responses and those that are routine events supporting and extending old knowledge. Finally, specific language features can be facilitated within naturally occurring conversations by means of the adults' use of focused contrasts, modeling, event casting, open questions, expansions, recasts, and redirects and prompted initiations.

ROLE OF THE TEACHER(S)

The LFC model has been implemented in a way that requires at least two adults to be in the classroom at all times. More adults may be needed depending on the number of children enrolled. These adults could be speech-language pathologists (SLPs), early childhood educators, special education teachers, or aides. In LAP, the lead teacher is a speech-language pathologist with early childhood training and the assistant teacher is an early childhood educator. If the teacher is not a speech-language pathologist, then a speech-language pathologist will be needed to do assessments, participate in individualized education programs (IEPs), and consult or collaborate with the teachers regarding the implementation of the program. We have found that a combination of speech-language pathologists and early childhood educators works well.

Facilitation of Language Acquisition

The role of the teacher(s) and/or SLP(s) in the classroom is crucial to the implementation of the concentrated normative model. First, the teacher or SLP has the role of a facilitator of learning, rather than one who directs learning by telling others (i.e., the children) what to do. Second, appropriate knowledge and techniques to provide the necessary facilitation are required. A facilitator provides assistance or support at the level needed by the learner in order to achieve knowledge or understanding. A facilitator recognizes that the learner must construct his or her own knowledge and helps make that constructive process possible. The emphasis, then, is placed on active learning. Thus, in this view, the adults in the classroom teach language by providing opportunities and models, directing attention to specific linguistic contrasts, helping set goals, and giving encouragement and feedback.

Tharp and Gallimore (1988) describe teaching as assisted performance and discuss this notion within a Vygotskian framework of mediated learning. In considering a child's ability to perform a task, Vygotsky (1978) identified a period of incomplete mastery, a time when a child could achieve success given adult assistance. This observation led Vygotsky to propose the zone of proximal development, defined as the distance between the level of accomplishment a child can achieve independently and the level attainable in conjunction with an expert adult or more capable peer (Bruner, 1986). Thus, learning is enhanced by adult (or peer) scaffolding or support.

In the case of language intervention in the classroom, the support from the adult may come through curricular planning (cf. Bunce, 1995), awareness of the linguistic abilities of each child, attunement to the intervention goals for particular children, and specific techniques of linguistic input including the use of focused contrasts. The adult must also be ready to take advantage of special moments of learning readiness (cf. K.E. Nelson's [1989] notion of "hot spots") as exemplified in the opening vignettes.

In describing clinical teaching based on a Vygotskian model, van Kleeck and Richardson (1986) outline the adult's and child's responsibilities. At an initial stage, the adult's role is to entice the child to take a risk to learn. The child's role is to take the risk of becoming involved in the learning. In the next stage, the adult must scaffold success. The child's responsibility is to learn the target response or become familiar with the structure. During the third stage, the adult needs to vary the task demands and slowly abdicate control of the task. The child's role is to stabilize his or her learning. In the last stage, the adult's role is limited to helping the child monitor his or her learning and generalize it to new contexts. The child's role is to monitor his or her learning and use it in appropriate contexts.

The various activities in the classroom are designed to entice the child to learn at a level that is comfortable. For example, during dramatic play activities, the adult may demonstrate the use of an interesting prop, or the adult may model a script with other children and then include the target child. At the art table, interesting materials, such as water, fingerpaint, glue, scissors, or Play-Doh, may be available. The block and quiet areas also have materials that are interesting to the child. Once the child is involved in an activity, the teacher then provides support to the learning whether it be new vocabulary, concepts, grammatical structures, or ways to interact with others. The intent is for the child to arrive at some new level of knowledge. As the child achieves success, the likelihood of further willingness to participate increases. When the child can perform the response with the support of the adult, the adult begins to withdraw the support until the child can perform without aid. Providing support for too long can be counterproductive. Therefore, the adult must be alert to optimal times to withdraw from the interaction.

Sometimes the support from the adult lies in the structure of the classroom and materials at a level removed from overt verbal interactions. For example, if peer–peer interaction is desired, providing the target child with control of a crucial prop (e.g., cash register in the grocery store activity) may result in more child–child interaction than if the adult participated as the cashier. Another example of how an adult may support children's interaction is in manipulating children's proximity (e.g., who sits next to whom at snacktime) or who shares play activities. In these indirect manipulations of children's verbal interactions, the teacher also influences children's opportunities to benefit from each other's skills. Children with specific language impairment can learn from children with typically developing language, if the situations are configured in a conducive manner.

Assessment

Another role of the teacher or speech-language pathologist is to assess the children's linguistic abilities. Following a referral, in LAP, a battery of standardized speech and language tests is administered to obtain basic information about each child's speech skills and expressive and receptive language abilities. In addition, information from the parents regarding birth, developmental, and medical histories is obtained. Further information is provided from a 100-utterance language sample collected in a free-play context. The language sample is analyzed for basic linguistic features such as mean length of utterance (MLU), number of different words, total number of words, grammatical morpheme acquisition, and pronoun usage. Other information from the language sample might include the proportion of the utterances that initiate a conversation or the number and type of questions used. Additional assessment information about children's verbal interactions with peers is gathered on an ongoing basis following enrollment in the program. The Social Interaction Coding System (SICS) (Rice et al., 1990), an on-line measure of a child's conversational initiations and responses while interacting with peers and adults, is one measure often utilized.

Thus, the child's linguistic system is the primary source of information about which particular language skills should be targeted. For expressive language goals, an attempt is made to select features that appear to be emerging in the child's language; for example, a grammatical morpheme with approximately 20%–30% accuracy in obligatory contexts would be identified as emergent. Furthermore, words and forms that the child is actively attempting to express constitute appropriate targets for work on production. For example, if a child talked about trucks, bikes, and motorcycles but did not use the specific labels for these objects (perhaps relying entirely on indefinite pronouns such as *it* and *that*), then, specific transportation vocabulary items would be an appropriate goal for that child. In addition, the normative sequence of various language skills is given consideration in the goal-selection process. Forms and grammatical constructions that appear later in development, such as passive sentences (e.g., Mary was kissed by John), would not be taught before the earlier-appearing forms, such as simple declarative sentences.

Language skills important to a child's parent are also given special attention. A frequent parental request is that a child be assisted in saying his or her own name intelligibly. We have explored the use of parental evaluations of their children's speech and language via a questionnaire developed for that purpose (Hadley & Rice, 1993). Parental judgments proved to correspond well with those of the SLP. Filling out the questionnaire helps alert the parent to the skills and competencies of interest to the clinician.

Monitoring Child Progress

A variety of procedures are used to monitor the progress of individual children; they are as follows:

1. In order to document gains in a child's performance relative to normative expectations, a battery of standardized speech and language tests is administered each year to all children. The findings from the routine standardized assessments are reported in Chapter 9; in general, children with speech and language impairments enrolled in LAP make gains in their communication abilities relative to their same-age peers.

2. Spontaneous speech samples are routinely analyzed at the beginning and end of each semester to note progress or change in the mean length of utterances, grammatical morpheme acquisition, number of different words used, total number of words used, and pronoun usage.

3. A classroom notebook is available for staff members to note anecdotal information regarding children's behavior and/or verbal productions. Of special interest are difficult-to-elicit grammatical forms, social uses of language, spontaneous use of targeted forms or skills, or personal strategies or preferences that are related to communicative functioning. These records can be used to document certain kinds of language gains or errors and to provide meaningful examples for parents. In addition, there is a similar notebook located in the observation room for parents to note interesting happenings or progress made by their children.

4. The SICS (Rice et al., 1990) is used to document the children's social use of language in the classroom. This information, collected intermittently, documents change in social interactions.

5. Specific progress on target goals is noted each day. Comments concerning the effectiveness of therapy are noted on the therapy plans so that the SLP can use the evaluation in planning the next day's therapy. The evaluation procedures might include a tally of the number of correct responses or the number of productions of a certain structure. Periodic probes may also be employed.

These sources of information regarding a child's progress are reported to parents in weekly summaries of their child's therapy progress. In this way, parents have current information about their child's status.

Application of Linguistic Techniques in the LAP Classroom

Communication among staff members is important in providing appropriate programming. First, the short-term goals for the children with specific language impairment are posted so that all staff members have easy access and knowledge of each child's target goals. Second, to help with planning and implementation, a curriculum notebook is readily available for staff members. In that notebook are the overall weekly plan of activities, daily planning guides, and lesson plans for specific dramatic play, art, and group activities. Two components of the classroom curriculum are particularly important in bridging the gap between daily plans and incorporation of language-enhancing strategies. First, *daily planning guides* are used to summarize each day's activities and to detail the specific linguistic, social, cognitive, and motor skills likely to be needed for participation in the day's activities. (An example of a daily planning guide is shown in Figure 1.) With respect to language intervention, then, these daily guides serve to highlight for classroom personnel the linguistic intervention opportunities they are likely to have, or may be able to construct, within a given day in the preschool classroom.

The second step in this curriculum interface is the development of *therapy guides*. (An example of a therapy guide is shown in Figure 2.) From the daily planning guides, classroom teachers and/or the SLP develop therapy guides for individual children with language impairments. In using the therapy lesson plan, the SLP first lists the child's goals. These goals then become the focus for planning the therapy. Second, the SLP studies the curriculum plan, noting suggested vocabulary and language structures. The SLP then uses the information to formulate a plan for therapy that focuses on the goals for that particular child and fits the activities planned for the classroom. Therapy guides outline specific times during the classroom day when teachers or clinicians will attempt to promote targeted linguistic skills, they describe the materials or props to be used, and, most importantly, they highlight specific language intervention strategies to be employed. In actual practice, therapy guides serve as preliminary plans; teachers and clinicians must adjust their therapy guides to the interests and activities of individual children and to the varied participants present in an interaction. At the same time, these therapy guides provide a type of base plan from which a teacher or clinician can work, with modifications of features such as materials, activities, and participants used as needed. At the end of the session, data concerning progress on specific goals can be noted on the therapy guides.

These two curriculum planning aids, daily planning guides and therapy guides, serve as the primary media through which methods of language intervention are integrated within the classroom curriculum. Daily lesson plans and therapy guides provide the link between classroom activities and language intervention strategies.

STRUCTURE OF THE LAP DAY

To provide a language-rich environment, we developed a language-focused curriculum (See Bunce [1995] for a more complete description of the LAP curriculum.) that follows conventional early childhood recommended practices, by means of developmentally appropriate activities (DAP) (cf. High Scope model [Hohmann et al., 1979]). Developmentally appropriate practices for preschool children involve recognition of the children's need to be actively involved in the learning process. The preschool child learns by doing, talking, and acting on objects, not just by passively listening and following adult direction. The preschool activities must be organized to provide structure and meaning for the child while maintaining the freedom to explore and learn.

In LAP, activities are planned on a weekly basis and are organized around a content theme of the week. The content themes provide coherence for language-learning opportunities throughout the day and across all classroom activities. The classroom is organized in a typical pre-

CURRICULUM: DAILY PLANNING GUIDE

Theme: Transportation

Week of: September 14, 1993

(Monday)   Tuesday   Wednesday   Thursday

Dramatic Play	Art	Story	Group	Song
Airplane	Paper airplanes	*The Trip*	Circles	I'm a Little Airplane

Language Skills Facilitated

- **Vocabulary** - transportation, airplane, pilot, flight attendant, baggage, suitcase, take-off, landing, seat belt, security check, ticket, seat, passenger, beverage, cockpit . . .

- **Verb Phrase Structures** - fasten your seatbelt, land*s* the plane, *is* land*ing*, land*ed*, *flew* the plane, serv*ed* food, check*ed* baggage, who's going on the plane? I *am* (incontractible auxiliary verb), I'*m* flying (contractible auxiliary) . . .

- **Adjective/Object Descriptions** - large plane, small plane, big suitcase, little bag, carry-on bag, blue ___, red ___, purple ___, . . .

- **Pronouns** - I, you, he, she, we, they, my, your, her, his, our, their, me, you, us, them

- **Prepositions** - In, on, under, over, near, beneath, next to, beside, around, inside, outside

- **Sounds** - /l/ lands, pilot, fill; /r/ ride, car; /s/ sit, talks; /k/ carry, ticket, pack; /f/ five, off . . .

Social Skills Facilitated:

- Initiating to peers and adults; responding to questions and requests from peers and adults
- Negotiating with peers for toys and materials
- Group cooperation—waiting for a turn in a group, taking a turn at the appropriate time

Cognitive Skills Facilitated:

- Problem Solving Skills—how to fold paper to make a plane
- Classification Skills—circle shapes
- Sequencing Skills—song, story
- Narrative/Story Structure—adventure

Motor Skills Facilitated:

- **Large Motor**—outdoor play activities: jumping, running, hopping, pedaling, climbing . . .
- **Small Motor**—writing, drawing, glueing, folding . . .

Figure 1.   An example of a daily planning guide.

THERAPY GUIDE

Child: S.B.

Clinician: L.D.

Date: 9/23

Theme: Transportation (Airplane)

Target Language Skill(s):

1. Increase use of specific vocabulary (focus on nouns, verbs, adjectives, and locatives).
2. Increase number of initiations with peers.
3. Increase use of present progressive (-*ing*).

When to Emphasize Target Skills:

During center time, snacktime, outdoor play, and free time.

How to Emphasize Target Skills:

Provide *focused contrasts* and *modeling* to elicit target structures and expand child utterances by:

- *Describing* what he is doing and providing labels for objects, actions, and locations (parallel talk) (e.g.,"D., you're buy*ing* a ticket . . . you are the pilot"; "You are mak*ing* an airplane," "He is fly*ing* the airplane fast", "It is land*ing* on the ground")

- *Joining in* the activities and also describing what the clinician is doing ("I want a *large* coke, "My seatbelt is on, "I'm go*ing* to Disneyland")

- *Commenting* on and *expanding* child utterances (e.g., "belt off," "yes, your belt is off," "I can fix it")

- Encourage *requesting* from a peer or teacher during snacktime, art, and sharing time. Encourage peer interaction through sharing the role of pilot or flight attendant. *Redirect* child to peers when appropriate.

Special Props and/or Materials Needed:

Utilize play materials child is using in dramatic play, art, block, or quiet areas.

Documentation of Progress (What Happened?):

[Describe on back of sheet success/failure of therapy procedures.]

- S. used -*ing* form three times (omitted it seven other times for a total correct use of 3/10). The -*ing* structure was modeled by the clinician 20 times during the course of the day.

- By the end of center time, S. used the term "pilot" twice instead of just pointing when he wanted to be the pilot. S. appeared to understand "behind" because he got behind another child on command while waiting for a turn.

- S. verbally initiated two times to an adult during a 10-minute observation.

Figure 2.   An example of a therapy guide.

school fashion with areas for free play (quiet area, block area, art area, and dramatic play area) and areas where children are grouped for teacher-directed activities. Each day's schedule includes the following activities (adapted from High Scope [Hohmann et al., 1979]): arrival time, circle/calendar time, center time, storytime, sharing time, outdoor time, snacktime, group time, and music time (see Figure 3 for the LAP daily schedule). The children attend LAP either in the morning or afternoon for 3 hours per day, 4 days per week. The make-up of the classroom includes children who are developing language skills in a typical fashion, children

DAILY SCHEDULE

Time/class

A.M.	P.M.	Activity
8:30–8:45	1:00–1:15	**ARRIVAL** Health checks and free play.
8:45–9:00	1:15–1:30	**CIRCLE TIME** Children and teachers greet each other; discuss helper of the day, today's date, and topic for the day; and choose where they will play.
9:00–9:50	1:30–2:20	**CENTER TIME** Children can play at one of four centers (art/science, blocks, quiet area, dramatic play).
9:50–10:05	2:20–2:35	**CLEAN UP/STORYTIME** Children clean up the toys. Then, they listen to a story.
10:05–10:15	2:35–2:45	**SHARING TIME** Children gather back in circle area to share information or toys. They take turns being the questioner or respondent.
10:15–10:45	2:45–3:15	**OUTSIDE TIME** Children play individual games, as well as organized group games (e.g., "Duck Duck Goose").
10:45–11:00	3:15–3:30	**SNACKTIME** Children assist in preparing snack. This is a good time to encourage conversation and table manners.
11:00–11:15	3:30–3:45	**SMALL/LARGE GROUP TIME** Each day different activities will be planned. Sometimes the children will be split into small groups during this time; on other days, the whole class will participate in a group project.
11:15–11:30	3:45–4:00	**MUSIC TIME** Children sing songs, play instruments, and/or dance.
		DISMISSAL Children sing a good-bye song and are dismissed.

Figure 3.   The LAP daily schedule.

who have speech and language impairments, and children who are learning English as a second language.

Teacher-Directed Versus Child-Centered Activities

The activities that comprise the LFC can be grouped according to whether they are predominantly teacher directed or child centered. Teacher-directed activities take place during circle/calendar time, storytime, sharing time, group time, and music time. The control of the activity primarily rests with the teacher. Child-centered activities occur during arrival time, center time, snacktime, and outdoor play. In child-centered activities, the children are free to participate in an activity for whatever length of time they choose and they can move freely among the activities. It should be noted that for approximately two thirds of the day, a child can choose how to spend his or her time. In this way, an optimal balance between teacher-directed and child-centered activities is achieved. The two types of activities fulfill different goals and it is important that both be included in the curriculum.

Teacher-Directed Activities

The teacher-directed activities help the children learn to attend to an adult while new concepts are presented in a structured format. The children learn to participate as part of a group. Teacher-directed activities are of short duration and are alternated with child-centered activities. In this way, the children are expected to attend in a group setting for only short periods of time each day.

Child-Centered Activities

The child-centered activities allow the children to focus on what is of interest to them. These activities are structured by the adult but the children decide their level of participation. It is during the child-centered activities that many language-learning opportunities occur. For example, during these activities adults can describe or comment on what the children are doing, thereby providing a language model for the children. Adults can provide focused contrasts, or expansions and recasts of the child's speech (as in the opening vignettes). The adults are providing language input about a child's topic, which may or may not result in child output. Opportunities for children to talk are provided many times during the day, but the children are not required to talk. It is recognized that children can learn from observation. However, as children hear language describing their own activities, they often begin to talk about the activities. Even if they do not talk, it is assumed that the children are still receiving information that is comprehensible within the activity of their own choosing.

Center Time

A very important daily event is that of the 50-minute center time. During this period of the day, children can choose to play in any of four areas: the *quiet area* with books and puzzles, the *block area* with different kinds of blocks and miniature toys, the *art area*, and the *dramatic play area.* The activities in the latter two areas change daily depending on the theme; there is greater constancy in the materials in the block and quiet areas. The classroom areas were adapted from the High Scope model (Hohmann et al., 1979). Some modifications were made in order to maximize language use and understanding. For example, in the High Scope procedures, the children are required to choose where they want to play and must ask permission to change areas. Our experience is that requiring children to ask permission to change areas appeared to break up the activities artificially. Children with low language ability were very hesitant to ask to change areas and the procedure required much teacher involvement to encourage children to ask first or to reprimand children for switching without asking. Instead, we focused on ways to enhance language usage and did not worry about limiting access to play areas. The point to be made here is that the reason the request procedure did not work well is that it was superimposed on the flow of children's play. Instead of the verbal request following a natural function, it became a part of the teacher directedness. So, we found other ways to work on developing children's request forms (e.g., during snacktime).

Thus, during center time, children may choose to play only in one area or they may move from area to area. For example, a child might choose to play in the art area for a time and then join the ongoing activity in the dramatic play area. Alternatively, a child might choose to spend all of center time playing in the block or quiet areas.

The different center time activities allow for different levels or amounts of verbal ability. In making an activity choice, the child is to a certain degree also choosing a level of verbal participation. In the quiet area, children may, but do not have to, talk. They may instead listen to a story or play with a puzzle. Similarly, playing with blocks and manipulative toys in the block area does not require the child to talk. Play can proceed by manipulating the objects. In the art area, children occasionally may need to ask for more materials, but most of the time the activities do not require talking. However, when in the dramatic play area, talking even at the one-word level will be more likely to ensure a child's acceptance into the activity and ability to participate. During outdoor play, similar levels of language use may occur. Little talking may be needed when riding a tricycle or playing in the sand pile; much more talking is needed when playing with others in active games such as pretending to be Ninja Turtles. In any case, the teacher or clinician can provide appropriate language-learning information to a child by describing what the child is doing, by engaging a child in conversations about the activity at hand, or by encouraging child–child interactions. Embedded in this language are the focused contrasts, expansions, and redirects tailored to a specific child's needs.

Routine Versus Variation

Activities in LAP can also be categorized according to whether they are a routine activity or whether they are an activity that changes daily. For example, circle time is a routine activity, whereas dramatic play activities change daily. Familiar, routine activities allow the children to practice new forms within a known format. Variations in activities allow new structures, vocabulary, and concepts to be modeled. Choice of activities allows the child control over the pace of learning. Teacher direction allows for stretching the child's knowledge and for support of new learning. The combinations of familiarity and change complement each other as language enrichment opportunities. It is the combination of activities, rather than one type of activity, that is crucial in the development of a concentrated normative model of intervention.

Routinized Activities

Two features associated with the routine activities are beneficial to the child's learning. One is the predictability of the sequence of the activities. The children can rely on the sequence and know what is to come and, therefore, be more likely to participate. Also, transitions between activities are made less stressful because the child knows what is to happen. The second feature is the routine use of linguistic forms and structures. The two features together create a way to highlight language forms and functions and provide a framework for learning. The combination of known sequence and known linguistic form allows the adult to support the children's language use. The routine activities, then, play an important role in facilitating the child's learning.

During circle time, a routine format is used each day to begin the day's activities. Roll call, calendar time, and introduction to the day's activities are part of each circle time. In addition to sequences within activities, the overall schedule of the activities provides a routine structure for each day. Children quickly learn the sequence of activities and can predict what will happen next.

Routinized Phrases

Another routine format is used during sharing time. Here the procedure involves the use of routinized phrases. One of the purposes of this activity is to teach children how to ask questions. Questions are important because of their social usefulness and their grammatical constructions. Being able to ask questions empowers children to obtain information when they desire it. However, children with language impairments often have difficulty constructing questions. During sharing time, one child asks another child a typical set of questions about an object brought from home or chosen from the classroom. The questions include, "What do you have?", "Where did you get it?", and "What do you do with it?" For some children, the questions may be reduced to one- or two-word phrases (e.g., "Have?", "Where get?", "What do?"). Other questions can be added, but these three form the core of the interaction between the two children. The repetitive format allows children to hear the appropriate grammatical constructions repeatedly in a socially appropriate context. The teacher's role is to facilitate the interaction and, if necessary, prompt the questions.

Snacktime is another routine activity in which stock phrases such as "More juice, please" are used. Other routine activities include playing with blocks, books, puzzles, and other manipulative toys typically available in the block and quiet areas of the classroom. Outdoor activities also can be viewed as routine in that the same types of equipment and toys are available each day and the rules for playing with toys or on the equipment remain the same each day. Phrases for sharing toys or playground equipment such as "My turn, please" or "You can have a turn in a minute" also become routinized. Routine activities allow for consolidating skills within a known format. Routine phrases such as "Clean-up time" or "More crackers, please" may become the first words some children learn.

Variation

In contrast, other activities vary from day to day. Dramatic play, art, and group activities change depending on the theme or weekly unit. Having activities that change allows for new concepts, vocabulary, and language structures to be introduced. The activities are interesting to the children because of their newness. They provide a challenge, stretching the children's intellect, language, social, and motor skills. Although this lack of predictability creates some communicative risks, the shared themes provide an important structure for the child. A *weekly planning guide* is shown in Figure 4. This guide is used to plan the curriculum activities that change on a daily basis. In LAP, the plans are developed by staff members under the direction of the director. The planning meetings take place the week before the target week. The weekly plan provides an overview of the activities for a particular week. Specific lesson plans are then developed (see Bunce [in press] for examples). The daily planning guides mentioned earlier are also developed at this time. After the plans have been completed, they are placed in a notebook for easy access by staff members. For each week, then, there are: 1) a weekly plan; 2) daily plans for each day; and 3) lesson plans for the dramatic play, art, and group activities.

Weekly Content Themes

To ensure that the children understand the basic notions of the theme and the underlying coherence of the activities, the teacher provides a preview each day. This is accomplished by introducing each day's theme-centered activities at the end of circle time. The activities take place during center time, at both the art center and the dramatic play center. First, the art activity is described and demonstrated. Then, the various props and possible enactments of the dramatic play are introduced. Although there are no memorized scripts, sample linguistic forms as well as actions are modeled by the adult with the help of one or two children. What is important is that the children understand the event, what it means, and how it unfolds. Then, the actual verbal productions can be left largely to the individual children.

Dramatic Play Activities

If the theme for the week is vacation, the dramatic play activity for the first day might be going on an airplane trip, the second day might be staying in a motel, the third could be about a stay at the beach or a trip to

CURRICULUM: WEEKLY PLANNING GUIDE

Semester Theme: Vacations

Weekly Theme: _____ **Week of:** June 13–16

	Dramatic Play	Art	Story	Group	Music
Monday	Airplane	Paper airplanes	*The Trip*	Measuring (how far planes flew)	I'm a Little Airplane
Tuesday	Motel	Water-color painting	*Jake Baked the Cake*	Letter "M"	Going to Kentucky
Wednesday	Beach	Aquariums	*A House for a Hermit Crab*	Color mixing (Mix primary colors to make secondary colors)	Bubble, Bubble, Bubble, POP
Thursday	Amusement park	Mural	*Here We Are*	Sound sequencing	Mickey Mouse Song

Suggested Props and Materials:

Monday	Seatbelts, luggage, tickets, counter, metal detector, rudder, instrument panel, paper, paper clips, markers . . .
Tuesday	TVs, rooms, keys, check-in desk, telephones, restaurant, table, food, pool, brooms, vacuum cleaners, water paints, paper, frames. . .
Wednesday	Sandboxes, beach towels, sunglasses, lifeguard stand, shovels, pails, shells, star-fish, tissue paper, fish shapes, yarn (for seaweed), blue cellophane, paper plates . . .
Thursday	Mural paper, bean bag toss, Sit & Spin, concession stand, trampoline, ball toss, clothespin drop, drum (for sound pattern sequencing) . . .

Figure 4. An example of a weekly planning guide.

an amusement park, and so forth. For the airplane trip dramatic play activity, the roles that the children might play include the pilot, co-pilot, flight attendants, passengers, and ticket agents. Verbal scripts might include "Ticket, please," "Do you want some coffee?", "Fasten your seatbelt," and "We will be landing in 2 minutes." Possible actions could involve packing, buying a ticket, getting into the airplane, fastening a seatbelt, serving refreshments, or piloting the plane.

Each dramatic play would have its own set of props, actions, and verbal scripts. Again, following a demonstration of possible actions and verbal scripts, the children would act out various roles appropriate for each dramatic play. The children determine who is playing what part so that a child might first be a pilot, then a passenger or ticket agent, and then return to being the pilot. The adult supports the dramatic play by assuming a role, describing the action, providing props, or facilitating the turn taking. (Figure 5 is a sample dramatic play activity plan for the airplane trip.)

The dramatic plays, although changed daily, are repeated within different themes. For example, the airplane trip dramatic play activity can also be part of a transportation theme. This planned redundancy is achieved without sacrificing the opportunity to provide new vocabulary or new concepts. Furthermore, each time the airplane dramatic play occurs, the children take a more active role in leading the enactment.

Other Daily Activities Associated with a Weekly Theme

The art activities each day would also change. For the vacation theme, the first day might be folding paper airplanes, the second day painting pictures (within a frame like a television for motel day), the third day making aquariums or sand pictures (for beach day), and so forth. Group activities would also change. For the first day, a measuring activity could be done by measuring the distance a child flew a paper airplane. For the second day, identifying a letter such as M (for motel) could be part of the group activity. For the third day, a color-mixing activity involving water could be done. Other group activities might include a classification or sequencing activity. Stories and songs would also vary so that they reflect the weekly themes (see Bunce [1995] for a listing of different themes, and the various dramatic play, art, and group activity plans that could be used in implementing these themes). During all of these activities, the adults provide language input tailored to the individual child's needs.

Thus, the activities in LAP can be categorized according to whether they are teacher directed or child centered, and according to whether they are routine or they change daily. In other words, some of the routine activities are teacher directed and some are child centered. In the same fashion, the activities that change may be teacher directed or child centered. The distribution of activities can be summarized in a grid as in Figure 6.

Developing Individualized Language Goals for Children

The information from the language assessment is used to identify possible linguistic and interactive target skills for the children with language

ACTIVITY PLAN

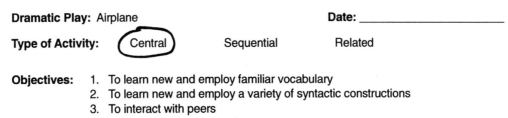

Dramatic Play: Airplane   **Date:** _____

Type of Activity: (Central)   Sequential   Related

Objectives: 1. To learn new and employ familiar vocabulary
                   2. To learn new and employ a variety of syntactic constructions
                   3. To interact with peers
                   4. To sequence familiar routines
                   5. To expand conceptual knowledge of the world

General Description of Activity

Introduce activity by reading the book *Going on an Airplane Trip.* An airplane trip involves purchasing a ticket, checking baggage at the counter, going through security check, and finally finding a seat on the plane. Seatbelts must be fastened for take-off. Food and beverages are served by flight attendants. When you arrive baggage needs to be reclaimed at the baggage area. Carry-on luggage can be stored under a seat.

Setting

- Airport
- Ticket office or counter
- Airplane facsimile (chairs arranged in rows behind a "cab" where a play dashboard is set up)
- Kitchen
- Cockpit
- Baggage claim area (optional)
- Metal detector (optional)

Props

- Tickets
- Chairs with seatbelts (men's ties can be used for seatbelts)
- Dashboard
- Luggage
- Food and drinks
- Trays
- Carts
- Dolls

Roles

- Pilot and co-pilot
- Flight attendants
- Passengers
- Clerks at the ticket counter
- Security people

_____

(continued)

Figure 5.   An example of a dramatic play activity plan. The theme for the week is vacation. The day's activity is an airplane trip.

Figure 5. (*continued*)

Verbal Productions

Level of linguistic complexity varies with the role or competence of the child playing the role.
- "We're coming in for a landing so fasten your seat belts" or "Plane's landing."
- "Do you want a beverage?" or "Drink, please."
- "May I see your ticket?" or "Ticket?"

Adult Facilitory Role

The adult's role is to assist the children in the role play and to help expand their language use. Emphasis on different structures and/or vocabulary may be necessary depending on the individual child's needs and abilities. The adult(s) may provide focused contrasts, model appropriate scripts, ask open questions, expand or recast the child's productions, redirect a child to request items from another child, or provide confirming feedback to a particular child.

impairments. The teacher or SLP, the director or educational coordinator (who oversees the implementation of the program), the family services coordinator, and the family members then meet together to determine specific target skills for each child with language impairments (see Chapter 8 on collaborating with families for a description of a typical individualized education program [IEP] conference).

In general, the SLP and parents come to the meeting prepared to generate goals for the child. The SLP provides testing information and information drawn from classroom observations. The parents are prepared for the IEP conference by the family services coordinator who encourages them to have thought about their child's strengths and weaknesses and what they would like to see the child learn. The conference starts with the parents providing information about their child and their desires. The staff members then provide information about the child's language skills and classroom interactions. After a period of discussion, specific long- and short-term goals are generated.

Goals across linguistic domains are often targeted concurrently. Typical long-term goals include improving intelligibility, increasing vocabulary knowledge, increasing sentence length and complexity, increasing correct pronoun usage, improving understanding and production of different question forms, and improving appropriate peer interactions. Because new IEPs are written each semester, goals and objectives are subject to automatic and continuous review and are revised frequently. However, children's progress does not necessarily follow the adult timing of conferences; therefore, the goals and objectives are revised as needed in collaboration with parents (via telephone, written notes, or mini-conferences). If year-long IEPs are used, then more objectives may have to be written and/or new objectives generated as children make progress.

The identification of specific linguistic goals for the children with language impairments does not preclude learning of other linguistic skills. On the contrary, the preschool classroom provides a rich linguistic environment across a range of phonological and language features. Children continually hear various aspects of language presented in a manner

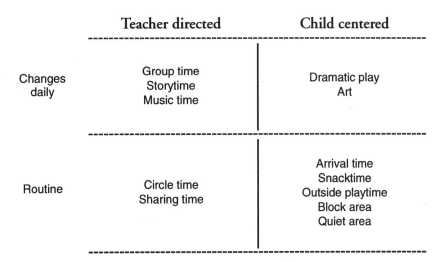

	Teacher directed	Child centered
Changes daily	Group time Storytime Music time	Dramatic play Art
Routine	Circle time Sharing time	Arrival time Snacktime Outside playtime Block area Quiet area

Figure 6. Types of activities in LAP, categorized by whether they are teacher directed or child centered and whether they change daily or are routine.

designed to enhance learning; thus, the opportunity is always present for each child to master both his or her own specific targets and those of his or her classmates. It is this aspect of LAP that makes language facilitation possible for all participating children, children with widely varying linguistic competencies—children with language impairments, children learning English as a second language, and children learning language typically.

Goals for a Typical Child with SLI

The process of goal setting can be illustrated with a typical child with SLI. John was enrolled in LAP at 4 years, 5 months of age. Assessment revealed that John had a severe articulation delay, receptive and expressive language delays exceeding 2 standard deviations below the mean, and limited social interactions with peers. Relatively long-term goals for John's enrollment in LAP included: 1) increasing John's correct production of selected sounds, particularly /k/, and production of final consonant sounds, particularly /s/; 2) decreasing John's use of nonspecific vocabulary (e.g., *it, that*) by increasing use of specific content words; 3) increasing John's use of past tense *-ed* forms; and 4) increasing the frequency of John's conversational initiations and responses with peers. In this way, specific goals were selected to address the specific needs and current linguistic tasks facing the child. Short-term objectives for John included the following:

1a. John will improve production of /k/ in initial positions in words to a level of 80% correct on probes taken during center time activities.

1b. John will produce /s/ correctly in the final position in words at the level of 80% correct on probes taken during center time activities.

2a. John will demonstrate understanding of 15 nouns and 5 verbs derived from the classroom activities at the level of 90% correct on probes taken weekly.

2b. John will produce 15 nouns and 5 verbs derived from classroom activities at the level of 90% correct on probes taken weekly.

2c. John will increase his usage of specific vocabulary by reducing the amount of nonspecific vocabulary (*it, that*) as measured by the postsemester spontaneous speech sample.

3a. By the end of the semester, John will demonstrate his knowledge of past tense by correctly labeling completed actions during child-centered activities at a level of 80% correct.

3b. John will increase his correct usage of past tense grammatical morphemes to the level of 80% correct as measured by pre- and post-semester spontaneous speech samples.

4a. John will increase the number of peer initiations during child-centered activities as measured by the SICS administered twice per semester.

4b. John will increase the number of peer responses during child-centered activities as measured by the SICS administered twice per semester.

This list illustrates some of the possible objectives for John. The important issue is that parents and staff members work together in developing the goals and objectives and in implementing the intervention. Furthermore, it is important that all adults in the classroom are aware of, and remember, the individual goals for each child. To facilitate this awareness, each child's goals are posted in a designated area in the classroom. The collaboration between parents and staff members is ongoing, in the ways described in Chapter 8.

CLASSROOM AND LANGUAGE INTERVENTION ACTIVITIES

The teachers and/or speech-language pathologists develop appropriate language-focused activities for each child, which may be group or individually implemented. The activities may be teacher-directed introductions of new concepts or teacher-responsive strategies. The ways in which techniques of linguistic input can be incorporated into classroom activities are virtually unlimited. Some possibilities are exemplified in the following:

1. In a dramatic play activity with the theme of clothes shopping, the learning of subjective and objective pronouns can be facilitated by modeling with a contrastive focus in utterances such as, "*I* am going to buy a blue sweater for *me* and a green one for *you*. Lisa wants a red dress. Please give *it* to *her*."

2. In an art activity involving pasting a collage of pictures, phonology can be emphasized by selecting pictures that all begin with the same *target sound*.

3. An art activity could also be used to develop the use of language as a social tool, or the use of questions, by requiring a child to *request* various items (e.g., "I need more glue," "Pass the scissors, please," "Can I paint?", "May I have the blue marker?").

4. Play with blocks and toys can become a setting for facilitating the learning of different *verb structures* when the task is to make a farm where the animals and people do things (e.g., the cow is riding in the truck, the chicken is sitting on the fence, the boy is running to the horse, the horse is jumping).

5. A reading activity is an obvious way to expand *vocabulary* and provide models of syntactic structure.

6. Sharing time can serve as an occasion to facilitate the use of *question asking* (one child asks another about the items brought for sharing—what do you have? where did you get it?, etc.).

7. A matching game can facilitate children's *learning of concepts* (e.g., same or different, big or little).

8. Even outdoor playtime can be valuable for language learning. During this time, adults can emphasize *prepositions* (e.g., *in* the sand, *on* the bike, *under* the table, *on* top of the house, *between* the airplanes) or *verb structures* (e.g., I *am running*, he *ran*, I *dropped* it, you *will ride* the bike next).

Further possibilities are available in *child–child interactions*, when adults prompt or encourage a child to interact with another or by setting up child–child situations and stepping out of the interactions. The point is that the activities of the classroom are rich resources for language facilitation, and there are endless ways to intertwine the two.

REFERENCES

Baker, N., & Nelson, K.E. (1984). Recasting and related conversational techniques for triggering syntactic advances by young children. *First Language, 5,* 3–22.

Bruner, J. (1986). The inspiration of Vygotsky. In J. Bruner (Ed.), *Actual minds, possible worlds* (pp. 70–149). Cambridge: Harvard University Press.

Bunce, B. (1995). *Building a language-focused curriculum for the preschool classroom. Vol. II: A planning guide.* Baltimore: Paul H. Brookes Publishing Co.

Carne, E. (1987). *A house for hermit crab.* New York: Scholastic.

Constable, C.M. (1986). The application of scripts in the organization of language intervention contexts. In K. Nelson (Ed.), *Event knowledge: Structure and function in development* (pp. 205–230). Hillsdale, NJ: Lawrence Erlbaum Associates.

Constable, C.M. (1987). Talking with teachers: Increasing our relevance as language interventionists in the schools. *Seminars in Speech and Language, 8,* 345–355.

Cross, T.G. (1984). Habilitating the language-impaired children: Ideas from studies of parent–child interaction. *Topics in Language Disorders, 4,* 1–14.

Duchan, J.F. (1986). Language intervention through sensemaking and fine tuning. In R.L. Schiefelbusch (Ed.), *Language competence: Assessment and intervention* (pp. 187–212). San Diego: College Hill.

Dudley-Marling, C., & Searle, D. (1988). Enriching language learning environments for students with learning disabilities. *Journal of Learning Disabilities, 21,* 140–143.

Fey, M.E. (1986). *Language intervention with young children.* San Diego: College Hill.

Gertner, B. (1993). *Who do you want to play with?: The influence of communicative competence on peer preferences in preschoolers*. Unpublished master's thesis, University of Kansas, Lawrence.

Hadley, P.A., & Rice, M.L. (1993). Parental judgments of preschoolers' speech and language development: A resource for assessment and IEP planning. *Seminars in Speech and Language, 14,* 278–288.

Hart, B., & Rogers-Warren, A. (1978). A milieu approach to teaching language. In R. Schiefelbusch (Ed.), *Language intervention strategies* (pp. 193–235). Baltimore: University Park Press.

Heath, S.B. (1986). Separating "things of the imagination" from life: Learning to read and write. In W. Teale & E. Sulzby (Eds.), *Emergent literacy* (pp. 156–172). Norwood, NJ: Ablex.

Hennessy, B.G. (1990). *Jake baked the cake*. New York: Scholastic.

Hoff-Ginsberg, E. (1986). Function and structure in maternal speech: Their relation to the child's development of syntax. *Developmental Psychology, 22,* 1–13.

Hoff-Ginsberg, E. (1991). Mother–child conversations in different social classes and communicative settings. *Child Development, 62,* 782–796.

Hoff-Ginsberg, E., & Shatz, M. (1982). Linguistic input and the child's acquisition of language. *Psychological Bulletin, 92,* 3–26.

Hohmann, M., Banet, B., & Weikart, D. (1979). *Young children in action*. Ypsilanti, MI: High Scope Press.

Johnston, J.R. (1985). Fit, focus, and functionality: An essay on early language intervention. *Child Language Teaching and Therapy, 1,* 125–134.

Keats, E.J. (1978). *The trip*. New York: Mulberry Books.

Lieven, E.V.M. (1984). Interaction style and children's language learning. *Topics in Language Disorders, 4,* 15–23.

Miller, L. (1989). Classroom-based language intervention. *Language, Speech, and Hearing Services in the Schools, 20,* 153–169.

Nelson, K. (1981). Social cognition in a script framework. In J.H. Flavell & L. Ross (Eds.), *Social cognitive development* (pp. 97–118). Cambridge: Cambridge University Press.

Nelson, K. (Ed.). (1986). *Event knowledge: Structure and function in development*. Hillsdale, NJ: Lawrence Erlbaum Associates.

Nelson, K.E. (1989). Strategies for first language teaching. In M.L. Rice & R.L. Schiefelbusch (Eds.), *The teachability of language* (pp. 263–310). Baltimore: Paul H. Brookes Publishing Co.

Nelson, K.E., Denninger, M.M., Bonvillian, J.D., Kaplan, B.J., & Baker, N.D. (1984). Maternal input adjustments and nonadjustments as related to children's linguistic advances and the language acquisition theories. In A.D. Pellegrini & T.D. Yawkey (Eds.), *The development of oral and written language: Readings in development and applied linguistics*. New York: Ablex.

Nelson, N.W. (1989). Curriculum-based language assessment and intervention. *Language, Speech, and Hearing Services in the Schools, 20,* 170–184.

Norris, J.A., & Hoffman, P. (1990). Language intervention within naturalistic environments. *Language, Speech, and Hearing Services in the Schools, 21,* 72–84.

Piaget, J. (1974). *The language and thought of the child*. New York: New American Library.

Rice, M.L. (1986). Mismatched premises of the communicative competence model and language intervention. In R.L. Schiefelbusch (Ed.), *Language competence: Assessment and intervention* (pp. 261–280). San Diego: College Hill.

Rice, M.L., Sell, M.A., & Hadley, P.A. (1990). The Social Interactive Coding System (SICS): A clinically relevant, descriptive tool. *Language, Speech, and Hearing Services in the Schools, 21,* 2–14.

Snow, C.E. (1984). Parent–child interaction and the development of communicative competence. In R. Schiefelbusch & J. Pickar (Eds.), *The acquisition of communicative competence* (pp. 71–107). Baltimore: University Park Press.

Snow, C.E., Midkiff-Borunda, S., Small, A., & Proctor, A. (1984). Therapy as social interaction: Analyzing the contexts for language remediation. *Topics in Language Disorders, 4,* 72–85.

Tallarico, T. (1988). *Here we go.* New York: Putnam.

Tharp, R.G., & Gallimore, R. (1988). *Rousing minds to life: Teaching, learning, and schooling in social context.* Cambridge: Cambridge University Press.

van Kleeck, A., & Richardson, A. (1986). What's in an error? Using children's wrong responses as language-teaching opportunities. *National Student Speech-Language-Hearing Association Journal, 14,* 25–50.

Vygotsky, L.S. (1978). *Mind in society.* Cambridge: Harvard University Press.

∼5∽

Speech Intervention in a Language-Focused Curriculum

Kim A. Wilcox and Sherrill R. Morris

Today is cooking day at the preschool. Charlie and several of his friends are busy making a fruit salad. Charlie becomes troubled and leaves his play group to tell his teacher something.

Charlie:	Daz nu a terry.
Teacher 1:	What?
Charlie:	(pointing to the kitchen area) Na tin.
Teacher 1:	The kitchen?
Charlie:	Nu terry tin.
Teacher 1:	You were working in the kitchen.
Charlie:	(turning to another teacher) Ni ma terry.
Teacher 2:	You need more what?
Charlie:	Terry.
Teacher 2:	Show me what you need.
Charlie:	Ta nu ma! (walks away)

There weren't any more cherries, so Charlie *couldn't* show the teacher what he needed!

Charlie is frustrated by his inability to convey his wishes. Much of what he says is unintelligible to the teachers and, as a result, they are at a loss for what to do. With few understandable words to go by, Charlie's teachers are only able to guess his needs. Although he has difficulties in several aspects of language, Charlie's primary communication difficulty is his inability to produce the sounds of speech accurately.

As noted in Chapter 1, speech-language pathologists have traditionally differentiated speech from language. In this traditional formulation, speech refers to the movements of the vocal and articulatory systems for making sound and language refers to the system of words and sentences that the sounds represent. Children can demonstrate impairments in speech, but not language; language, but not speech; or impairments in both domains. Although speech and language represent two distinct domains, errors in the two areas are often seen together in young children. In fact, there are as many children with specific language impairment (SLI) who have difficulties in both speech and language as there are children with problems in only one of these two domains (Ruscello, St. Louis, & Mason, 1991; Shriberg & Kwiatkowski, 1982). Thus, it is important that intervention procedures targeting speech problems be compatible with those targeting language impairments, in order to provide efficient and effective intervention to the largest group of children.

The basic intervention principles of the language-focused curriculum (LFC) apply to both speech and language intervention. Nevertheless, some special considerations are necessary when speech is the target of intervention. This chapter describes the ways in which an LFC, and therefore the concentrated normative model (CNM), can be applied to the development of speech skills. We first provide an overview of the sound system of the language and the social and developmental consequences of speech impairments. This is followed by a description of the speech intervention techniques we have developed in the Language Acquisition Preschool (LAP) setting. A special feature of this intervention is that *all* intervention is incorporated into the daily activities of the classroom.

PHONOLOGY

Phonology refers to the study of the sound system of language. More specifically, the phonological system dictates which sounds are acceptable in a language, how those sounds are produced, and in what ways they can be combined with each other. Each language has its own unique sound system, just as it has its own unique system of words and sentence forms. For example, French and English differ in several ways: Semantically, the two languages use different words (e.g., "plume" and "pen"); syntactically, they place the words in different orders (e.g., "plume rouge" and "red pen"); and phonologically, they rely on different sounds (notably the increased nasalization present in French vowels relative to English ones).

Basic Units of Language

The basic phonological units of a language are referred to as phonemes. The total number of phonemes in English varies slightly by dialect and by system of linguistic analysis. Forty-two—17 vowels and 25 consonants—is the number most often attributed to the Standard American dialect. Remember from elementary school that our alphabet is composed of 26 letters—5 vowels (a, e, i, o, u) and 21 consonants. As a result, the 26 letters of our alphabet are used in various combinations to represent the 42 different phonemes of English. For example, the letter "a" is used to represent two different vowel sounds in "pass" and "sofa" (as well as several others). Similarly, the letters "s" and "h" typically represent different phonemes individually (e.g., "see," "hit") than they do in combination (e.g., "she"). To accommodate this lack of one-to-one correspondence among the phonemes of the language and the letters of the alphabet, speech-language pathologists rely on the International Phonetic Alphabet (IPA) to symbolize the sounds of the language. Within the IPA, every speech sound has its own symbol. These symbols are usually placed within vertical slashes to differentiate them from letters of the alphabet. Thus, "pass" becomes /pæs/ and "sofa" becomes /sofə/. "See," "hit," and "she" become /si/, /hɪt/, and /ʃi/, respectively. A complete listing of the phonemes of English is provided in Table 1.

Vowel and consonant phonemes differ in several respects. These differences are important to our discussion because in young children consonant errors are much more prevalent than vowel errors (Weiss, Gordon, & Lillywhite, 1987). By definition, vowels serve as the nuclei of syllables; with relatively few exceptions, every syllable has one vowel and every vowel corresponds to one syllable. Consonants, by contrast, tend to cluster around vowels in various combinations, such that some syllables have no consonants at all and others have a variety of consonants preceding and following the vowel nucleus (e.g., "a," "say," "stay," "stray," "aid," "aids," "spades"). During the process of articulating (i.e., pronouncing) individual speech sounds, vowels become characterized by

Table 1. Phonemes of American English

Consonants		Vowels	
Sound	Key word	Sound	Key word
p	pie	i	beet
b	boat	ɪ	bit
t	top	e	bait
d	dog	ɛ	bet
k	kite	æ	bat
g	gate	a	father
f	fine	ɔ	law
v	vase	o	boat
θ	thumb	ʊ	book
ð	that	u	boot
s	soup	ʌ	but
z	zoo	ə	sofa
ʃ	shoe	ɝ	bird
ʒ	treasure	ɚ	brother
h	house	aɪ	buy
t	church	ɔɪ	boy
d	judge	aʊ	how
m	man		
n	now		
y	sing		
ʍ	white		
w	water		
j	yellow		
l	lion		
r	run		

relatively open mouths and consonants by relatively closed mouths. As a result, vowels are generally longer in duration and greater in intensity, or loudness, than consonants. Furthermore, consonants generally demand greater articulatory precision than vowels, in that they often require rapid movements that can be easily misinterpreted if not correctly executed. Remember, too, that there are only 17 vowels in English, compared with 25 consonants. Thus, young children must not only master more consonants than vowels, but these consonants are likely to be shorter in duration, more motorically demanding, and harder for them to hear than the vowels. It is also much more difficult to predict how many (if any) consonants might appear in any given syllable, while each syllable has one and only one vowel. As a result, it is not surprising that young children typically have more difficulty producing consonants than vowels.

Combining Phonemes into Words

In addition to learning to produce all of the phonemes of his or her language, a child must also learn the rules for combining those phonemes into syllables and words. This occurs in much the same way that children learn both the words of the language and the rules for combining those words into meaningful and coherent sentences. Although few speakers can identify or describe the phonological rules of their language, these rules are nonetheless an important part of a speaker's linguistic competence. For example, when native speakers of English are asked if "splude" is a word, they will generally indicate that it might be a word, but that they have never heard it before. By contrast, when the same speakers are asked if "lpsude" is a word, they will recognize that such a combination of sounds, or letters, cannot occur in English. Quite simply, the phonological rules for combining English phonemes do not allow /l/, /p/, and /s/ to occur in that order at the beginning of a word; even though that same order is permitted at the end of a word (e.g., "helps"). Furthermore, when sounds are placed adjacent to one another, they tend to interact in specific ways. For example, the /p/ in "splude" is systematically different from the /p/ in "spray" and the /r/ in "spray" is systematically different from that in "ray" (Shriberg & Kent, 1982). Many of these modifications are dictated by the phonology of English, and each modification results in a different allophone, or variant, of the original phoneme.

Although phonology deals primarily with speech sounds, it is but one part of a highly integrated language system. Within this system, phonology interacts more closely with morphology than the other components. In fact, in many cases, changing a single phoneme transforms one morpheme into another, as in "bid" and "bad," "bad" and "mad," "mad" and "mat," and so forth. Furthermore, many morphemes are represented by only one phoneme, as with the "s" in "cats." Thus, when even one phoneme becomes unintelligible, the identity of an entire morpheme may be lost to the listener.

The rules of morphology and phonology also interact in very specific ways. In Chapter 1, subject–verb agreement marking was used as an example of the rules of morphology. In that example, "s" must be attached to "go" to produce "he goes," but it is not added to "go" in "I go," "you go," and "they go." Although denoted by the letter "s," the agreement marker in "goes" is actually a /z/. (To test this, say "goes" and hold out the last sound as both an /s/ and a /z/.) However, when that same agreement marker is added to "sit," it is both alphabetically and phonemically an /s/, not a /z/. Thus, for present tense markers in English, the final phoneme of the word (e.g., the /o/ in /go/ or the /t/ in /sɪt/) determines which phoneme is used to represent the agreement morpheme.

In summary, English-speaking children must learn the basic set of 42 phonemes, all of the acceptable allophones of each of those phonemes, and the rules that govern the combination of those allophones to make acceptable words and sentences. Problems in any of these areas can result in reduced intelligibility, loss of meaning, or both.

PHONOLOGICAL IMPAIRMENTS

Although we often refer to speech development separately from language development, much of speech development is phonological acquisition or mastery of a portion of grammar. We must remember, however, that what makes speech different from language is that speech also involves the movement of the muscles of the throat and mouth to make audible sounds. Much like learning how to ride a bicycle or tie shoe laces, mastery of the speaking task requires coordination and practice. The early years are a time of speech practice and a time to refine articulatory accuracy (Edwards, 1992; Kent, 1976; Smith & Kenney, 1994).

Some children, such as those with cerebral palsy, have speech difficulties that are primarily the result of problems in muscle movement or coordination. These children may understand much of the phonology of the language, but their bodies are simply unable to make the precise movements necessary for clearly articulated speech. By contrast, the speech problems of children with SLI are thought to result primarily from phonological, rather than motor, problems. These children do not fully understand the role of individual phonemes and allophones in representing the meanings of specific morphemes and words. As a result, they may fail to produce some phonemes (e.g., "da" for "dog"), to contrast one phoneme with another effectively (e.g., the child's production of "pea" sounds like "bee" to most listeners), or to correctly apply the combinatory rules of the language (Shriberg, Kwiatkowski, Best, Hengst, & Terselic-Weber, 1986).

In many cases, these apparent errors may be as much in the ear of the listener as in the mouth of the speaker. Remember that each phoneme has many allophones. Given this range of choices, children often produce incorrect or nonstandard allophones when attempting to mark a particular phoneme (Weismer, 1984). If a listener is familiar enough with a child's speech, these nonstandard allophones may be interpretable as standing for the correct phoneme. For example, if you know that a child uses /t/ in place of /k/, then "toat" is readily understood to mean "coat." However, if you are unfamiliar with the child's speech, you might have great difficulty figuring out the intended message. It is not uncommon for young children to present exactly this type of situation. Many children who are unintelligible to strangers are easily understood by parents or siblings. These children have succeeded in developing a structured communication system. Unfortunately, however, it is not the standard system.

Phonological errors such as these can result in speech that ranges from mildly aberrant to completely unintelligible, depending on the nature and the extent of the phonological confusion, as well as the familiarity of the listener and the specific conversational situation.

Consequences of Phonological Impairment

Phonological, or speech, problems are particularly important because of their impact on other aspects of the language system. Some minimum level of intelligibility is necessary for verbal communication. If the individual sounds of speech are not understandable to the listener, then the message is lost. As a result, children with robust lexical, morphological, and syntactic skills are at a communicative risk if their phonological problems prevent them from being understood.

In addition to having a potentially broad effect in the linguistic system, phonological errors are also very noticeable. Even a relatively unfamiliar listener can usually identify a child with a phonological problem, while many semantic and syntactic problems may go unnoticed. The effects of phonological problems on intelligibility, combined with their ready detectability, can lead to difficulties in social and pragmatic development for these children. In the opening vignette, both Charlie and his teachers were extremely frustrated by his inability to communicate. There are many ways in which children respond when repeatedly faced with these kinds of communicative breakdowns. Many children become quiet and careful about when and to whom they speak (Rice, Sell, & Hadley, 1990); others learn which sounds, words, or sentences are most likely to be understood correctly by their listeners and they shape their conversations accordingly (Schwartz & Leonard, 1982); still others support their verbalizations with gestures or contextual cues in order to increase the likelihood of communicative success. Although these strategies produce a range of success across various children, they each can have a negative impact on linguistic and social development.

One of the key aspects of the concentrated normative model is that a primary component of language learning is the opportunity to practice new skills in meaningful contexts. To be good at describing your grandmother, you must practice describing your grandmother; to be good at talking your buddy out of his toy tractor, you must practice talking your buddy out of his toy tractor; and to be good at conning your friends out of an extra turn, you must practice your justification for moving to the front of the line. Through these experiences, children build their semantic, morphological, syntactic, *and* phonological systems. Children who are not easily understood, who adopt a strategy of nonparticipation, or who avoid some sounds or words are not likely to be full participants in the verbal interactions necessary for optimizing language growth. The following vignette illustrates one possible impact of a severe phonological impairment on a child's interactions.

Three children, Ben and Sally, who are developing language typically, and Max, who has a phonological disorder, are playing veterinarian.

Ben:	"My dog has been coughing."
Sally:	"Bring him over here."
	"Let me listen to him."
	(to Max) "Give me the stethoscope."
	(Max hands her the stethoscope.)
	"Thanks." (Listens to sick dog)
Ben:	"Will he be OK?"
Sally:	"Yes, he needs medicine."
	(to Max) "Get some medicine for the dog and give it to Ben. Tell him how much to give."
Max:	(hands medicine to Ben) "Take two."

This short vignette illustrates the tendency for linguistically adept children to take the lead in interactions with their peers. Not only are Max's comments limited in number, but they also serve a supportive, rather than central, role in the interaction. These two consequences, limited participation and assuming secondary roles, are typical for many children with phonological impairments.

TRADITIONAL ARTICULATION THERAPY

The practice of speech-language pathology traces some of its earliest roots to a cadre of dedicated teachers in the early part of the 20th century (Paden, 1970). These teachers were particularly concerned about the speech problems of their students, the majority of whom either stuttered or had speech sound problems. For both groups of students, a direct instructional approach was considered the appropriate treatment strategy. Thus, children were taught to position and move their lips, tongues, and jaws correctly in order to produce accurate and fluent speech. Because this work developed primarily in the public schools, it is not surprising that most articulation therapy programs were designed to address the prevailing problems seen in school-age children, including many relatively mild cases of misarticulation, such as children who say "wabbit" for "rabbit" or "thoup" for "soup." The clinical insights of these professional pioneers were largely correct for this age group. As a result, school-age children have, for many years, benefited from direct instruction in the articulation of the allophones of English.

As these articulation therapy programs developed, they were heavily influenced by two areas of study. The first of these was the growing field of experimental and applied phonetics. As sophisticated instrumentation became available, scientists were able to observe and describe the fine aspects of the motor movements of speech. This, in turn, enabled the specification of the crucial elements for the correct production of various sounds and sound combinations. These details were used by early speech-language pathologists to delineate plans for instruction and documentation of speech improvement. The second influence on articulation therapy came from behavioral psychology, which promoted teaching strategies with tightly controlled stimuli (often the instructor's spoken model) and predefined and carefully administered feedback. The well-defined surface forms of speech lend themselves nicely to such a teaching paradigm. Thus, there are numerous articulation therapy programs that systematize intervention activities and emphasize the documentation of specific changes in a child's speech (e.g., Baker & Ryan, 1971).

The influences of experimental and applied phonetics and behavioral psychology had several additional consequences. First, in most articulation therapy programs, a premium was placed on massed practice. The idea was that in order to master a new motor task, one must practice it repeatedly. Furthermore, each practice item was generally seen as equivalent to every other item. There was no allowance for the possibility that one carefully chosen production might be more useful to a child than some other production. Second, articulation therapy emphasized the importance of overt responses on the part of the child, as in the "I say–you say" drills referred to in Chapter 2. Given the assumption that the correction to be made was primarily motoric, it followed that the most appropriate remediation involved observable, motor responses from the child. Third, practice was organized from the articulatorily simple to the complex. Sounds were practiced in isolation, then in syllables, then in words, then in phrases, and so forth. At each level, drills usually focused on a small number of representative items (e.g., 10–20 words at the word level), and when these were mastered therapy advanced to the next level of complexity. In many therapy programs, students only moved to "real" practice (i.e., practice in meaningful conversations) after mastering all of the preceding levels. This general organization schema allowed speech-language pathologists to monitor performance carefully while also making the motor demands of the speaking task more manageable for the student.

Finally, in order to encourage participation in the necessary drills, an elaborate system of artificial reinforcement was often needed. Targeted responses were positively reinforced, and undesirable responses were negatively reinforced or punished (e.g., "Say all 10 of these /s/ sounds correctly and you will get a gold star"). Although the logic behind these reinforcement systems is straightforward, their necessity underscores the artificiality of many therapy programs. In natural consequences, children learn to speak because communication is self-reinforcing. By reducing speech to forced drills, the self-reinforcing aspects of the process were removed.

It has been only since the 1970s that speech-language pathology has begun integrating phonological theory into the planning and implementation of articulation therapy (Elbert, Dinnsen, & Weismer, 1984; Fey, 1985; Hodson & Paden, 1983). With this integration, the term "articulation therapy" has given way to the term "phonological remediation," reflecting an expanded focus on both the motor movements of speech and the underlying sound system of the language. Many practitioners now routinely consider the role of phonemes and allophones in the phonological system of English before they select a target for treatment. Similarly, many therapy programs are now specifically designed to share the importance of particular phonological contrasts with the child. However, most phonological therapy continues to rely on motor practice and drillwork, with the primary focus on repeated oral attempts of a targeted sound until mastery is achieved.

In contrast, the premise of the approach used in LAP is that many children can benefit from therapy focused on acquiring an understanding of the sound system rather than on the development of motor skills. It is true that children must master the motor movements of speech and that this mastery, as well as much of the understanding of the phonological system, must be acquired through verbal practice. Similarly, a good portion of phonological knowledge can be acquired by listening to other speakers in the environment. The challenge to present and future speech-language pathologists is to create a comprehensive phonological intervention program that assists the child in discovering and understanding the phonological system and that is sufficiently self-reinforcing to ensure its own use.

THE LANGUAGE-FOCUSED CURRICULUM INTERVENTION PROGRAM

As noted at the beginning of this chapter, most of the basic facilitation principles of the LFC, and the CNM, apply to both speech and language. If language is a set of interrelated components, then the activities that facilitate growth in one aspect of that system should facilitate growth in the other aspects as well. In other words, phonology should benefit from many of the same activities that support morphological and syntactic development. The 10 principles that underlie the LAP program and guide facilitation efforts in both speech and language are summarized in Table 2.

Taken together, the principles of the CNM describe a highly embedded and interactive facilitation model, with the children (and their parents) viewed as primary players in their own remediation programs. It is important to note at the outset that this philosophy of intervention is not necessarily compatible with the long tradition in articulation therapy, which emphasizes the repeated practice of a small number of iso-

Table 2.   Operational guidelines for concentrated normative model

1.	Language intervention is best provided in a meaningful social context.
2.	Language facilitation occurs throughout the entire curriculum.
3.	The language curriculum is rooted in content themes.
4.	Language intervention begins with the child.
5.	Verbal interaction is encouraged.
6.	Passive language learning and overt responses are encouraged.
7.	Children's utterances are accorded functional value.
8.	Valuable teaching occasions can arise in child-to-child interactions.
9.	Parents are valuable partners in language intervention programming.
10.	Routine parent evaluations are an integral part of the program.

lated tokens. Indeed, one of the most frequently asked questions of the LAP staff is: "How do you treat phonological problems in the classroom?" The idea that phonological therapy can be embedded in classroom activities is alien to many speech-language pathologists. The same individuals who endorse vocabulary practice incorporated into play themes as a means of enhancing semantic development are troubled by the idea of embedding allophonic practice into play themes as a means of enhancing phonological development.

In order to highlight the special considerations that affect phonology, the following three additional guiding principles are offered that apply to phonological therapy in classroom contexts:

1. *Little emphasis is placed on eliciting correct productions.* Children receive few instructions on the correct placement of their articulators for producing particular sounds. So, for example, there are no long periods spent in front of mirrors examining the placement of the tongue tip during production of /t/. Instead speech-language pathologists work from the child's own utterances, building on correct productions and contrasting those with errors.

2. *Not all trials are equal.* In the course of the school day, a child is likely to produce hundreds of tokens (correct and incorrect) of any given phoneme. It is impossible to control or monitor all of these occurrences; instead, clinicians attempt to highlight and shape selected utterances throughout the day. Some productions of a given phoneme are naturally more important to a child than others. The relative importance is affected by a number of factors including the nature of the adjacent sounds in a word and the role of the sound or word in an activity. For example, "stop" (and by extension, /s/) becomes highly salient for the child who is the traffic cop and whose classmates are all potential speeders.

3. *Therapy success can be measured in ways beyond the number of correctly produced phonemes.* Correct production of all of the phonemes of the language is the ultimate goal for all children receiving intervention. However, given the interrelationship between phonology and other aspects of the language system, and the social implications of misarticulation, a simple count of the number of correctly produced phonemes in a speech sample may not fully reflect a child's phonological development. Progress in morphology or syntax is also important indicators of phonological advancement for many children. Given that phonological skill is needed to mark much of morphology and syntax, increases in morphological ability are often associated with increases in phonological skill.

Similarly, an increase in the number of verbal interactions, especially those with peers (see Chapter 4), experienced by a child can be an important indicator of language gains. Even in cases in which few phonological changes are apparent, an increased willingness to enter into play activities and conversations (in other words, an increased willingness to take verbal risks) can be an important sign of growth. This increase in verbal participation can often facilitate even greater phonological gains, in that access to conversations provides access to new opportunities for practice and for language learning.

TEACHING STRATEGIES

Experience in the LAP classroom has led to the development of phonological intervention strategies consistent with the three principles enumerated above. Insofar as phonological experiences are a part of all speaking activities, the range of possible options available to speech-language pathologists goes far beyond the examples provided here. Thus, the following strategies are to be regarded as illustrative for practitioners who will see ways to extend them in naturalistic settings.

The strategies are organized into two categories, individual teaching strategies and sound games. Although the individual teaching strategies are described in terms of one-to-one interactions and the sound games are typically group events, neither category is limited to only one type of interaction. Instead, individual teaching strategies can be included in group activities and sound games can be played by individual dyads of adults and children. In the LAP classroom, it is relatively rare to have a one-to-one teaching situation. Instead, the children are usually engaged in play with several peers at any given time. Thus, the typical case is to have more than one child participating in any activity.

Individual Teaching Strategies

Focused Contrasts and Re-embedding

Focused contrasts and *re-embedding* are two of the most important strategies used for phonological, as well as morphological, semantic, and syntactic instruction in LAP. Usually appearing together, focused contrasts and re-embedding refer to the process of drawing a child's attention to a particular sound or utterance and then attempting to incorporate that item back into the child's ongoing activity. Although the procedure can take many forms, the following are two typical examples:

Sue: "All washed. Now I'll -omb your hair."
Teacher: "Thank you for the shampoo. Please Comb it nicely. I love to have my hair Combed."
          "Ooh, don't pull my hair with the Comb. It hurts."
Bill: "My turn."
Teacher: "I think Bill needs to have his hair Combed. Ask him if it needs to be Combed."
Sue: "You wanna be combed?"

Gary: "I don't like shish."
Teacher: "It's a Fish, Fish. It's a Fish. I don't like Fish either."

Depending on the situation and the specific skills of the child, the teacher might expect the child to use the target in the ensuing conversation, as in the first example, or might expect no verbal attempt from the child. When no verbal response is expected, the teacher typically uses his or her own productions both to focus on the targeted form and to re-embed it into its appropriate place in the conversation. The two examples above also illustrate different levels of explicitness of the focusing and of the degree to which the model is removed from the play conversa-

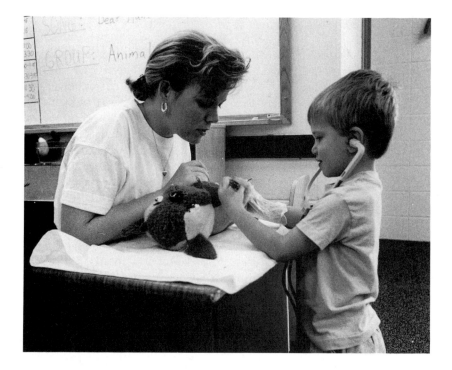

tion. In the first interchange, focus is drawn to the /k/ sound in "comb" by emphasizing the sound within the word. In this example, there is the expectation that the child will recognize this emphasis and benefit from it. In the second case, the teacher has identified more explicitly the fact that an error has occurred and where it is located.

Regardless of the explicitness of the instruction, the targeted item is usually selected from the child's own speech. Sometimes, however, the target is initially produced by the teacher, based on her knowledge of the child's particular speech problems. In either case, the best items for focusing are sounds or words that are central to some aspect of the activity at hand. In this way, the child's interests are incorporated into the activity, and it is easier to re-embed the target into the conversation.

There are two key components to successful focused contrasts and re-embedding. First is the identification of good candidates on which to focus. This requires the adult to be familiar with the child's phonological system and the specific goals of his or her treatment program. In addition, the speech-language pathologist must monitor the play situation for potential exemplars of the child's goals and he or she must continually assess the potential value of various exemplars as candidates for intervention. Among other factors, the relative facilitory value of an item will vary by situation, allophone type, position in a word or phrase, linguistic import in the activity, and so forth. The second key component to successful focused contrasts and re-embedding is the orchestration of play situations to increase the number of obligatory contexts for an item. Obligatory contexts are those linguistic situations where the rules of the language require the use of the targeted item. Such orchestration is often necessary to ensure an ample number of opportunities for speech practice. It is important, however, that all of the created contexts be as natural a part of the ongoing play as possible.

Minimal Contrasts

Minimal contrasts were first utilized therapeutically by Cooper (1968). His work represents one of the initial attempts to employ lexical meaning as a central part of articulation therapy. In LAP, this translates to selecting intervention targets for which the child's typical error produces significant semantic contrast (e.g., a child who intends to say "glue" but produces "blue"). Selection of such intervention targets means that potential errors become salient in the semantic domain, thereby increasing their likelihood for identification by the child. Minimal phonological contrasts are also useful when produced solely by the teacher, during playtime and group time, as a means of highlighting the nature and form of various allophones.

Focused Practice

Focused practice of targeted phonemes is used sparingly in LAP. Generally, it occurs at less structured times, such as the beginning of the day before all of the children have arrived. In these cases, speech-language pathologists work individually with children and practice the production of selected syllables or words. Although this appears to resemble traditional articulation therapy, it differs in several respects. First, the focus in LAP is on highlighting the forms for the child and not on accuracy of production. Children are not held to, or rewarded for, an expected standard of correct performance, but instead are given an opportunity to practice some of their sounds. One of the important consequences of the focused practice sessions in LAP is that children come to learn "their sound" and the types of words in which their sound appears, so that they are more receptive to other types of instruction throughout the day.

Second, focused practice sessions often take the form of sound play, in that the format is relatively unstructured and peers are often eager (and encouraged) to participate. Third, speech targets are drawn from the child's interests and the materials are usually of the child's choosing. So, for example, if two children are working puzzles before school starts, the speech-language pathologist might join them and encourage some sound practice centering around the puzzle or its pictorial theme. Fourth, practice proceeds from the child's level of ability, but seldom if ever does it include practice of isolated sounds. Instead syllables and words are often the targets. In particular, sound play using consonant-vowel (CV) and vowel-consonant (VC) syllables and the vowels /a/, /i/, and /u/ is a common focused practice activity. Fifth, most focused practice sessions last only a minute or two. There is no long regimen of drillwork.

Sound Games

Sound games are simply overt manipulations of phonological patterns. It is our shared knowledge of the regularities of the phonological system that allows us, even as adults, to enjoy sound and word games. In a classroom these games are a means of sharing the systematicity of the sound system with the children. Like most of the other teaching strategies employed in LAP, little effort is made to force participation in sound games. This is because active listening by the children is considered just as important as speaking, and also because the nature of the games themselves makes them appealing to the children. Most sound games are one of three types: *alliteration, rhyming,* and *syllable manipulation.*

Alliteration and Rhyming

Most people are familiar with alliteration and rhyming, with the proviso that we are discussing sounds not letters ("tongue" rhymes with "sung"; "thin" and "thumb" are examples of alliteration, but "thin" and "there" are not). Opportunities for reciting a litany of rhyming words, or words that start with the same phoneme, abound in a preschool. With just a bit of creativity, a string of words such as "fire,","Frank," "fuel," "flame," "favorite," "five," "firehouse," "forever," and "fat" is easily embedded into playing firehouse. Or "rung," "hung," "lung," and "young" can be embedded into the same setting with perhaps the teacher pantomiming hitting the firebell ("rung"), arms overhead as if hanging from a window ledge ("hung"), administering cardiopulmonary resuscitation ("lung"), and holding her hand down low, indicating a child's height ("young"). It is also possible to continue that string of words with "gung," "jung," "blung," "krung," and so forth. The latter have the advantage of sharing the productivity of phonological rules while eliciting giggles. Opportunities for both alliteration and rhyming can be increased by means of careful selection of available toys or play themes.

Syllable Manipulation

Syllable manipulation refers to the systematic creation or disintegration of words. Thus, "she" can be transformed into "sheep," or "more" into "Mortimer," by simply adding on to the end of the original word. Syllables may also be manipulated in ways much like alliteration and rhyming, where words are grouped together based on the similarity of the first or last parts of the word or syllable. In fact, creating rhyming words is really a type of syllable manipulation. To produce a word that rhymes with "rung" (/rʌŋ/), the final portion of the syllable (/ʌŋ/) is attached to a different initial consonant (/z/ + /ʌŋ/ = "zung"). The same process of combining word parts to create rhymes can be done with multisyllabic words, as in "rotation," "notation," "elimination," "excitation," and so forth. Other syllable manipulations create similar, yet non-rhyming words, as in "exciting," "excitable," "excitement," and "excitation." Both of these sets of words reflect some of the ways that English words are generated and the systematic phonological and morphological changes that are a part of that process. As with any type of word game, syllables can be manipulated to create real words as well as nonsense forms that conform to the phonological rules of the language.

Another syllabic activity involves counting, or tapping, in time to the syllables in a word or to the words in a nursery rhyme. Remember that in English there is generally a one-to-one correspondence between vowels and syllables. As a result, syllable-counting activities provide the child with direct clues to the number and placement of vowels in a word or sentence.

Opportunities to Play Sound Games

Alliteration, rhyming, and syllable manipulation are embedded throughout the classroom day in LAP. There are some aspects of the curriculum, however, that offer special opportunities to play sound games. Some of those specific occasions are described below.

Classroom Routines   *Classroom routines* provide a unique opportunity to practice the sound system. For example, at the beginning of each day the children in LAP greet each of their classmates by name. They then participate in a choral speaking exercise identifying the month, the date, the day of the week, the season, and the prevailing weather pattern. The order of this information is fixed and the list of acceptable responses in each category is limited. As a result, the children soon learn the sequence of events and the best possible response to each of the teacher's queries. In this type of situation, all of the participants know what to expect next in the interaction. As a result, they can, as a group, turn their attention to the form, as well as the content, of the message. This means that later in the school year the children can begin to appreciate that Bobby's and Billy's names start with the same sound; and later still, that both names start with the same letter, as well. Similarly, group time, snacktime, outdoor time, and going-home time have their agreed-upon verbal routines that can be opportunities for shared phonological experiences.

Children's Stories   *Children's stories* provide numerous instances of repetition and verbal routines. Anyone who has spent time with a young child appreciates how much children enjoy repetition. As a result, many children's stories include a simple refrain that is repeated over and over throughout the story. These refrains are ideal for highlighting sounds, syllables, or words. For example, the familiar "I'll huff and I'll puff and I'll blow your house down" can be useful in teaching /h/, /p/, /b/, /bl/, /f/, /d/, /s/, and /o/, or any number of combinatory phonological rules. The utility of such strings can also be enhanced by adding intonational cues, changing speaking rate (e.g., slow down and elongate the /f/ production), or adding gestures (e.g., raising a finger to note something important during the prolonged /f/).

Children's Songs   By their very nature, most *children's songs* also include repetition and rhyming. Some songs, however, have special phonological value. The following LAP favorite is one example of overt phonological manipulation.

> "I like to eat, I like to eat, I like to eat, apples and bananas."
> "I like to ite, I like to ite, I like to ite, ipples and bininis."
> "E leke to eat, E leke to eat, E leke to eat, eepples and beeneenees."
> "A lake to ate, A lake to ate, A lake to ate, aepples and baenaenaes."
> "Oo luke to ute, Oo luke to ute, Oo luke to ute, oopples and boonoonoos."
> "Oh loke to ote, Oh loke to ote, Oh loke to ote, opples and bononos."

Other songs, such as the Cookie Monster's "C Is for Cookie, It's Good Enough for Me" and the traditional alphabet song, also offer special phonological training opportunities.

Noises Not all sound games need words. Many noises are potential sources for phonological experience. "k,k,k,k,k,k . . ." can be a handy noise for a helicopter or a rusty old truck. Adding sounds to large motor activities helps make the play more fun and provides an outlet for children's exuberance and the tendency to yell and scream while making big movements.

Given the emphasis of U.S. society on literacy, many sound games in the popular children's media include alphabetic relationships and these relationships are often included in the classroom. In the classroom, literacy is considered much like the rest of the child's evolving world. It is something to explore and, for children with a special interest, it may be a domain in which speech and language training is undertaken. Since the 1980s, researchers have begun to appreciate the role of phonology in reading development, with recent studies indicating that phonological skill can actually predict eventual reading level in children (Catts, 1991). Thus, the sound games described here are likely to enhance phonological development and, in turn, later reading ability.

The combined result of the activities outlined above, and those employed within the other language domains, is a classroom where children manipulate and think about the language system. All of the children, whether they are typically developing, are learning English as a second language, or have a language impairment, are accustomed to stopping in the middle of their play and focusing on a sound or group of sounds. In a sense, such an occurrence is no different for them than stopping in the middle of play to look at a beetle. It is just another part of the child's world that warrants examination. By extension, there is relatively little stigmatizing of children with phonological impairments for having to "work on their sounds." Through the course of the year, many of the children do become aware of each other's sound goals, and in some cases peers take on the role of clinical aides by reminding each other of their speech errors. We conclude this chapter with two short scenarios that illustrate the level of phonological awareness of some of the children in LAP.

At one of the end-of-the-year parent productions, Justin was cast as one of the three little pigs. Right in the middle of the production, Justin stopped with, what was to him, an exciting discovery that he felt compelled to share with a friend.

Justin: "You can't get us in this house. It's made of sticks, not bricks."
(Aloud, but to himself)
"Sticks . . . bricks . . . sticks . . . bricks."
(Turning to a classmate) "Hey, Cristina, sticks rhymes with bricks!"

At the beginning of the year, Betsy's phonological difficulties made her speech nearly unintelligible. Near the end of the year, her speech had improved markedly, but she still had several errors, including difficulties with many of the allophones of /s/. On this particular day, Betsy and Jacob were playing gardener.

Betsy: "If it's not lunny, the plants won't grow."
Jacob: "Say 'sunny,' not 'lunny.'"

And from then on, Betsy did.

REFERENCES

Baker, R.D., & Ryan, B.P. (1971). *Programmed conditioning for articulation.* Monterey, CA: Monterey Learning Systems.

Catts, H.W. (1991). Facilitating phonological awareness: Role of speech-language pathologists. *Language, Speech, and Hearing Services in Schools, 22,* 196–203.

Cooper, R. (1968). The method of meaningful minimal contrasts in functional articulation problems. *Journal of the Speech and Hearing Association of Virginia, 10,* 187–190.

Edwards, J. (1992). Compensatory speech motor abilities in normal and phonologically disordered children. *Journal of Phonetics, 20,* 189–207.

Elbert, M., Dinnsen, D.A., & Weismer, G. (Eds.). (1984). *Phonological theory and the misarticulation child (American Speech and Hearing Association Monograph No. 22).* Rockville, MD: American Speech and Hearing Association.

Fey, M. (1985). Articulation and phonology: Inextricable constructs in speech pathology. *Human Communication Canada, 9,* 7–16.

Hodson, B.W., & Paden, E.P. (1983). *Targeting intelligible speech: A phonological approach to remediation.* San Diego: College Hill.

Kent, R. (1976). Anatomical and neuromuscular maturation of the speech mechanism: Evidence from acoustic studies. *Journal of Speech and Hearing Research, 19,* 421–447.

Paden, E.P. (1970). *A history of the American Speech and Hearing Association, 1925–1958.* Washington, DC: American Speech and Hearing Association.

Rice, M.L., Sell, M.A., & Hadley, P.A. (1990). The Social Interactive Coding System (SICS): An on-line clinically relevant descriptive tool. *Language, Speech, and Hearing Services in the Schools, 21,* 2–14.

Ruscello, D.M., St. Louis, K.O., & Mason, N. (1991). School-aged children with phonological disorders: Coexistence with other speech-language disorders. *Journal of Speech and Hearing Research, 34,* 236–242.

Schwartz, R.G., & Leonard, L.B. (1982). Do children pick and choose? An examination of phonological selection and avoidance in early lexical acquisition. *Journal of Child Language, 9,* 319–336.

Shriberg, L.D., & Kent, R.D. (1982). *Clinical phonetics.* New York: John Wiley & Sons.

Shriberg, L.D., & Kwiatkowski, J. (1982). Phonological disorders I: A diagnostic classification system. *Journal of Speech and Hearing Disorders, 47,* 226–241.

Shriberg, L.D., Kwiatkowski, J., Best, S., Hengst, J., & Terselic-Weber, B. (1986). Characteristics of children with phonologic disorders of unknown origin. *Journal of Speech and Hearing Disorders, 51,* 140–161.

Smith, B.L., & Kenney, M.K. (1994). Variability control in speech production tasks performed by adults and children. *Journal of the Acoustical Society of America, 96,* 699–705.

Weismer, G. (1984). Acoustic analysis strategies for the refinement of phonological analysis. In M. Elbert, D.A. Dinnsen, & G. Weismer (Eds.), *Phonological theory and the misarticulation child (American Speech and Hearing Association Monograph No. 22,* pp. 30–52). Rockville, MD: American Speech and Hearing Association.

Weiss, C.E., Gordon, M.E., & Lillywhite, H.S. (1987). *Clinical management of articulatory and phonologic disorders* (2nd ed.). Baltimore: Williams & Wilkins.

~6~

A Language-Focused Curriculum for Children Learning English as a Second Language

Betty H. Bunce

It is the first day of preschool. Three-year-old Paulo Trujillo holds tightly to his mother's hand and looks shyly at the teacher. Mrs. Trujillo speaks very little English and also appears shy and hesitant while her husband does the talking. The other children mill around. Some are playing with blocks, others with small toys, and still others are coloring. It is a typical first day with lots of excited, but apprehensive, children and adults. Mr. Trujillo hands over Paulo to the teacher and explains that Paulo, having just arrived from Mexico, speaks only Spanish. The teacher smiles and assures Mr. Trujillo that Paulo will be fine. Paulo is then gently directed over to the play areas and, through gestures, is encouraged to join the other children. He looks worried, but does not cry. He slowly picks up a crayon and begins to draw. Thus begins the story of Paulo and his parents' 2-year adventure in the Language Acquisition Preschool (LAP).

PAULO'S ENROLLMENT

Mr. and Mrs. Trujillo had heard about LAP from friends who were living next to them in the graduate student apartments. They came over to the LAP office to check on enrolling Paulo. The LAP family services coordinator and the director met briefly with Mr. and Mrs. Trujillo to explain LAP's policies and show them the classroom. The staff members also explained that, if possible, a university student who spoke Spanish would be available during the first few days to help explain the classroom routine to Paulo. Paperwork for enrolling Paulo was then completed.

THE REST OF PAULO'S FIRST DAY

A flick of the light switch signals that arrival time is over and play items are to be put away. Paulo looks up startled, but Carla, his interpreter, explains that it is time to put his crayons away and his drawing into his cubby. He is then shown where to sit for circle time. When his name card is held up by the teacher, he is helped to raise his hand to show that he is present. The teacher then helps the children count on the calendar to determine what the day is. A child puts up the number and the whole class sings a song about the days of the week. Paulo just watches.

The teacher then demonstrates what can be done at the quiet, block, art, and dramatic play areas. Books and puzzles are available in the quiet area; blocks, cars, trucks, dollhouses, and other small toys are available in the block area. For art, a water-painting activity is demonstrated. Finally, the water-play activity, where children can pour and pump water, play with boats, and wash baby dolls, is demonstrated. The teacher then lets the children choose where they want to play.

Paulo chooses the art area and begins to paint a picture. Periodically, he looks over at the children at the water table. Finally, with the encouragement of his interpreter, he approaches the table, while watching the other children. One child moves away and Paulo begins to play with the pump. Every once in a while, other children will hand him a toy or indicate that they want a turn with the pump. At first, Paulo's interpreter explains what is needed, but soon Paulo seems to know what to do without the interpreter's explanation. Again, the light flashes to signal a change. Paulo helps dry the toys and put them away. He then goes back to the circle for storytime. Paulo no longer looks worried. He sits quietly as the other children gather around the teacher. And so the day continues.

One third of the children enrolled in LAP are, like Paulo in the vignette above, learning English as their second language (ESL). The other children are monolingual speakers of English with one third having speech and language impairments and the other third having language skills within the typical range. The children who are learning English as their second language are limited in their knowledge of English but are competent speakers of another language. A range of first languages are represented by the children enrolled in LAP. Children whose first languages include Chinese, Japanese, Polish, Spanish, Urdu, and Serbo-Croatian have attended LAP. Since LAP was created, speakers of 15 different language groups have attended. In any given semester, five or six language groups are usually represented.

When LAP was in the planning stages, it was decided that children of graduate students and professors in attendance at the University of Kansas should be recruited. This sample ensured linguistic diversity, and, generally, a parental interest in their children's academic and linguistic progress. The intent was to include preschool children who were new to the United States (i.e., in residence less than 4 months) and who were limited in their knowledge of English (typically had no prior experience with English). Our interest was in how these children would go about the problem of learning a second language, how they would participate in and contribute to a language-facilitating classroom, and how they would progress in learning English. Our expectation was that a language-focused curriculum (LFC) based on a concentrated normative model (CNM) would be helpful to all three of the groups we had targeted for enrollment—children learning English as a second language, children with speech and language impairments, *and* children with expected language acquisition milestones.

ISSUES RELATING TO SECOND LANGUAGE ACQUISITION

Many issues arise with regard to acquiring English as a second language and the participation in preschool of children new to the United States. Over the years, parents have articulated many of these issues, with a few occurring repeatedly. Because these concerns are important and interesting, this chapter is organized around them. Observations of the children in LAP are used to illustrate key points. The key questions to be addressed here are as follows:

1. How does a child learn a second language?
2. Are there individual differences in the ways children learn a second language?
3. How long does it take for a child to become proficient in the second language?

How Does a Child Learn a Second Language?

Parents often want to know more about how children learn a second language. To many people, the acquisition of a second language by children is viewed as no problem. Children who travel to different countries with their parents often are reported to learn the new language quickly. Through their interactions with native speakers, they just seem to "pick it up." There appear to be striking parallels between the ways children learn their first language and their acquisition of a second language, especially if the children are young (see Hakuta, 1986, for a general review of issues in bilingualism; and Ellis, 1986, for a discussion of theories of second language acquisition). As the youngsters interact verbally with native speakers, they come to work out the semantic, grammatical, and pragmatic conventions of the new language. However, a significant caution is important here and is addressed in detail later in this chapter. That caution is that although oral language skills can appear with some readiness in young children, the development of competency with more formal, academic properties of language can require much more time to establish (cf. Cummins, 1984).

What seems to be crucial in the process of second language acquisition is the opportunity for children to experience *comprehensible* linguistic input in the second language (cf. Wong Fillmore, 1989). What makes a new language comprehensible to a youngster? Much of the input becomes understandable through the context in which the language is used. The context can provide clues about meaning even if the language is unknown.

Tabors and Snow (in press) describe two nonverbal processes that are important as preschool children learn a second language. The first process, "spectating," occurs when children actively observe peers and adults using the target language. There is a focus on making sense of the English input. "Rehearsing" is the second process, in which children repeat phrases heard but do not use the repetitions in a communicative manner. Rather, they appear to be practicing the productions of the new language, which in LAP is English.

In LAP, children learning English as their second language have contact with English-speaking children and adults within the context of a preschool classroom. They have many opportunities to "spectate" and to rehearse phrases they hear. Routine activities help provide support for understanding what is being said. For example, pointing to the hook inside a child's cubby can help the child understand that a coat needs to be hung there. This is understood even more readily if other children are hanging up their coats, too. Other routine activities such as snacktime, sharing time, and circle time can provide excellent opportunities for them to hear specific vocabulary and sentence structure where the intent of the communication is apparent. These activities tend to have similar sentences produced over and over, day after day. For example, phrases such as "more crackers, please" and "more juice, please" are often heard during snacktime. Children learning English as a second language may at first practice, or rehearse, saying these phrases even when they have plenty of juice and crackers. Soon, they learn to use the phrases to get their needs met. As children play during child-centered activities, labels can be provided without direct teaching. Use of gestures to identify objects can be very helpful in the child's understanding of what is said. The context of the activity helps support the child's understanding and ability to make sense of the input. In this way, then, the language-focused curriculum provides contact with English speakers in naturalistic interactions, and comprehensible input, both of which are likely to facilitate second language acquisition.

Are There Individual Differences in the Ways Children Learn a Second Language?

Second language acquisition may not be uniformly easy. Research with young children learning a second language has shown wide variability in how quickly children acquire new languages and the levels of competency reached (Hatch, 1978; Snow, 1983; Wong Fillmore, 1979, 1989). For example, some children may be silent in the classroom for long periods of time before beginning to talk (Ervin-Tripp, 1981; Hakuta, 1978; Tabors, 1987; Wong Fillmore, 1989). These children may use a variety of nonverbal means to communicate (Saville-Troike, 1988). Other children begin speaking right away, but rely on routine expressions or sentence patterns such as "I wanna play," "Lookit," or "How do you do dese?" (Wong Fillmore, 1979, pp. 211–213). This usage of routine expressions is called "formula" or "formulaic" speech by some researchers (Rescorla & Okuda, 1987; Wong Fillmore, 1979). Rescorla and Okuda note that children differ in the ways they use this strategy. For example, they may use it with peers and not adults, or vice versa. Other children might choose not to learn the second language, to reject the entire process. So, although there may be typical patterns of second language learning, there are also differences among children. An obvious consequence is that there can be considerable variation in how quickly children learn a second language. This difference appears to be related more to issues bearing on a child's individual personal traits, such as a willingness to take risks, than on more general traits of speakers of a certain language group. Thus, individual differences seem to be better characterized in terms of Child A versus Child B instead of speakers-of-Spanish versus speakers-of-Chinese (Wong Fillmore, 1979, 1989).

These observations about individual differences have also been noted in the acquisition of English by children in LAP. The differences in style and rate of acquisition do not appear to be due to a particular language group; rather, observed differences appear to be related more to the individual child's personality. For example, two 3-year-old Chinese children used different styles in acquiring English. One child, Bao, was very outgoing and sociable. He first used a strategy of imitating whatever the teacher said. After about 3 weeks, he would use sentence formulas such as "I want the _____" or "What do you have?" After Bao had been in the program approximately 6 months, he appeared to go through a "semi-silent" phase in which he did less talking and used less complex sentence structure than he had used earlier. However, his sentences were more spontaneous and not formulaic. At the end of his first year in LAP, he routinely used three- and four-word sentences. After 2 years, Bao was fluent in English and scored within typical limits for native English speakers on both receptive and expressive standardized tests.

Another Chinese child, Sheng, followed a different pattern. He appeared shy and was hesitant to join in some of the classroom activities. Sheng was silent for approximately 5 months. He carefully observed classroom activities and communicated his needs nonverbally. His first words involved food and were part of the snacktime routine (e.g., "More crackers, please"). However, once Sheng started talking, he relied less and less on routinized phrases. By the time he had been in the classroom 10 months, he was generating novel two- to three-word sentences. A child who spoke Indonesian followed a pattern similar to Sheng, waiting for 7 months before saying his first word in English.

Paulo, the child in the opening vignette, was silent for approximately 3 months. He was also very observant and participated nonverbally in most of the classroom activities. When he did begin to talk, he used one- to five-word utterances and did not appear to rely on routinized phrases. Although Paulo did not talk very much, when he did speak, his sentences were well formed. After 2 years in the program, Paulo also scored within typical limits for native English speakers on both receptive and expressive standardized tests.

Thus, our conclusion is that the length of time in the program and the personality of the children appear to affect the learning of English more strongly than the child's first language. Great individual differences are evident among children with the same native language, and there are similarities among children of different native languages.

How Long Does It Take for a Child to Become Proficient in the Second Language?

Cummins (1984) noted that elementary-age children who began learning English at age 5 appeared to achieve good conversational skills after 2 years. However, he also suggested that it may take 5–7 years for children speaking English as their second language to reach the same level of competency as native speakers on verbal academic tasks (e.g., tasks involving written language). This has important educational policy considerations. Hakuta and his colleagues (Stanford Working Group, 1993) have begun to address some of these issues and suggest that language-minority students must be provided with an equal opportunity to learn the same content and high-level skills that are advocated for all students. For children in preschool classrooms, conversational skills are the main focus. There is not the gap involving the academic skills between the second language learners and the native speakers that is sometimes the case for the older children.

Most children who are enrolled in LAP for 2 years can communicate effectively in English. Often their proficiency approaches that of native speakers (Bunce & Shirk, 1993). For example, children who have been in the program 2 years or longer are usually, but not always, fluent and score within typical limits on standardized testing using norms for monolingual speakers of English. Children who attend LAP for only 1 year are usually able to express their needs using short sentences. Their vocabulary and use of complex sentence structures, however, can be restricted. One child appeared to actively choose not to learn much English during the 2 years he was in LAP. When he was questioned by his parents about why he was not using English, he said he did not want to learn English because he knew they would be returning to Korea soon. However, most children do learn to communicate effectively in English.

FACILITATING ACQUISITION OF A SECOND LANGUAGE

In the first section of this chapter, issues about how children acquired English as a second language were addressed. The focus of this section is how second language acquisition can be facilitated. Again, parents have asked questions about this process; some of these questions include the following:

1. What are effective ways to teach or facilitate the learning of a second language?
2. Are interpreters needed? If so, what is their role?
3. Is it helpful or is it a problem to have children who speak the same first language in the classroom where English is to be learned?
4. How can the first language be maintained?
5. What is the academic progress of children in LAP who are learning English as a second language?

What Are Effective Ways to Teach or Facilitate the Learning of a Second Language?

As discussed in Chapter 1, children, at least in their acquisition of a first language, are not *taught*, but rather *acquire* language through interaction with their environment, through making sense of the linguistic codes, and through their need to communicate with others. A supportive environment, although not a requirement, can enhance children's ability to use cognitive, linguistic, and social information to acquire language. When helping children construct their new linguistic systems, such a supportive environment may be more crucial in second language learning than in first language learning. Children need comprehensible input and opportunities to interact with others to develop expertise in the new language. Ways to provide this input include facilitating semantically contingent talk, talk embeddded in familiar routines or activities, and child-centered talk (i.e., talk about what the child is doing). Opportunities to interact with other children occur spontaneously in naturalistic settings such as a classroom. Both Wong Fillmore (1989) and Lindfors (1987) advocate similar positions in facilitating second language learning.

Wong Fillmore (1989) describes a model of language learning that consists of three parts—the learner, the speakers of the target language, and the setting. She has noted that each of these components plays crucial roles in the cognitive, linguistic, and social processes involved in learning a language. How a program addresses the different roles is important because the philosophy of the program and the staff members determine the development of procedures to facilitate learning of a second language.

Lindfors (1987) describes two views that are based on different assumptions about the learner, the task to be learned, and the setting. One view can be characterized as a conventional drill-and-practice approach. The other view can be characterized as learning language through natural interactions. In the first view, the second language learner is perceived as one who must be taught new forms, preferably in isolation. Therefore, language learning is first broken into parts and practiced and then the pieces are put together. The teacher controls the learning by controlling the presentation of the new forms. The learner's role is to practice the forms until the new forms are established. This is done through structured drill with immediate correction of errors. After correct forms are learned, they can be used in more natural communicative situations. Cummins (1984) refers to this view as the *transmission model* because the teacher transmits the information and the learners receive it (see also Richard-Amato, 1988, for a review of different types of programming for children learning English as their second language). The content of the lessons and the pace of learning is primarily controlled by the teacher.

In contrast, Lindfors's second view advocates a more active role for the learner in determining what is learned and how the learning is achieved. The role of the learner is to engage in natural interactions. The natural interactions, then, provide the comprehensible input necessary for the learning of a second language. Forms are learned within the communication, not apart from it. Content, form, and use of language are embedded in each interaction. Cummins (1984) would label this the *reciprocal interaction model* of language learning. This model also would be consistent with theories of development that suggest that learners construct their own knowledge from acting on their environment (e.g., Piagetian theory) and from social interactions (e.g., Vygotskian theory). This view is also consistent with the language-focused curriculum used in LAP.

In the LFC as we have implemented it in LAP, the language learner is provided with adults and children who speak the target language, interesting activities to talk about, and preacademic activities to stretch cognitive skills. The operational guidelines of the concentrated normative model are listed in Table 1. The general language facilitation strategies described in Chapter 4 and summarized here also apply to children learning English as a second language.

- Provide opportunities for language use and interaction.
- Include familiar classroom routines to support language learning.
- Use dramatic play activities to build world knowledge and accompanying language.
- Encourage social interaction among children.
- Provide ongoing information to parents regarding daily activities and intervention needs.

In addition to providing a general environment for language learning, the following specific techniques are used to facilitate focused stimulation of particular language features (see Chapter 4 for elaboration on these techniques):

- Focused contrasts
- Modeling of target sounds, words, and forms
- Event casting (i.e., ongoing descriptions)
- Open questions
- Expansions
- Recasts
- Redirects and prompted initiations
- Scripted play

Strategies for facilitating second language learning in the classroom hinge on providing an environment in which many opportunities for natural language use and interaction occur. There must be opportunities for both child–child and adult–child talk. In addition, there must be activities that provide new information and concepts that require new re-

Table 1. Operational guidelines for the concentrated normative model

1. Language intervention is best provided in a meaningful social context.
2. Language facilitation occurs throughout the entire curriculum.
3. The language curriculum is rooted in content themes.
4. Language intervention begins with the child.
5. Verbal interaction is encouraged.
6. Passive language learning and overt responses are encouraged.
7. Children's utterances are accorded functional value.
8. Valuable teaching occasions can arise in child-to-child interactions.
9. Parents are valuable partners in language intervention programming.
10. Routine parent evaluations are an integral part of the program.

sponses, as well as routine activities that support and extend old knowledge. Finally, specific language features can be facilitated in naturally occurring conversations using the specific techniques listed above.

Are Interpreters Needed? If So, What Is Their Role?

Including interpreters as adjunct personnel is sometimes advocated. This may serve to ensure the child's comprehension of information spoken in the unfamiliar language. Interpreters are also used when assessment of a child's language skills is needed. Research on the use of interpreters in the classroom has been sketchy. In the implementation of the LAP classroom, we have experienced different levels of participation by interpreters. During a child's first year in LAP, the interpreters usually spent 1–2 hours in the classroom on a daily or twice-weekly basis. Their role was to be a special friend to the child learning English as a second language and to help in the child's adjustment to the class by explaining or translating information into the child's first language. Although children's reactions to, and use of, the interpreters varied, most children relied on the interpreter during the initial weeks of enrollment. After that, they began to move away from the interpreter and toward other children or adults. After a few months, some children welcomed being with the interpreters as long as they could still play with their friends. In contrast, other children actively ignored the interpreters. Following the child's first year in LAP, the amount of interpreter participation was reduced, and a more informal arrangement was followed. As of 1995, LAP's 9th year, interpreters were present for the first week of classes for 1–2 hours each day. Their role is still to ease the child's initial adjustment to the classroom by explaining the routine and aiding in interactions with other children and adults. After the first week, the interpreters no longer come into the classroom, but are occasionally present for parent conferences or special activities. The abbreviated use of interpreters appears to work well and the children do not usually have difficulty adjusting to the classroom setting.

Is It Helpful or Is It a Problem to Have Children Who Speak the Same First Language in the Classroom Where English Is to Be Learned?

Some researchers (Lambert, 1981; Richard-Amato, 1988) have described programs in which children speaking the same first language are placed in classrooms where the students speak one language but are taught in a different (i.e., target) language. The teachers are usually bilingual and bicultural. These types of programs are called *immersion programs*. Usually the children share a similar level of proficiency in the second language. The data from the immersion programs are, in general, positive for both academic progress and for proficiency in the second language. Some of the reasons cited for the effectiveness of immersion programs is that the acquisition of the second language is not viewed as supplanting the first language and that it has the support of the parents and community. One problem noted by Richard-Amato is that "errors" caused by interference from the first language may persist somewhat longer than ex-

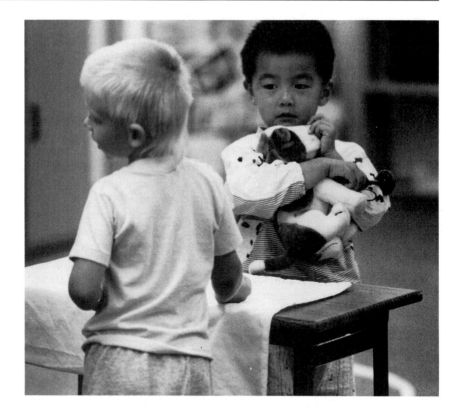

pected; this is believed to be because, without much contact with native speakers, these errors may be tolerated for a longer period of time.

It is also possible that when children of one language group are together, acquisition of English may be more difficult. The supposition is that children can communicate with each other and are less inclined to learn English. However, other factors, such as the children's motivation and learning styles or the status of the minority language in the community, may affect whether the children choose to reject learning English (Hakuta, 1986; Wong Fillmore, 1989).

During the time of our observations, in the configuration of the LAP classroom, two or more children from one language group were often present. In this setting, children rarely speak their first language with anyone other than their parents or an interpreter. The children are not discouraged from speaking their first language and there are certainly plenty of opportunities during the child-centered times for them to do so. We have asked children (through their parents and directly) why they do not use their home language with their friends. The response has been that English was to be spoken at school and the first language at home. Parents report that even when children are playing outside in an apartment complex playground, they tend to use English rather than the first language. It also may be that five or six children speaking the same language need to be present before much talking would be done. At one point, there were five Chinese children present in one LAP class. Three of the children did speak some Chinese to each other, mostly when one child was "bossing" the other two during center time activities. On occasion, we have specifically asked a child to talk to a new child in their native language. Some children will comply readily, but others refuse. Part of the reason may be personality factors such as shyness. Another reason may be that the child does not understand the task. Some children also may begin to reject the first language and, therefore, do not want to demonstrate they can speak it.

Shin was a Chinese child who would readily speak in Mandarin to another child when requested to do so. He would translate for the other child. He also was quite willing to do a direction-following game for which he gave directions in Mandarin to another Chinese child. Ching, another child from China, had been in LAP a year longer than Shin. Ching would not speak Mandarin in the classroom. When a new child was upset and Ching was asked to find out what was the matter, he refused saying he did not know what it was that the child wanted. It could be that he could not understand the crying child; however, it appeared that he understood but did not want to translate. It was interesting to note that he also refused to participate in the direction-following game for which he was to tell another child in Mandarin where to place some objects. His parents report that his usage of Mandarin at home is excellent.

How Can the First Language Be Maintained?

Several researchers (e.g., Cummins, 1984; Grosjean, 1982) have noted that there are various levels of bilingualism. For many people, it is difficult to be a balanced bilingual (i.e., one whose fluency in two or more languages is essentially the same). More often, one language becomes dominant because it is used more often by the person in day-to-day contact. Language proficiency of children is a dynamic process, so there is also a real possibility that the first language will be lost. Fantini (1985), in describing his son's acquisition of three languages, noted that different languages may be used for different purposes. One may be used during informal family gatherings, another when dealing with the outside community. Numerous factors, including the setting, purpose, audience, and emotional state, contribute to when one language versus another is used and whether proficiency in both languages is maintained. Crucial to maintaining bilingualism is the opportunity to use both languages.

In LAP, parents and children are encouraged to maintain and develop their first language further (cf. Chapter 8). Because English is used at school, the parents are advised to use the first language at home in order to provide opportunities for the first language to continue to develop. In addition, parents are encouraged to visit the classroom and share information about their culture and language by participating in a variety of activities. For example, sometimes a parent will read a story in one of the languages spoken by a child or children in LAP. The children who can understand the story really enjoy the activity. The story is translated page by page into English so others can understand. Sometimes a traditional song is sung or traditional dress, food, or other customs are described. These activities all add to the richness of the language-learning environment. LAP, then, provides the environment for the acquisition and use of English and the home environment supports the acquisition and use of the first language.

What Is the Academic Progress of Children in LAP Who Are Learning English as a Second Language?

By the end of 2 years in LAP, most of the children learning English as a second language demonstrate competency in preacademic skills at a level similar to monolingual English speakers. For example, they can recognize and recite the alphabet, have good sound–letter recognition, can write their names, and can identify and count to 20 or more.

Because some of the children return to their home countries after their attendance in LAP, information about their subsequent academic achievement is not often available. For the 12 children who have entered the local educational system as of the writing of this book, none have received ESL services. In addition, parents report that their children are succeeding in the classroom and have not received any other special services.

REFERENCES

Bunce, B.H., & Shirk, A. (1993, November). *Children learning English as a second language: Classroom language facilitation.* Poster session presented at the American Speech-Language-Hearing Association Convention, Anaheim, CA.

Cummins, J. (1984). *Bilingualism and special education: Issues in assessment and pedagogy.* San Diego: College Hill.

Ellis, R. (1986). *Understanding second language acquisition.* Oxford: Oxford University Press.

Ervin-Tripp, S. (1981). Social process in first and second language learning. In H. Winitz (Ed.), *Native language and foreign language acquisition* (pp. 33–47). New York: The New York Academy of Sciences.

Fantini, A.E. (1985). *Language acquisition of a bilingual child: A sociolinguistic perspective.* Boston: College Hill.

Grosjean, F. (1982). *Life with two languages.* Cambridge, MA: Harvard University Press.

Hakuta, K. (1978). A report on the development of the grammatical morphemes in a Japanese girl learning English as a second language. In E.M. Hatch (Ed.), *Second language acquisition: A book of readings* (pp. 132–154). Rowley, MA: Newbury House.

Hakuta, K. (1986). *Mirror of language: The debate on bilingualism.* New York: Basic Books.

Hatch, E.M. (1978). Discourse analysis and second language acquisition. In E.M. Hatch (Ed.), *Second language acquisition: A book of readings* (pp. 383–400). Rowley, MA: Newbury House.

Lambert, W.E. (1981). Bilingualism and language acquisition. In H. Winitz (Ed.), *Native language and foreign language acquisition* (pp. 9–22). New York: The New York Academy of Sciences.

Lindfors, J.W. (1987). *Children's language and learning* (2nd ed.). Englewood Cliffs, NJ: Prentice Hall.

Rescorla, L., & Okuda, S. (1987). Modular patterns in second language acquisition. *Applied Psycholinguistics, 8,* 281–308.

Richard-Amato, P.A. (1988). *Making it happen: Interaction in the second language classroom.* New York: Longman.

Saville-Troike, M. (1988). Private speech: Evidence for second language learning strategies during the "silent period." *Journal of Child Language, 15,* 567–590.

Snow, C. (1983). Age differences in second language acquisition: Research findings and folk psychology. In K. Bailey, M. Long, & S. Peck (Eds.), *Second language acquisition studies.* Rowley, MA: Newbury House.

Stanford Working Group. (1993). *A blueprint for the second generation.* Stanford, CA: Stanford University.

Tabors, P.O. (1987). *The development of communicative competence by second language learners in a nursery school classroom.* Unpublished doctoral dissertation, Harvard University, Cambridge, MA.

Tabors, P.O., & Snow, C.E. (in press). English as a second language in preschool programs. In F. Genesee (Ed.), *Reading, writing, and schooling.* New York: Cambridge University Press.

Wong Fillmore, L. (1979). Individual differences in second language acquisition. In C.J. Fillmore, D. Kempler, & W.S.Y. Wang (Eds.), *Individual differences in language ability and language behavior* (pp. 204–228). New York: Academic Press.

Wong Fillmore, L. (1989). Teachability and second language acquisition. In M.L. Rice & R.L. Schiefelbusch (Eds.), *The teachability of language* (pp. 311–332). Baltimore: Paul H. Brookes Publishing Co.

～7～

"Come buddy, help, help me!"
Verbal Interactions with Peers in a Preschool Language Intervention Classroom

Pamela A. Hadley and C. Melanie Schuele

Today is the first day Freddy came to school. Freddy came to introduce the day's dramatic play. The teachers wanted to include dental hygiene as part of the week's health curriculum, but they certainly did not want the children examining each other's teeth. What could they do? Freddy provided a creative solution! Freddy is not a dentist from the community; he is a puppet, a bright blue dog with two rows of teeth and an oversized red tongue. During circle time, the teacher brushed Freddy's teeth and talked about what happens at a dentist's office. As the children left the opening circle activity, they identified themselves as pet owners, veterinarians, or receptionists. The pet owners made appointments with the receptionists to have their pets' teeth cleaned. Ben had just finished giving a checkup to an ordinary stuffed puppy when Freddy caught his eye. To Ben's dismay, Freddy was already being examined by another vet.

Ben: Another one dog. Another dog.
Teacher: You need another dog?
Ben: Yeah, right there.
Teacher: Well, maybe you could ask Nelson if he would like to come over and help you.
Ben: Nelson, come buddy, help, help me.
Teacher: Can you go over and talk to Nelson?
Ben: Nelson, other one.

Teacher:	Ben, can you (say) ask Nelson if you can help. Say "Can I help?"
Ben:	Will you help? You help?
Teacher:	Ask him. Say "Can I help?"
Ben:	You help? (Ben directs this request to another adult.)
Teacher:	Talk to Nelson.
Ben:	Nelson? I help?

This scene illustrates some of the peer interaction difficulties children with limited communication skills, like Ben, experience amid the bustle of activity in the preschool classroom. As we have discovered, children with limited communication skills often rely on adults to mediate their interactions with peers. Rather than talking directly to his peer, Ben first expressed his desire for "another dog" to his teacher. What is also apparent is the considerable amount of teacher support required for Ben to join in Nelson's play with Freddy, the prized dog. The teacher coaches Ben step by step—first suggesting that Ben approach Nelson, and then telling him exactly what to say. Unfortunately, Ben's initial attempts to interact with Nelson fail. Nelson remains fully focused on his own doctoring efforts, ignoring each of Ben's requests. Relative to other children with limited communication skills, Ben shows a great deal of persistence and eventually Nelson and Ben begin playing together. Yet too often, initial attempts to engage in peer interaction fail and children with limited communication skills may retreat into familiar, comfortable interactions with attentive adult partners. Although adult–child interactions provide rich opportunities for facilitating communication skills as described previously (see Chapter 4), it is essential for children to be able to use verbal skills effectively in interactions with peers.

In this chapter, we examine the relationship between verbal interactive skills and the way these skills are put to use in the context of peer interactions. The importance of verbal interactive skills in peer interactions and peer relationships can be thought of using the following metaphor: Consider verbal interactive skills as the currency of the preschool. With this currency, children buy, sell, and trade goods and services with peers. The more currency a child possesses, the more goods and services he or she is likely to acquire. In addition, these everyday transactions serve as the bedrock for the evolution of friendships. Thus, children with limited verbal interactive skills may be less able to obtain the riches of the preschool and, in turn, fewer opportunities may exist for building social relationships with their trading partners.

Peer interactions provide an important context for language learning and forming peer relationships. More capable peers can provide a rich source of linguistic input to children with limited communication skills (Nelson, 1989). Similarly, during peer interactions, children learn to resolve disputes, persuade peers to change play activities, and so forth. These are necessary learning experiences for managing the rough-and-tumble reality of peer culture and cannot be simulated authentically by an adult conversational partner. Moreover, the process of gaining acceptance in peer groups is an important facet of child development (cf. Hartup, 1983). Children who have had difficulty with peer interactions and establishing peer relationships as preschoolers are not likely to develop peer relationships effortlessly when they enter elementary school. It is important, then, to recognize that verbal interactive skills are not only essential for negotiating for prized toys or a turn to be the McDonald's cashier, but they are also vital for cultivating friendship relations in peer group settings. Therefore, an appreciation of the interaction between the linguistic and social domains is required in any preschool intervention effort.

Importantly, it does not appear that optimal peer interactions and peer relationships can be achieved simply by enrolling children with communicative limitations in classroom settings with typically developing children. Rather, adults continue to play a crucial role in facilitating peer interaction by helping children with communicative limitations play together in a verbally interactive way. When promoting peer interaction, an adult's facilitory role shifts from carrying on an isolated conversation with an individual child to supporting verbal interactions between two or more children. Thus, adults are actively involved in the children's play, providing support when necessary for children with more limited abilities to engage in the play of the peer group.

This chapter is organized in the following manner. First, the verbal interactive skills of children with typically developing language skills are described. This is followed by an overview of what we have learned about verbal interactive skills from the children in the Language Acquisition Preschool (LAP). Our findings indicate that placement of children with communicative limitations in a preschool classroom with typically developing children and children learning English as a second language does not facilitate verbal interactions with peers in and of itself. Thus, we discuss the implementation of a specific teaching strategy designed to facilitate children's verbal initiations to peers in the context of ongoing classroom activities.

VERBAL INTERACTIONS WITH PEERS

When children enter traditional preschool classrooms around the age of 3, most are able to participate in simple verbal interactions. They are able to take one or two conversational turns but have much to learn about maintaining lengthy conversations with peers (cf. McTear, 1985). In classroom settings, opportunities for individual children to engage in lengthy conversations with teachers may be somewhat limited, particularly when the ratio of children to teachers is high. Therefore, verbal interactions with peers provide the majority of opportunities for children to develop and refine their verbal interactive skills.

The verbal interactions of two preschool language users differ substantially from adult–child interactions where adults provide a considerable amount of conversational support (Hartup, 1983). Peer partners present children with greater conversational challenges than adult partners. For example, children differ in their background knowledge of conversational topics, making some topics more difficult to talk about (Nelson & Gruendel, 1979). Also, when peer partners do not understand a child's message, they may be less inclined to ask the child to repeat or rephrase the message. As a result, breakdowns in the flow of conversations may be frequent. It has been speculated that because children must work harder to carry on a conversation with peers, verbal interactions with peers may drive the development of new conversational skills, such as establishing relevant background information and making and responding to requests for clarification.

For most children, verbal interaction skills emerge with little difficulty during the preschool years. The rates of peer interaction and verbal initiations to peers increase developmentally, especially between 2½ and 4 years of age (Greenwood, Walker, Todd, & Hops, 1981; Holmberg, 1980; Howes, 1987; Mueller, 1972; Mueller, Bleir, Krakow, Hegedus, & Cournoyer, 1977; Rueter & Yunik, 1973). By age 3, children initiate about half of their peer interactions and are highly successful in eliciting conversational responses from their partners. When children's attempts to start a conversation fail, it is often because their first comment or question was hard to understand or did not make sense (Mueller, 1972). By 4 or 5 years old, most children are able to maintain verbal interactions over multiple conversational turns (cf. McTear, 1985). This is demonstrated in the following example: Two children with age-appropriate conversational abilities, Hannah, age 4.7, and Don, age 4.5, are planting flowers in an indoor sandbox. Although the general conversational topic revolves around gardening (e.g., flowers, worms, digging, burying), this example represents a number of relatively short verbal interactive exchanges punctuated by periods of silent play. In this example, the children both take responsibility for initiating verbal interactions. The first exchange (1:1–1:2) consists of an initiation and a verbal response, and then the children turn their attention back to digging. Next, Don and Hannah each attempt to start the conversation again. Neither gets an immediate response. In the final exchange (6:1–6:3), the children are able to maintain the interaction over three conversational turns. What may not be immediately apparent, but is important to emphasize, is that these two children are able to interact verbally with one another without support from an adult.

Hannah (1:1):   Let's take a flower and put it in, then dig it up.
Don (1:2):   Mine is over here.
                 (The children continue digging in the sand.)
Don (2:1):   Hey. Hannah, let's bury it.
Hannah (3:1):   No! No! No! No! No! We gotta plant it.
                 (Hannah takes flower from Don; the children continue digging.)
Hannah (4:1):   Don't bury my all sweet flowers up. Don't bury all my sweet flowers up.
Don (4:2):   And you don't bury all my sweet flowers up.
                 (The children continue digging.)
Don (5:1):   I found worms. Worms camed out of the ground.
                 (Hannah does not respond.)
Don (6:1):   Let's dig for worms. I found a worm.
Hannah (6:2):   Let's bury all the worms up.
Don (6:3):   No, Hannah. Let's keep them.

Not only do strong conversational skills appear to make peer interaction less effortful, but they are also linked to the social status of children in preschool settings. In two recent studies, preschool children identified as well liked by their classmates demonstrated more effective and coherent conversational skills than children identified as disliked (Black & Hazen, 1990; Hazen & Black, 1989). Black and Hazen noted that well-liked children were more inclined to direct initiations clearly to their conversational partner. With regard to conversational responsiveness, the well-liked children responded more often, and did so more appropriately, than did the disliked children. Among elementary school-age children, appropriate conversational skills continue to influence ratings of social status among peers (Place & Becker, 1991) and also contribute to teachers' positive impressions (Becker, Place, Tenzer, & Frueh, 1991).

In summary, basic facility with conversational skills is necessary for the development of sustained verbal interaction with peers. Moreover, these skills contribute to children's social acceptance among peers and the formation of positive impressions among teachers. These findings suggest that children with limited communication skills are at a marked social disadvantage relative to peers with age-appropriate communication skills.

Rice (1993) proposed that before children with specific language impairment (SLI) enter kindergarten, it is possible for them to be caught in a negative social spiral. Children with SLI may be highly sensitive to repeated instances of communicative failure. Rice suggested that in response to their own social awareness of their communicative difficulties, these children may withdraw from peer interactions or rely more on adults to mediate peer interactions as Ben did in the opening vignette in this chapter. Yet these types of behavioral adjustments may bring with them potentially negative social consequences. First, withdrawing from peer interactions may restrict the development of peer relationships. This, in turn, may restrict access to important peer socialization experiences. A second potential consequence is that children's reluctance to interact with peers may be misperceived by teachers as an indication of social immaturity. It seems kindergarten teachers rely on estimates of social maturity when making kindergarten retention decisions (Walsh, 1989). This may be particularly true of teachers' impressions of children with limited communication skills. In a sample of kindergarten children with significant language impairments, Catts (1990) noted that 17 of 35 children were retained in kindergarten or placed in "developmental" or "transitional" first-grade classrooms. Catts reported that, in most cases, the nonpromotion decision was based on the children's perceived social immaturity. Similarly, our own work suggests that when asked to rate various child attributes, kindergarten teachers judge children with SLI as less socially mature than children with age-appropriate communication abilities (Rice, Hadley, & Alexander, 1993).

We have become increasingly aware of the negative social consequences that children with limited communication skills may experience in their interactions with teachers and peers in classroom settings. Our sensitivity to these consequences has been heightened as we have come to understand the subtle, but consistent, patterns of peer interaction and peer preferences revealed in the LAP classroom. In the next section, we summarize the empirical studies of peer interaction and social acceptance conducted in LAP and highlight the clinical implications of the findings.

LESSONS LEARNED IN THE LAP CLASSROOM

The initial studies of social interaction in the LAP classroom investigated the verbal interactive skills of the three groups of children—children with specific language impairment, children developing language typically, and children learning English as a second language. Although the children with communicative limitations were physically enrolled in a program that did not segregate them from their peers, it was important to document the extent to which they were socially integrated. In other words, did the children with communicative limitations engage in social interactions with typically developing peers? Given that one purported educational benefit of inclusive programs is that typically developing peers can serve as valuable language models, it was particularly important to determine the extent to which children were engaging in *verbal* interactions with one another.

When we began these studies, peer interaction difficulties had been documented previously for children with mental retardation and hearing impairments (cf. Guralnick, 1990; Odom & McEvoy, 1988; Vandell & George, 1981). The general conclusion drawn from these studies was that, in inclusive settings, typically developing children tended to interact more frequently with peers who were also typically developing or peers with mild impairments rather than with peers with moderate or severe disabilities. We were interested in whether this same pattern of social segregation would be apparent among children whose *only* disabling condition was SLI. Additionally, the children learning English as a second language were an important comparison group for the children with SLI. Although their communication skills were also limited, the children learning English as a second language had histories of using their native language as a successful social tool.

Patterns of Verbal Interaction

Observations of the children's verbal interactions occurred during center time. This was a time when children moved freely between four different classroom areas. Children could play in the block area with blocks or toy vehicles or in the quiet area with puzzles or books. Activities in the other two areas changed on a daily basis. Children could work on an art project at the art table or engage in make-believe dramatic play. The patterns of verbal initiations, responses, and the conversational partner of choice were recorded as children engaged in play with peers and teachers (for more complete details about the Social Interactive Coding System [SICS], refer to Rice, Sell, and Hadley, 1990, 1991).

The results of two cross-sectional, observational studies in the LAP classroom indicated that children's facility with communication skills influenced several dimensions of verbal interaction (Hadley & Rice, 1991; Rice et al., 1991). First, the typically developing children appeared

to be the preferred partners for all children's peer initiations. All children, perhaps quite unknowingly, gravitated toward peers in the classroom with the strongest communication skills. Second, conversations involving a child with SLI as one of the partners were more likely to break down. If the youngsters with SLI tried to begin the conversations, peers ignored them more often than they ignored the typically developing children. In contrast, when peers initiated conversations with the children with SLI the children with SLI were less responsive to these interactive overtures than their typically developing classmates. Finally, when compared to their typically developing classmates, both children with SLI and children learning English as a second language were less likely to initiate to peers than to adults. Only one third of the initiations by children with SLI and children learning English as a second language were directed to peers, whereas 50% of the typically developing children's initiations were.

We have also examined changes in verbal initiations to peers in a longitudinal sample of children (Hadley, Rice, & Wilcox, in preparation; Rice, Wilcox, Hadley, & Schuele, 1993). From a clinical perspective, it was important to determine whether children made considerable gains in the percentage of verbal initiations directed to peers over the course of preschool enrollment or whether specific intervention procedures were necessary to facilitate this facet of social interaction skills.

The peer interactions of 17 children were examined across four consecutive semesters of preschool enrollment, equivalent to approximately 18 months. The typically developing and SLI groups each consisted of six children; five children formed the English as a second language group. It should be noted that children in the latter group were significantly younger ($M = 34$ months) than the children in the other two groups ($M = 43$ months, and $M = 39$ months, respectively).

The longitudinal observations revealed an increase with age in the rate of peer interactions and verbal initiations to peers. This generalization applied to all three groups of children. However, it was not until the fourth semester that the frequency of peer interactions and peer initiations by the children with SLI and the children learning English as a second language began to approximate the initial rates for the typically developing children during the first semester of preschool enrollment.

Group differences were also apparent in the percentage of initiations that were directed to peers over time. These differences were most salient at the time of initial enrollment in the program. During the first semester of preschool enrollment, the typically developing children directed approximately 40% of their initiations to peers ($M = 40.5$, range = 14%–58%). As might be expected, the children learning English as a second language, with virtually no English skills, relied completely on the adults in the classroom. Four of five of the children learning English as a second language did not direct any initiations to peers. The children with SLI fell in between the other two groups of children, directing an average of 12% of their initiations to peers (range = 0%–44%).

During the fourth semester, all typically developing children except one directed more than 50% of their initiations to peers ($M = 59\%$, range = 26%–78%). In contrast, the children with SLI remained below this level, with an average of 43% peer-directed initiations (range = 22%–78%). Importantly, four children with SLI still only initiated to peers about one third of the time. Only two children with SLI directed more than half of their verbal initiations to peers. The children learning English as a second language increased their percentage of peer initiations to an average of 36% (range = 15%–52%). Recall, however, that the children learning English as a second language were 6–10 months younger than the children in the other two groups, and many were still eligible for another year of preschool programming. For the three children who remained in the program, a steady increase in peer-directed initiations continued in the third year.

To summarize, the descriptive measures indicate that children with limited language skills are reluctant participants in peer interactions and rarely initiate to peers upon entry into preschool intervention programs. Although all groups demonstrated an increase in the percentage of peer-directed initiations over time, a considerable increase in peer-directed initiations was evident among the typically developing children during their fourth and final semester of preschool enrollment. In contrast, the percentage of initiations among the other two groups remained relatively constant. We return to the clinical implications of these findings in a later section.

Peer Friendships

Peer preferences, similar to those revealed indirectly from the classroom observations, were also evident in a recent study designed to examine social status more explicitly (Gertner, Rice, & Hadley, 1994). We asked the children to identify peers they liked to play with during dramatic play. The typically developing children were chosen as preferred playmates more frequently than the children with SLI or the children learning English as a second language. Furthermore, when we inspected the children's nominations for evidence of mutual friendships (i.e., pairs of children who identified each other), the typically developing children had the greatest number of mutual friends and the children with SLI had the least. This study suggests that communication abilities may play a central role in social acceptance and perhaps even the formation of friendships. It follows then that children with communicative limitations may be at risk for low social status in inclusive classroom settings. External teacher pressures to elevate "popularity" are not likely to be effective strategies to counteract social biases. From our perspective, we believe that by facilitating children's communication skills in the context of verbal interactions with peers, we equip them with basic tools to elevate their social status independently.

The peer preference findings, in combination with the results of the observational studies of peer interaction, suggested that the children with limited language skills were not completely woven into the social tapestry of the LAP classroom, despite our commitment to immersion. First, children with SLI and children learning English as a second language showed a greater dependence on adult conversational partners, perhaps as a compensatory strategy to make up for their communicative difficulty in peer interactions. Second, peers were less likely to engage in verbal interactions with children with limited communication skills. And third, peers were less likely to identify children with limited communication skills as preferred playmates. Together these findings indicate a need to facilitate verbal interactive skills *with peers* as part of comprehensive preschool intervention efforts.

Clinical Implications for Facilitating Verbal Interactions with Peers

When we first initiated the studies of peer interaction, we did not expect children as young as 3 or 4 years of age to be so systematic in selecting to whom they wanted to talk and with whom they wanted to play. Our increased sensitivity to the children's subtle, but systematic, preferences have influenced a number of general classroom practices. For example, we are more sensitive to the need to support the peer interactions of children with SLI and the children learning English as a second language throughout the classroom day. For example, the LAP curriculum provides a number of routine activities such as sharing and snacktime that can be structured in ways to support peer interactions (see the second volume in this series, *Building a Language-Focused Curriculum for the Preschool Classroom, Volume II: A Planning Guide* [Bunce, 1995]).

More specifically, we have been able to identify general expectations for children's patterns of peer interaction in this particular preschool setting. The generalizations drawn from the *group* patterns of peer interaction have enabled us to interpret *individual* children's rates of peer interaction and relative conversational assertiveness with peers, and therefore, to identify individualized goals for intervention. It is interesting to note that across the set of observational studies, we have found repeatedly that the 50% mark appears to be an informative index for capturing differences between children enrolled in the typically developing group and children enrolled in the other two groups. In both the cross-sectional and longitudinal observational studies described above, we have found that only the typically developing children initiate to peers more than 50% of the time (Hadley & Rice, 1991; Hadley et al., in preparation; Rice et al., 1991; Rice et al., 1993). We do not wish to imply that teachers and clinicians should use this as a normative index. It is quite likely that measures of peer interaction will differ considerably across different preschool classrooms. However, this 50% index has provided us with an estimate with which to form general interpretations of individual children's patterns of peer interaction.

Finally, the findings from our longitudinal study of peer interaction suggest that for 3- to 4-year-old children in their first year of preschool enrollment, primary peer interaction goals may focus on general increases in the frequency of verbal initiations, regardless of whether they are directed to adults or peers. In fact, our experience with one 3-year-old child who we attempted to include in an intervention study provides support for this recommendation. We found that it took twice as long to observe 50 initiations from the 3-year-old in comparison to the 4-year-olds we retained in the study. In contrast, for 4- to 5-year-old children with SLI who show a marked preference for adult conversational partners throughout their second year of preschool, goals may focus more explicitly on increasing the percentage of these initiations directed to peers. This may be particularly important for 5-year-old children who are facing the transition to kindergarten. The kindergarten transition may be especially difficult for children who rely predominantly on adults to mediate their social interactions insofar as the accessibility to adult conversational partners becomes greatly restricted in most kindergarten classrooms. Therefore, for these children, it is particularly important to develop classroom practices to minimize such consequences and set a positive social and academic spiral in motion. Much of the foundation for establishing peer interactions is embedded in the LAP classroom curriculum (see Bunce, in press). However, for some children, specific intervention may be helpful, if not necessary, to facilitate *verbal* interactions with peers. In the next section, we discuss a specific intervention strategy that can be used to increase children's verbal initiations to peers that are compatible with the child-centered philosophy and guiding principles of the concentrated normative model.

VERBAL INTERACTION INTERVENTION: THE REDIRECT STRATEGY

Angie and Michelle, two children with SLI, were playing in the block area, reenacting a portion of *The Three Little Pigs*. The teacher sat nearby, ready to assist the children as needed. Michelle was in the "house" and Angie, as the wolf, was getting ready to "blow the house down."

Angie: Knock, knock, let me in little pig.
Michelle: Not by chinny chin.
Angie: Then I'll blow your whole house. (Angie knocks down the bricks.)
Angie: I wanta be a little pig (to the teacher).
Teacher: Okay. Well you have to tell Michelle that and ask her to be the big bad wolf.
Angie: Michelle, can I be the pig? Can I be the little pig?
            (The girls change roles.)

Angie's interaction style is typical of the children with SLI in LAP. As discussed previously in this chapter, children with SLI tend to rely on adults to mediate their interactions with peers. In the above interaction, Angie clearly had a message to convey—she wanted to change roles with Michelle. This exchange could have been negotiated directly with Michelle. Instead, Angie initiated to the teacher, seemingly as an indirect request for the teacher to tell Michelle to change places with Angie. In instances such as these, the teacher could deflect the child's initiation and suggest that the child initiate to a peer, as the teacher did in the above interaction. In LAP, we explored the feasibility of using this teaching technique, a redirect strategy, to facilitate the abilities of children with SLI to initiate to peers verbally.

An opportunity to redirect arises when a child initiates to an adult. Following the child's initiation, the adult redirects the child to initiate to a peer. The adult's redirect consists of a hint, suggestion, or model of how to initiate to a peer. A crucial component of the redirect strategy is that it follows a child's adult-directed initiation.

The need for techniques to facilitate interactions among peers has been recognized in the special education literature (cf. Odom & Brown, 1993; Odom, McConnell, & McEvoy, 1992; Odom & Strain, 1984). Many different techniques (e.g., peer confederate training, teacher prompts, social skills training) have been implemented with varying levels of success. Whereas our interest in facilitating interactions among peers was not new, our implementation of redirects addressed new dimensions not always a part of procedures previously described in the literature. First, our focus was on *verbal* peer interactions, specifically verbal initiations. Second, redirects were implemented in the course of the ongoing routine of classroom activities. There was no special training time or setting. Therefore, the children's initiations could be redirected throughout the day. Additionally, all classmates were potentially participants in the intervention. Any child could be redirected and any peer could be the recipient of the child's redirected initiation. Third, because the children with SLI relied on adults as conversational partners, there was ample opportunity to build on the child's discourse needs. By making the implementation of the teaching technique contingent on a child's verbal initiation, any subsequent initiation to a peer related to the child's expressed desire to communicate. Furthermore, the child, not the adult, established the topic of the interaction. For example, in the above interaction, Angie expressed a desire to change roles; the teacher did not have to set up or pose the communicative opportunity. Building on the child's discourse needs not only maintains a child-centered philosophy but also capitalizes on the child's own motivation to interact with others in the classroom.

An Investigation of Redirects

An investigation of the effectiveness of the redirect strategy was conducted in LAP. Four boys participated in the study. Three were 4-year-olds and in their second year in LAP; one was a 5-year-old and in his third year in LAP. These children had advanced to the point that they verbally initiated consistently albeit more often to adults than to peers. Their average rate of verbal initiation was one to two initiations per minute. Thus, they appeared to be appropriate candidates for redirects. Their verbal assertiveness was established, and it needed to be generalized to initiations with peers.

In the first semester of the study, the subjects' patterns of interaction were observed in the absence of any specific intervention to alter initiations. In the second semester, the assistant teacher in LAP was trained to implement the redirect strategy. She redirected the boys' initiations during center time (50 minutes per day) for 9 weeks.

The results indicated that the redirect strategy is a promising strategy to increase the peer initiations of preschool children. Because the study is reported in detail elsewhere (Schuele, Rice, & Wilcox, in preparation), the description here highlights the main findings. Although prior to training the teacher rarely redirected (less than 3% of the four boys' initiations), after a brief training session, the teacher redirected about one third of their initiations. The boys tended to respond positively to a redirect; when redirected they initiated to a peer after about half of the time. They generally received a conversationally appropriate response from peers.

Although not intended, training the teacher to redirect was also associated with an increase in the frequency with which she *prompted* verbal initiations to peers. In contrast to redirects, prompted initiations were defined as instances in which the teacher initiated an interaction with a child, and then prompted the child to initiate to a peer. Hence, during the 9 weeks of intervention, the teacher facilitated peer-directed initiations with redirects as well as prompted initiations.

In addition to positive responses to the teacher's redirects, the intervention period was associated with positive changes in the boys' proportion of spontaneous initiations addressed to peers. The measure of spontaneous initiations excluded any initiations that might have been prompted or redirected. Virtually no change in the proportion of peer initiations ($M = .01$) was demonstrated during the nonintervention semester. In contrast, the proportion of peer initiations increased for all of the boys in the intervention semester. The average proportion of peer initiations prior to intervention was .35 and after intervention was .59. Note that the redirect intervention led to the boys' mean proportion of peer initiations approximating the 50% mark characteristic of the typically developing group, as discussed previously.

In sum, a teacher was able to redirect children after a brief training session. Subjects responded to the redirects by initiating to peers. Furthermore, introduction of redirects by the teacher was associated with a gain in the proportion of initiations addressed to peers. In this study, this gain can be interpreted as a generalization of the effects of the teaching technique to situations in which a teacher is not facilitating peer initiations via redirects. Given that redirects appear to be a promising strategy to facilitate peer initiations, the following sections provide a more in-depth discussion of the teaching strategy.

Types of Redirects

A redirect can take one of three forms—a model, an explicit redirect, or a hint (Table 1). These forms vary in the level of support the adult provides the child. Different types of redirects may meet the needs of children with varying levels of linguistic and interactional competencies. Additionally, variables in the play context may influence which type of redirect is effective for a child in a particular context. However, it should be noted that in our study there was no attempt to match the type of redirect to situational demands or variables. In the classroom, the teacher used her discretion as to the type of redirect employed. Future investigations might explore the relationship among children's verbal interaction capabilities, contextual variables, and the success of varying types of redirects.

A redirect with a model, the strongest prompt, not only tells the child to initiate to a peer but provides an utterance to be repeated verbatim. For example:

Ben: I got some for me.
Teacher: Hey, tell Sam to come over and eat with us. **Say, "Sam, would you like to eat with us?"**

Situational characteristics may make a modeled redirect appropriate. In difficult communicative interactions, such as conflict negotiations, the child may benefit from an utterance to repeat. Similarly, in unfamiliar situations (e.g., a new dramatic play), a modeled redirect may simplify the task of peer initiation. Unfamiliar activities present additional chal-

Table 1.   Forms of redirects

Form	Definition	Example
Model	Adult provides the child with a specific utterance to repeat to a peer	"Tell Paul, 'I want the suitcase please.'"
Explicit	Adult overtly suggests the child initiate to a peer	"Ask Penny for the money."
Hint	Adult hints to the child to initiate to a peer	"I think John has what you want."

lenges because children do not have previous experience to guide them in initiating and maintaining verbal interactions in that activity. An individual child's language skills may suggest the need for a modeled redirect. If provided an utterance, children with limited verbal skills may be able to initiate to peers verbally. Providing a model may also facilitate the use of emerging linguistic skills (e.g., newly learned linguistic structures, more complex sentences). In the following example, the redirect enables Nelson, a typically developing child, to use a more linguistically sophisticated sentence in initiating to a peer.

Nelson: I caught the same yellow fish.
Teacher: The same yellow fish. Well, why don't you go tell Saul what you've been doing. Say, "I've been catching the same yellow fish all the time."
Nelson: **I've been catching the same yellow fish all the time.**

An explicit redirect consists of a suggestion to initiate to a peer and perhaps, specifies the peer, but the adult does not provide the child with a specific utterance to repeat. Rather, the child must take the adult's redirect and formulate an utterance from the information given. This level of redirect was most frequently used in our study. It assumes that the child has the linguistic ability to take the adult's suggestion and formulate a verbal initiation to a peer. For example:

Jane: I can't get out of here.
Teacher: You can't get out of there? Well, you better ask Ben for help.
Jane: Will you push the button?

From the adult's redirect, the child could have formulated a variety of utterances such as, "Help me, please" or "Ben, help me" as well as the utterance formulated.

The most subtle type of redirect is a hint. For example:

Jimmy: Knock, knock, knock. Knock, knock, knock.
Teacher: Yes?
Jimmy: This is the house cleaning. Um, may I come in, please?
Teacher: Well, I'm kind of busy right now. Could you come back later?
Jimmy: Yes.
Teacher: Okay. Maybe you, maybe some of those other rooms need to be cleaned. You might want to knock on their doors.
Jimmy: Knock, knock. May I come in? This is the house cleaning.
Phil: Um, I'm doing, I'm getting ready to, I'm really busy and right now.

Children may need some sophisticated cognitive and social skills to act on this hint. Following up on a hint draws on a child's ability to infer the adult's intent. Without such skills, a child may not pick up on the hint, but rather may treat the adult's utterance as a turn in the conversation, as in the following example. The adult's second utterance is a hint to the child. In this play activity, other children were acting as vets and this child might have initiated an interaction with any of these children to get assistance for her pig. But, as can be seen, the child did not pick up on the adult's hint and, rather, continued the conversation with the adult.

Jane: Betty (*the teacher*), he roll over.
Teacher: Did the pig roll over? Did you want her to roll over?
Jane: Yeah.
Teacher: Well, maybe she's sick. Maybe she doesn't feel good and needs a doctor.
Jane: Yes, she feels good! She roll over.

Redirects that consist of hints are most appropriate for children who have language and social abilities that enable them to interact easily with peers in the particular context that the redirect occurs. The effectiveness of this prompt relies on the child's ability to interpret a subtle hint, a task that may be quite difficult for many children with SLI. Yet for some children with SLI interpretation of hints such as this may be a skill to be targeted. Inferential abilities of this nature are certainly necessary in many discourse situations they encounter or will encounter. Hence, for some children working toward picking up on these hints may be desirable.

In sum, three types of redirects have been identified—a model, an explicit redirect, and a hint. These forms of redirects provide the child with differing amounts of support. The appropriateness of each type of redirect depends on the child's abilities and needs in the specific context in which he or she is redirected to initiate to a peer. Next, we address several issues the adult might consider in implementing redirects.

Implementing Redirects in Classroom Activities

Redirects seem to be a relatively simple, straightforward means to facilitate initiations to peers. Interestingly, our observations before we started our study in LAP as well as other preschool intervention and typical preschool classrooms indicated that teachers were not likely to redirect children's adult-directed initiations. Less than 3% of the initiations were redirected. Training a teacher to redirect can be done in a relatively brief period of time. We conducted a 2-hour training session that included discussion and videotaped examples of children's adult-directed initiations and redirects. After defining redirects, several implementation issues were discussed.

The first issue to consider is whether or not the child's initiation is one that is appropriate to redirect. Is the topic of the child's conversation of interest to his or her peers? Can the adult assist the child in formulating an initiation to which a peer is likely to respond? Typical opportunities for adults to redirect initiations might include adult-directed initiations that are bids to play (e.g., "You be the mommy"), requests for materials (e.g., "I need a horse"), comments on what happened (e.g., "We built a road"), and requests for instructions (e.g., "How do I make it?"). These are just a few examples; speech-language pathologists and teachers no doubt can identify many more in their own classrooms.

Many times children initiate to adults to obtain approval or praise; for example, when showing an art project, the child may say, "Look at this." We have found that when the adult redirects this type of initiation (i.e., tells the child to tell a peer to look at the picture), the peer's response often has been a lack of interest. However, with a little creative thinking, sometimes the adult can use the redirect to develop or expand the topic. In turn, this will assist the child in the formulation of an initiation to which a peer might be likely to respond. In this way, redirects can be used to further a child's discourse skills. For example:

Eddie: Look my picture.
Teacher: Hey, that's a great picture. Maybe you can tell Julie how you made that picture.
Eddie: I make green paint.
Julie: (points to green paint on her picture).

In this example, the adult's manipulation of the topic, from looking at the picture to telling how it was made, provided the peer with something specific on which to comment. Obviously, there are times when a child initiates to an adult with a request that only the adult can fulfill (e.g., requests for materials that are out of reach of children or requests for assistance a peer cannot provide). These instances would not be appropriate times to redirect. A redirect is contingent upon a child's adult-directed initiation and thus, the frequency of adult-directed initiations determines the opportunities for redirects. In this respect, the adult has minimal control over how often a child is redirected. On a particular day, a child may not initiate to adults very often. There is no concern if the lack of initiations to adults comes about because the child is initiating to peers; the goal has been met. If, in contrast, few opportunities to redirect come about because a child is not very interactive on a given day, then another day may bring more opportunities to redirect.

A second issue to consider is that redirects need not immediately follow the child's initiation to the adult; that is, the child and adult may carry on a conversation and embedded in this conversation may be the adult's redirect. The adult can make a brief comment before redirecting, as in the previous example where the teacher initially remarked "Hey, that's a great picture." Alternatively, a few turns may be taken by each partner before the adult redirects, as in the following example:

Wes: Look!
Teacher: What'd you find?
Wes: A tape recorder.
Teacher: Is there a tape in there?
Wes: Yeah. We listen?
Teacher: Sure, but maybe some of the other children would like to listen, too. Maybe you can ask Tina or Peter to come over and listen with you.
Wes: Peter to come over and listen with you. Tina, wanna listen? Come here.

Embedding the redirect in an extended adult–child conversation may be very beneficial. The conversation can provide a practice opportunity for the child before he or she initiates to a peer. The child has the opportunity to converse with the adult and then the topic is developed and extended into a child–child interaction. Also, the adult can introduce new information into the conversation, which may provide the child with more information to share with a peer. The adult–child turns can build up the child's conversational skills, which are then immediately applied in a peer interaction.

A third issue adults should consider carefully is to whom they redirect the child. We want to redirect children to peers who are most likely to respond to the redirected initiation so that children have a maximal chance for a successful peer interaction. Good candidates for receipt of redirected initiations are peers who are physically close by, such as a peer sitting next to the child rather than a peer at the other end of the table. A peer who shares a common interest, for instance, or who is engaged with similar materials or in a similar activity, is also a likely candidate. For example, a child who just began fishing can be redirected to a peer who also is fishing. Or a child needing help on an art project can be redirected to a peer who has completed the project. Also, a peer who is not otherwise engaged may be receptive to an initiation. For example, a peer observing the play of others is likely to respond favorably to a bid to join that play.

When two or more children are playing closely together, they may not be receptive to the child's redirected initiation unless it relates to what they are already doing. Similarly, a peer who is engaged in another type of activity may not be receptive to an "off-topic" initiation. For example, a peer reading books in the quiet area may not be receptive to another child's request for assistance in building with blocks. Redirects may be more successful if the child's initiation to his or her peers is related to the activity in which those peers are presently engaged. Much in the same way that adults strive to follow a child's lead, initiations that are relevant to the peers' play activity and/or topics of conversation may be better received than tangential initiations.

In our study, the teacher reported that her attempts to redirect children led to a greater awareness of the children's behaviors throughout the classroom. In anticipation of redirecting, she found herself making quick scans of what the children were doing so as to identify to what peers a child might be redirected. This increased awareness perhaps influenced the effectiveness of redirects and prompted initiations and probably contributed to the success of redirects.

One further issue to consider is the support given to children regarding nonlinguistic aspects of initiating. Children need more than just the right words to initiate successfully to others. It is important to speak loudly enough, to gain the intended listener's attention, to wait for a response, and so forth. In the course of redirecting children, adults can incorporate support for these aspects of initiating into a redirect. Instead of saying "Go ask Paula for the spoon," the adult might say "Paula has the spoon. Say her name and then ask for the spoon" or "Remember to say it so Paula can hear you." In this way, the child's attention has been focused on these important components of successful communication when there is an immediate need to consider these components; that is, the opportunity to learn what makes successful initiations has arisen because of an immediate need to communicate successfully. The teacher has not arbitrarily chosen to "teach" a particular social skill. In the interaction shown at the beginning of this chapter, the teacher provided this support when she responded to the child's unsuccessful initiation attempts with "Can you go over and talk to Nelson?"

Responses for Redirects from the Child and the Peer

A child initiates to an adult and the adult redirects; the desired response from the child is that the child initiates to a peer. Then, we hope, the child receives a response from the peer. Several things might occur that interrupt this chain of events.

There may be no response after the adult's redirect. Rather, the child may end the interaction. In this case, the child had indicated a lack of interest in initiating to a peer. It seems wise to respect the child's choice to not follow through on the redirect.

Sometimes it may seem that the child has chosen not to respond to the redirect. However, the child may take a brief period of time to coordinate his or her efforts to initiate to a peer, as in this example:

Gina asks Joanne, the teacher, if she wants some hot chocolate. Joanne replies "No, but Sally might." Sally is sitting on Joanne's lap. Seemingly uninterested in initiating to Sally, Gina turns to walk away. However, she walks across the play area to the dishes, fetches a cup, and returns, offering Sally the cup, "Here's some hot chocolate."

The teacher had resisted her initial urge to call Gina back. In the end, what appeared initially as Gina ignoring the redirect was instead Gina's preparation to initiate to Sally. By not jumping in, the teacher let the natural course of events occur, which in this case resulted in the child appearing to initiate an interaction with a peer.

It is also possible that the child may not directly comply with the redirect but may continue the interaction with the adult. There then may be an opportunity for the adult to redirect a second time. In the next example, the first redirect is ignored but the teacher takes advantage of a second opportunity to redirect.

Wes: I gonna be the dad.
Teacher: Maybe Erica can be the mom. Ask her.
Wes: I fix diaper. Hold baby for me.
Teacher: Ask Erica to hold the baby.
Wes: (to Erica) Hold baby please.

In our experience any more than two consecutive redirects following an initiation rarely resulted in the child initiating to a peer. Further redirects can await subsequent adult-directed initiations.

Once the child initiates after a redirect the peer's response becomes of interest. For the most part, we have not concerned ourselves with intervening to ensure that a peer responds to a child's redirected initiation. Rather, we have opted to let the natural consequences of the interaction prevail. Frequently, the peer is close by and hears the adult's redirect. This may indirectly suggest to the peer that a response to the child's initiation is expected, increasing the likelihood of a peer response. Occasionally though the adult may find it beneficial to elicit a response from the peer, perhaps prompting the peer to respond. For example, after the child initiates to the peer, the adult might say to the peer, "Wes just asked you for that." In our view, successful responses are equivalent to conversationally appropriate responses, whether they are negative or positive. If the child asks a peer for a favorite toy, the child needs to learn to respond to "yes" as well as "no."

If the child initiates to a peer but the peer does not respond immediately, further intervention by the adult may take away the opportunity for the child to work through the many nuances of successful peer initiations. In the next example, Eddie has the opportunity to figure out on his own a more effective means of initiating to Gina.

Several children are engaged in water play with plastic fish, sharks, whales, and boats. Following a redirect, Eddie verbally initiates to Gina, trying to draw her attention to his shark. No response comes from Gina. Eddie pauses and then very deliberately reaches over, taps Gina on the head, calls her name, and then repeats his comment. Gina then responds enthusiastically.

Why Redirects Might Work

There are many reasons redirects might ultimately result in increasing the spontaneous initiations of children with SLI to peers. These reasons relate to why we believe the peer initiations of children with SLI are less frequent than those of typically developing children. To initiate to peers successfully, children must possess both the skills required by the task as well as the desire to execute the task. A child may have the linguistic skills to initiate to peers successfully but for some reason his or her first inclination is to initiate to adults. To initiate to peers, a child may need extra encouragement or an incentive. Alternatively, a child may have the social motivation to initiate to peers but not believe him- or herself capable of initiating to a peer successfully. The redirect from an adult can provide the needed support by supplying the child with words to use in initiating to a peer or by telling him or her which peer to approach. It can help the child maneuver into an established interaction or remind the child that a peer is an available conversational partner. This support or assistance may make the task of initiating easier and, therefore, help the child to initiate to a peer successfully. Over time, these successful initiations to peers provide the child increased positive peer interaction experiences and thus, ultimately, may lead the child to initiate to peers spontaneously more often—that is, when adult assistance is not available.

CONCLUDING REMARKS

Interaction with peers is an important part of development for preschool children. It is impossible to think about a child's social skills without considering the crucial role verbal skills play in a child's ability to initiate and maintain interactions with peers. Very young children's social interactions are supported by the more competent adult partner; this is not the case in interactions between peers. Thus, a child with communicative limitations is likely to encounter difficulties becoming a competent participant in the social network of peers. It is exactly in this network though that each child must play, compete, work, and learn. We believe that it is extremely important for intervention programs with preschool children to facilitate children's competence in interacting with peers, and thus, this is a central aspect of the LAP philosophy and curriculum.

It seems that environmental and curricular modifications can begin to make peer interaction more likely and to provide a supportive environment for children who are not likely to meet with much success in interacting with peers. However, we have found that some children with communicative impairments need more direct intervention; they benefit from a teacher more directly facilitating initiations to peers. This also may be true for typically developing children and children learning English as a second language who are reluctant interactors. We have described the teacher-implemented strategy of redirects and issues to consider in redirecting children. We have found that merely placing children together does not ensure interaction between peers. Peer interaction for children with communicative limitations is something that must be planned for and facilitated by adults. Thus, we believe that adults must be facilitators, and not just supervisors, of children's social interactions during play.

REFERENCES

Becker, J.A., Place, K.S., Tenzer, S.A., & Frueh, B.C. (1991). Teachers' impressions of children varying in pragmatic skills. *Journal of Applied Developmental Psychology, 12,* 397–412.

Black, B., & Hazen, N.L. (1990). Social status and patterns of communication in acquainted and unacquainted preschool children. *Developmental Psychology, 26,* 379–387.

Bunce, B.H. (1995). *Building a language-focused curriculum for the preschool classroom. Vol. II: A planning guide.* Baltimore: Paul H. Brookes Publishing Co.

Catts, H. (1990). *Promoting successful transition to the primary grades: Predictions of reading problems in speech and language handicapped children* (Project 3.1 of the Kansas Early Childhood Research Institute Annual Report). Lawrence: University of Kansas. (USDE Grant No. H024U280001)

Gertner, B.L., Rice, M.L., & Hadley, P.A. (1994). The influence of communicative competence on peer preferences in a preschool classroom. *Journal of Speech and Hearing Research, 37,* 913–923.

Greenwood, C.R., Walker, H.M., Todd, N.M., & Hops, H. (1981). Normative and descriptive analysis of preschool free play social interaction rates. *Journal of Pediatric Psychology, 6,* 343–367.

Guralnick, M.J. (1990). Peer interactions and the development of handicapped children's social and communicative competence. In H. Foot, M. Morgan, & R. Shute (Eds.), *Children helping children* (pp. 275–305). New York: John Wiley & Sons.

Hadley, P.A., & Rice, M.L. (1991). Conversational responsiveness of speech and language impaired preschoolers. *Journal of Speech and Hearing Research, 34,* 1308–1317.

Hadley, P.A., Rice, M.L., & Wilcox, K.A. (in preparation). *Longitudinal change in peer-directed initiations.*

Hartup, W. (1983). Peer relations. In W. Kessen (Ed.), *History, theory, and methods: Vol. 1. Handbook of child psychology* (4th ed., pp. 103–196). New York: John Wiley & Sons.

Hazen, N.L., & Black, B. (1989). Preschool peer communication skills: The role of social status and interaction context. *Child Development, 60,* 867–876.

Holmberg, M.C. (1980). The development of social interchange patterns from 12 to 42 months. *Child Development, 51,* 448–456.

Howes, C. (1987). Peer interaction in young children. *Monographs of the Society for Research in Child Development, 53*(1), serial no. 217.

McTear, M. (1985). *Children's conversations.* New York: Basil Blackwell Ltd.

Mueller, E. (1972). The maintenance of verbal exchanges between young children. *Child Development, 43,* 930–932.

Mueller, E., Bleir, M., Krakow, J., Hegedus, K., & Cournoyer, P. (1977). The development of peer verbal interaction among two year old boys. *Child Development, 48,* 284–287.

Nelson, K., & Gruendel, J.M. (1979). At morning it's lunchtime: A scriptal view of children's dialogues. *Discourse Processes, 2,* 73–94.

Nelson, K.E. (1989). Strategies for first language teaching. In M.L. Rice & R.L. Schiefelbusch (Eds.), *The teachability of language* (pp. 263–310). Baltimore: Paul H. Brookes Publishing Co.

Odom, S.L., & Brown, W.H. (1993). Social interaction skills interventions for young children with disabilities in integrated settings. In C.A. Peck, S.L. Odom, & D.D. Bricker (Eds.), *Integrating young children with disabilities into community programs: Ecological perspectives on research and implementation* (pp. 39–64). Baltimore: Paul H. Brookes Publishing Co.

Odom, S.L., McConnell, S.R., & McEvoy, M.A. (Eds.). (1992). *Social competence of young children with disabilities: Issues and strategies for intervention.* Baltimore: Paul H. Brookes Publishing Co.

Odom, S.L., & McEvoy, M.A. (1988). Integration of young children with handicaps and normally developing children. In S.L. Odom & M.B. Karnes (Eds.), *Early intervention for infants and children with handicaps: An empirical base* (pp. 241–267). Baltimore: Paul H. Brookes Publishing Co.

Odom, S., & Strain, P. (1984). Peer-mediated approaches to promoting children's social interactions: A review. *American Journal of Orthopsychiatry, 54,* 544–557.

Place, K.S., & Becker, J.A. (1991). The influence of pragmatic competence on the likeability of grade-school children. *Discourse Processes, 14,* 227–241.

Rice, M.L. (1993). "Don't talk to him; he's weird": A social consequences account of language and social interactions. In A.P. Kaiser & D.B. Gray (Eds.), *Enhancing children's communication: Research foundations for early language intervention: Vol. 2. Communication and language intervention series* (pp. 139–158). Baltimore: Paul H. Brookes Publishing Co.

Rice, M.L., Hadley, P.A., & Alexander, A. (1993). Social biases toward children with specific language impairment: A correlative causal model of language limitations. *Applied Psycholinguistics, 14,* 445–471.

Rice, M.L., Sell, M.A., & Hadley, P.A. (1990). The Social Interactive Coding System (SICS): An on-line clinically relevant descriptive tool. *Language, Speech, and Hearing Services in Schools, 21,* 2–14.

Rice, M.L., Sell, M.A., & Hadley, P.A. (1991). Social interactive skills of speech and language impaired children. *Journal of Speech and Hearing Research, 34,* 1299–1307.

Rice, M.L., Wilcox, K.A., Hadley, P.A., & Schuele, C.M. (1993, November). *Social skills for preschool and kindergarten success.* Miniseminar presented at the annual meeting of the American Speech-Language-Hearing Association, Anaheim, CA.

Rueter, J., & Yunik, G. (1973). Social interaction in nursery schools. *Developmental Psychology, 9,* 319–325.

Schuele, C.M., Rice, M.L., & Wilcox, K.A. (in preparation). *Redirects: A strategy to increase peer initiations.* Manuscript under review.

Vandell, D.L., & George, L.B. (1981). Social interaction in hearing and deaf preschoolers: Successes and failures in initiation. *Child Development, 52*(2), 627–635.

Walsh, D.J. (1989). Changes in kindergarten. Why here? Why now? *Early Childhood Research Quarterly, 4,* 377–391.

~8~

Collaborating with Families

Julie F. Sergeant

Five people are gathered around a circular table in a small conference room to write an individualized education program (IEP) for a 3-year-old named Alex. The speech-language pathology student is telling the others how Alex enjoys being "Helper of the Day." Alex's mother, Kathy, sits quietly in her chair listening, her purse clenched tightly in her lap. Stiffly seated next to her is Alex's father, Craig, and next to him, LAP's family services coordinator. The student finishes her description of Alex eagerly climbing onto a chair to flip the lights on and off and proudly announce, "Keen-up tine!" The final member of the IEP team, the lead teacher, then introduces everyone to Alex's father, who, unlike his wife, had not met everyone.

Because this will be Alex's first IEP, the lead teacher explains the purpose of the meeting and suggests the team begin by listing Alex's strengths, or what he does well. "We usually give the parents a chance to start, since you know your child better than anyone else—so I'll let you begin," she says, turning the floor over to Alex's parents.

"Well," Kathy nervously ventures, glancing at her husband for support, "I was amazed at how well he got used to LAP. I was afraid he was going to have trouble separating from me."

Everyone readily agrees that his easy adjustment to the program is a major strength for Alex. After the IEP team generates several strengths, including Alex's ability to follow directions, his interest in learning language, and his active imagination, the lead teacher suggests the team shift focus and try to think of things for Alex to work on.

The family services coordinator prompts Kathy, "You mentioned to me that Alex does not play with others at his play group."

In response, Kathy explains that she has noticed this hesitation more at Alex's play group than at LAP.

Kathy and Craig proceed to provide valuable information about Alex's language use at home. One of Alex's proposed goals is to acquire the plural -s ending, and Kathy relates an anecdote from home clearly demonstrating that he does understand the concept of plurality. Craig comments that

Alex rarely uses -s in conversations to designate plural. The team decides to write an expressive language goal concerning Alex's use of plural -s endings, since this appeared to be an emerging skill. As Kathy and Craig are drawn into the team atmosphere, both visibly relax and begin to contribute enthusiastically.

After goals have been written for each of Alex's relative weaknesses, the lead teacher asks his parents, "Is there anything else you would like to talk about?" Kathy expresses frustration with getting Alex to do things for himself—things she knows he is capable of doing, such as getting dressed. She believes he is too dependent on others, especially her! After discussing ways his parents can encourage him to be more motivated at home and things staff members can do at school to foster independence, the team writes an IEP goal addressing Kathy's concern. With the goals completed and the IEP signed by everyone present, the lead teacher promises to make a photocopy for Kathy and Craig.

Since the 1980s, family systems theory and naturalistic philosophies have influenced researchers and practitioners in the fields of speech-language pathology, special education, and early childhood education. The literature in these fields has stressed the importance of involving families in therapeutic and educational programs for their children (Andrews & Andrews, 1990; Donahue-Kilburg, 1992; Dunst, Trivette, & Deal, 1988; Galinsky, 1988; Schrader, 1989; Turnbull & Turnbull, 1990). Children are affected by their family system. When supported by a family-focused program, family functioning, parental coping, and caregiving effectiveness are improved, and the time parents spend with their children is increased. Children are, therefore, in a better position to benefit from services, and their developmental competence is likely to grow as a result (Mahoney, O'Sullivan, & Dennebaum, 1990). Family-centered early intervention may be distinguished from traditional programs as focusing on the child in the context of the family, recognizing the strengths and needs of all family members, including family members in the assessment process, and involving family members in the child's intervention program to the extent the family desires and circumstances permit (Donahue-Kilburg, 1992).

LAP'S FAMILY-FOCUSED PHILOSOPHY

In this chapter, the family service model developed in the Language Acquisition Preschool (LAP) is described. Aspects of these services are illustrated in the vignette described above. One particular conference, however, does not adequately convey the ways in which LAP family services are tailored to the needs of individual families. IEP conferences vary in length, participating team members, degree of family involvement, and topics of discussion. Although LAP staff members encourage family participation and work actively to help family members feel comfortable in their collaborative role, the degree of family involvement in the development of IEPs and in the LAP program varies from family to family. The main point to be conveyed here is the importance of individualized service for each family across a range of service options.

LAP's Model of Family Collaboration

Families are an integral part of LAP's concentrated normative model (CNM), in which an emphasis is placed on the child's use of language at home as well as in the preschool environment. The child is seen as a member of a family system; therefore, whatever affects the child will affect the family just as dynamics within the family will affect the child. Outside influences on the family also filter through the family system and affect family members. These outside influences emanate from the family's ecological environment and include friends, work environments, child care arrangements, governmental policies, and cultural background (Bronfenbrenner, 1986). It is through collaboration and the sharing of information between families and staff members that children are best served.

LAP staff members view primary caregivers as central to language facilitation and child development and well-being. The CNM promotes opportunities for parent involvement in all aspects of LAP programming. Through personal contact, newsletters, and conferences, staff members work to inform family members about their child's progress and participation at school, child language development, and language facilitation techniques. Specific goals for these interactions with families are listed in Table 1. These goals and the roles of staff members are described later in this chapter. The family services coordinator and other staff members actively seek frequent contact with the children's primary caregivers to obtain feedback about school activities, the child's behavior at home, and the family's goals for the child. This exchange of information between school and home facilitates the generalization of language skills across settings.

Realizing that family preferences and needs vary and that degree of involvement will differ from family to family, LAP offers a range of activities and services in which families may participate as they wish. This model of family support is a fluid process that is dependent on interactions between families and staff members to provide individualized, informal supports; it is in contrast with prepackaged family support programs that dictate the types of support families are to receive. The LAP model allows flexibility for changing family dynamics and expects the degree and type of family involvement to change over time.

Table 1.   Goals for working with family members to enhance children's language acquisition

- Acquaint family members with the typical stages of language development.
- Help family members recognize their child's progress in speech-language development.
- Help family members understand their role in their child's speech-language development.
- Increase family members' use of modeling, repetition, expansions, and recasting when interacting with their child.
- Increase family members' awareness of the manner in which they verbally interact with their child.
- Increase family members' verbal interactions with their children throughout the day by encouraging them to follow their child's interests and to rely on daily routines.
- Decrease family members' use of commands and yes/no questions when verbally interacting with their child.

This individualization and flexibility are accomplished through a combination of formal and informal supports. The formalized supports in this model address child and caregiving issues and service coordination and focus on enhancing language acquisition. These supports are based on parents' interests, are preplanned, and are offered to all families on a regular basis (e.g., a group parent night, a weekly newsletter). The formal supports provide the framework through which informal supports evolve. Informal supports are individualized and are often provided on the spur of the moment as the need arises with each family. It is not unusual for the family services coordinator to spend unscheduled time visiting with a mother who is struggling with the decision to return to work or listening to a father's description of his son's social interactions during their weekend rollerskating outings. Both formal and informal supports encourage two-way sharing of information. This information exchange is essential in a collaborative relationship.

Some basic principles guide staff interactions with families. First, use of family supports is optional. Family members are encouraged to take advantage of the formal support options by, for example, attending scheduled family events or using the observation room. Families are given suggestions for facilitating their children's language skills and are offered informal supports as the occasion arises, but each family determines whether or not it wants to take advantage of these opportunities. Second, staff members are open to suggestions and requests from parents. This feedback has led to changes in the format of IEP conferences, new parent nights on specific topics, and locating specific information to post in the observation room. Third, suggestions for working with children at home are designed to be easily incorporated into the course of the child's daily routine and to be fun for both the parent and the child. For example, talking about sequencing can easily be done at bath time— "First, I washed your face, then your arms, then your tummy. I washed your feet last." It is necessary for staff members to learn about family routines through conversations and/or home visits. Finally, any support that requires active involvement on the part of family members is designed in collaboration with the families and with their schedules in mind. For example, a suggestion for parents to label their child's food at dinnertime will not work if the child eats dinner at a babysitter's house.

The Family Unit

The individuality of each family unit, including roles of family members, varying personal characteristics, interactions among family members, life changes being experienced at any given time, and outside influences, affects interactions between LAP staff members and family members. LAP's model of family collaboration, which is derived from family systems theory, is represented in Figure 1. (For more information about the application of family systems theory with families of children with special needs, see Andrews & Andrews, 1990; Donahue-Kilburg, 1992; and Turnbull & Turnbull, 1990.) Andrews and Andrews combine family systems theory and family therapy techniques with speech-language intervention, creating a family-based treatment model. Turnbull and Turnbull

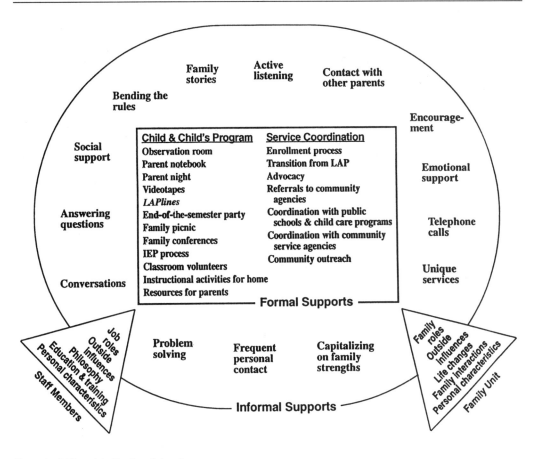

Figure 1.   LAP model of family collaboration.

discuss the family unit within a family systems conceptual framework drawn from literature in the field of sociology and special education. Donahue-Kilburg outlines family systems theory, discussing the family's role in language development; describes models of preventive intervention and how families are included in these models; and discusses assessment and evaluation of family-focused programs. The family is seen as a medium for communication growth. Providing many opportunities for interaction, motivating the child to communicate needs and desires, modeling language, and responding to the child's communicative attempts are all ways that families influence children's language acquisition (Donahue-Kilburg, 1992).

Influences on the Family System   In the LAP model of family collaboration, *family roles* involve aspects of day-to-day family functioning, such as caring for children, working outside of the home, housekeeping, and so forth. The division of these roles within the family helps to determine which family members will interact most with their child and with the professionals who work with their child.

Personal characteristics in the family unit include family size, cultural background, presence of a speech-language impairment or other disability, income, educational background, number of children, and individual personality traits of family members. Each of these personal characteristics influences the interactions between family members and staff members. In LAP, one third of the children enrolled have a speech-language impairment. Most of the families of these children received this diagnosis during the evaluation upon enrollment after a self-referral or after a referral through a local screening program.

Interactions in the family unit encompass relationships between parents, parents and children, brothers and sisters, nuclear family members and extended family members, and family members and nonfamily members.

Life changes include transitions to preschool or kindergarten and the public school system, diagnosis of a speech-language impairment or other disability, progression of child development stages, moving in or out of a foreign culture, divorce, and addition of new family members.

Outside influences on the family unit come from a child's babysitter, early intervention program or preschool, residential neighborhood, church, community, and even governmental policies.

Staff Members and Their Roles

Just as the family unit influences interactions between family members and staff members, roles and traits of staff members also affect the type and form of collaboration between individual staff members and family members. Job role; background in education, training, and philosophy; outside influences; and personal characteristics of staff members all influence these interactions.

Family Services Coordinator   At LAP, the family services coordinator establishes and maintains the liaison between each child's home and the classroom by arranging an environment that fosters information sharing, formal and informal support, and service coordination to families. The family services coordinator talks with family members about their goals for their children, serves as parent advocate, answers questions, provides information about community resources, and recognizes family strengths as important resources for the program as well as for the children. LAP's family services coordinator keeps records of information relevant to children's language programs and encourages family members to share information. Comments such as "Grandma talked to him on the phone last night and understood the entire conversation" shows progress that would be noted. The family services coordinator steers questions and issues that are better addressed by another staff member or agency to the appropriate individual and follows up to ensure that resolution occurred. The coordinator's flexible schedule allows her to be available to talk with families at drop-off and pick-up time or at a moment's notice when the telephone rings to discuss parenting issues or answer questions. The coordinator ensures that all families have equal access and opportunity to interact with staff members and to participate in their child's program as they desire. She helps overcome barriers (e.g., cultural differences) to interactions between home and school and encourages other staff members to take the initiative to do so as well.

On a daily basis, the family services coordinator helps staff members to recognize that their tendency will be to interact most often with the families whose values, lifestyle, and educational and cultural backgrounds are similar to their own (Galinsky, 1988). With increased awareness about the necessity of reaching out to all families in the program, staff members are encouraged to make, for example, the effort to ask a foreign-born mother about birthday celebrations or educational programs in her home country. This mother, although reluctant to initiate a conversation, may actually be eager to share stories with someone who has the patience to decipher her pidgin English. The information gained from the conversation may give insights into the nature of interactions between family members and the school staff. Staff members are encouraged to take the time to talk with parents whose lifestyles are radically different from their own, and to see the strengths they bring to their relationship with their child. Helping staff members encourage volunteer assistance from a family member who is too shy or too busy to be the first to sign up ensures that all families have equal access for involvement. This also avoids the trap of overburdening the same parent who can always be counted on to volunteer and is asked to do so over and over again. The coordinator intervenes when classroom staff members groan about assistance from a primary caregiver whose interactions with her child may not be, from their perspective, "appropriate." She helps them to see this situation as an opportunity for modeling discipline techniques, encouraging positive interactions between the primary caregiver and the child, and exchanging important information about the child's skills at home and at school.

Although the family services coordinator's primary job is to work directly with LAP families, this contact is not the exclusive province of the coordinator. All staff members recognize the important role that families play in children's development. LAP's director supervises the educational and therapeutic programs for each child and is cognizant of the specific level of language development of each child in the classroom in relation to developmental patterns. In frequent contact with LAP families, the director involves family members when evaluating children and answers questions pertaining to speech and language development and classroom behavior. Other staff members, such as the speech-language therapists, the assistant teacher, and the educational psychologist, interact with family members during family activities, at conferences, and as children are dropped off and picked up from school.

Staff Backgrounds LAP's staff members have varying educational and training backgrounds. Staff members hold degrees in levels from bachelor's to doctorate in fields ranging from speech-language pathology to early childhood education to special education. As previously noted, each staff member's area of emphasis helps define the type of interactions he or she has with families.

In spite of their varied educational backgrounds, LAP staff members share similar philosophies about child development, discipline, therapy techniques, and home activities. These philosophies are embodied in the

10 operational guidelines for the concentrated normative model (CNM) listed in Chapter 3, and focus on: 1) following the child's lead to choose activities that encourage developmental skills at school and at home, 2) using naturally occurring positive reinforcement for behavior problems, 3) conducting intervention in a naturalistic setting, and 4) encouraging naturalistic methods of generalization from school to the home. These philosophies are sought in job candidates and are promoted through a new employee inservice and ongoing staff meetings. Because of this shared set of values, families receive consistent messages from all LAP staff members.

Influence of Outside Factors on Interactions   Constraints and assistance originating from outside sources also affect how staff members interact with family members. Funding resources may limit the amount of money available to set up a resource library of books and videotapes or may prevent the program from hiring babysitters during a parent night. Time constraints placed on staff members who have responsibilities outside of work may limit the number of parent conferences held in the evenings or on weekends. When transitions to other classrooms are considered, the list of potentially limiting constraints grows. For example, an eligibility requirement for a special program such as a language-based kindergarten may limit enrollment to children scoring 1.5 standard deviations below the mean on an evaluation. This may frustrate a parent whose child scores 1.25 standard deviations below the mean.

The role of staff members is to operate under these constraints while working around busy schedules of staff members and family members, educating family members about eligibility requirements, and eliciting donations or setting up scholarship funds when necessary. Being willing to work together and compromise enables staff members to overcome these outside constraints, tap into available support from outside sources, and allow for a wider range of available supports for families. It is important that outside constraints do not become an excuse to avoid providing individualized family support. Programs must constantly search for ways to collaborate with outside agencies to provide the best possible services to families and their children.

Personal Characteristics and Experiences   Personal characteristics and experiences of LAP personnel, such as age, experience with foreign languages and cultures, being a parent, and personality traits, will affect the interaction between individual staff members and family members. Professionals' educational level and parenting experience have been shown to affect their attitudes toward parents. Sociodemographic differences among parents affect professionals' views of parents' child-rearing abilities. These differences may even affect the amount of support that parents receive (Kontos, Raikes, & Woods, 1983; Kontos & Wells, 1986). A possible bias in a preschool setting with highly educated staff members might be that written materials are the best way to provide information about children's developmental sequences, while a family member for whom reading is difficult may prefer to receive information through informal conversations and another family member may prefer to receive information via videotape.

One's culture influences the way he or she communicates. Communication styles vary widely from family to family and from professional to professional. A service provider must avoid the trap of thinking that a family's culture is "different." This is a two way street—from the point of view of the family, it is the professional's culture that is different! When interacting with families, early interventionists must be aware of their own cultural background. Lynch and Hanson (1992) stress this point:

> When we are out of touch with our own culture and its influence on us, it is impossible to work effectively with people whose cultures differ from our own. Only when we examine the values, beliefs, and patterns of behavior that are a part of our own cultural identity can we distinguish truth from tradition. Such an examination is not easy: It requires a consideration of all of the things that we have learned from childhood and an acknowledgment that those beliefs and behaviors represent only one perspective—a perspective that is *not* inherently "right." (p. 21)

Culture influences our choice of professional or casual clothing; formal or informal greetings; amount of eye contact; the family member sought out for interactions; and the method used for gathering information—verbal versus written attempts, or highly structured versus open-ended questions (Lynch & Hanson, 1992). An awareness of personal characteristics and cultural influences on the part of professionals will ease barriers to communication with families. This awareness will help ensure that all families involved in early intervention programs have equal access to family support.

Informal and Formal Family Supports

The third major component of the LAP model of family collaboration, as seen in Figure 1, is family support, which includes both informal and formal types of support. Traits of the family unit and professional staff members as described above affect interactions and the type of support families receive. The remainder of this chapter focuses on these informal and formal supports.

INFORMAL SUPPORT ACTIVITIES

Informal supports are not preplanned or structured but evolve as the relationship between LAP staff members and family members develops. Once this relationship is established, informal interactions tap into social support networks allowing an exchange of resources among family members and the friends, relatives, neighbors, and professionals with whom they are in contact. Utilizing social support networks allows social service agencies to provide families with a menu of supports from which families may choose to meet their individual needs (Deal, 1991). It is these individualized and unique informal interactions that make the difference in a quality family-focused program.

LAP strives to create an environment that facilitates informal support. Families must feel free to ask for unique types of support or staff members must know family members well enough to initiate informal support when they believe it is appropriate. Listening to the cute (or frustrating) thing a child did and appreciating it (or sympathizing) is an important part of providing informal support to families. Individually, LAP staff members have facilitated contact among families for purposes of carpooling or sharing of like experiences, worked to increase families' awareness of their own strengths, and assisted families in using their network of extended family or friends to help with a problem. This is done through telephone conversations, answering questions, frequent personal contact, home visits, family events, problem solving, and active listening. Informal support includes bending the rules and offering unique services to individual families—services that would be impossible to offer equally to all parents because of limited resources and time. In the past, staff members have combed out headlice nits, lent $5 for gas, walked a child to a program in the next building, jump-started a dead car battery, and allowed a child to attend both the morning and afternoon sessions for a week while his mother was unexpectedly hospitalized.

Informal support may take the form of helping a parent identify steps to ease stress in a child's or family's life, and then encouraging the parent to take these steps. Professionals must respect the parent's role as ultimate decision maker for his or her child. At some point, the professional must step back and wait for the parent's decision to act, no matter how anxious the professional is about instigating change. The following story illustrates this point. It also documents how family support instigating change in a child's environment away from school can affect behavior in the classroom.

Corey is 4 years old and has the ability to steal the hearts of his teachers despite challenging behaviors that often left bruises up and down their legs. Staff members began to suspect that some of these behaviors might be resulting from the quality of care he received from his sitter. Corey's grandmother believed that the children this sitter tended were often left to fend for themselves, and his father suspected that Corey was fed little or nothing from the time he was dropped off at the sitter's at 5 A.M. until he arrived at preschool at 1 P.M.

After sharing these concerns with Corey's mother, we learned that she took Corey to this sitter because she tolerated the mother's varying and odd work hours. She was affordable to Corey's mother, who was a single parent. She also believed that Corey was happy with this sitter because he would give her hugs when he saw her. LAP staff members began to give Corey a snack upon arrival at school and continued to document his behavior swings—associating them with the days he was dropped off at preschool by his sitter.

On the day that the sitter dropped Corey off wearing pants that had been urinated in, but left on so long that they were almost dry, the family services coordinator decided she had enough substantial information to discuss the situation with the health department's family child care licensing agent for the county. The health department personnel knew of this particular sitter, who managed to operate just within the letter of the law. They strongly recommended that the mother change sitters and offered to provide her with a list of family child care providers in her neighborhood.

The family services coordinator passed this recommendation along to Corey's mother along with the name of a sitter recommended by another LAP parent. Corey's mother did call the new sitter and made arrangements to meet with her, but was unable to keep the appointment. At this point, the family services coordinator discussed the health department's recommendation with Corey's grandmother and father and called the potential new sitter to encourage her to hold an opening for "a wonderful boy who needs quality and consistent child care." For several weeks, the family services coordinator acted as a liaison, relaying messages between the potential sitter and Corey's mother, continuing to encourage Corey's mother to take the step to change sitters.

This story does have a happy ending. Corey's mother eventually called the new sitter and enrolled her son. Within 3 weeks, Corey's behavior in the classroom changed dramatically. He began to learn to keep himself under control, and he discovered that hitting and kicking will not get him what he wants but that using words will. He attended and asked appropriate questions at group time. He looked healthier and was happier—laughing and telling jokes.

With these changes in his child care situation and subsequent improvements in behavior, Corey was better able to target his energies toward speech and language acquisition, which also benefited him significantly. Thus, with some subtle negotiations with the family, caregivers, and community agencies, the stage was set for Corey to benefit fully from the LAP curriculum.

Informal support is essential in a program designed to facilitate children's language use at home as well as at school through strong relationships with families. A program that offers frequent personal contact with parents, provides encouragement, answers questions, uses active listening techniques, and recognizes the importance of these types of informal supports greatly benefits families and, in turn, their children. Authorizing staff members to bend the rules on occasion also facilitates informal support to individual families. Programs must regard informal support to families as a priority and incorporate strategies facilitating informal support into day-to-day interactions with families.

FORMAL SUPPORT ACTIVITIES

Formal support forms the backbone of LAP's family-focused programming. These supports are listed in the center of Figure 1. Formal supports are systematically planned in advance and are either part of required service coordination for children with speech and language impairments or are offered equally to all families. An IEP conference is an example of a formal support for families of children with speech and language impairments.

Families are comfortable with these formal supports. They are traditional types of interactions between family members and educational professionals that help parents understand their child's preschool routine and how school and home activities facilitate their child's language and other areas of development. Some families feel that many nontraditional supports are intrusive, particularly when they relate to family matters not directly affecting the child's program. One grandmother, whose granddaughters were making a transition into a program in a neighboring school district, told our staff:

I don't like their program. They don't listen to me like you all do. The first day I was over there, they started asking me all these questions about why the girls were not living with their mother. I didn't know this man and there were four other people in the room. It wasn't any of his goddamn business!

The point of this example is that building a relationship with families takes time and sensitivity. Listening to families and supporting their decisions will result in a trustful, established relationship, which will allow professionals to approach sensitive issues. Formal family support services at LAP address child and caregiving issues, including the enhancement of language acquisition, or focus on coordination of services.

Initial Contact with Parents and the Enrollment Process

Locating quality child care that parents can trust is one of the most difficult and stressful tasks of parenting young children. For children with special needs, this is further complicated by decisions that must be made regarding therapy and service options. Staff members recognize this and take steps to ease the transition. Before a child is actually enrolled, parents have spoken with LAP staff members on the telephone and visited the classroom. They are encouraged to bring their child to the classroom for a visit while the children are present. If LAP has no openings or if the child's parents seem uncomfortable with the CNM; the service, research, and training combination; or with other aspects of the program, the family services coordinator refers the parents to other local preschools or to the school district for alternative service options. Parents who pay tuition (i.e., whose children are not eligible for mandated special services) are informed about the possibilities of a scholarship or funding through social and rehabilitative services.

Each child's speech and language skills are evaluated before enrollment. Before the evaluation, parents are told what to expect. A family member observes the administration of the formal assessment tools and gives feedback on the observed performance and the child's skills at home. Family members are asked to complete a case history form and discuss the child's development with the director. Evaluation results are discussed with family members immediately, and copies of the results and written report are available if the parents are interested. The child attends LAP for a trial period during which a language sample is collected and the child is eased into the program. Once the language sample is analyzed, the IEP team meets and the parents sign the forms to formalize their child's enrollment in LAP.

Diagnosis of a Speech or Language Impairment

Families whose child has recently received a diagnosis of a speech or language impairment are dealing with an onslaught of emotions. Families' lives at this time are further complicated by changes in services, including the adjustment to their young child's enrollment in preschool, the details of IEP documents and the special education system, and having professionals (who are, until this point, strangers) inquire about their lives. For some parents, a diagnosis may confirm observations that their child's speech and language skills were not quite what they should be. For an astute parent who has been trying to find a professional who will take his or her observations seriously, a diagnosis may be somewhat of a relief and confirmation of his or her parenting skills. Stages of grieving after the diagnosis of disability in a child have been described as shock, realization, retreat, and acknowledgment (Webster & Ward, 1993). An analysis of a family's progress through stages of grief is not what family members need at this time. Family members may want support, understanding, and compassion, in addition to information about the disability and child management when coping with a new diagnosis or other crisis (Webster & Ward, 1993). Listening to family stories is supportive and gives professionals important information. Linking together parents with similar experiences is another example of support that can be particularly helpful during this period immediately following the child's diagnosis. LAP staff members believe that these early supportive interactions with parents lay the groundwork for a positive and collaborative relationship.

Managing Guilt

One theme that is closely linked with the diagnosis of speech or language impairment is guilt. Many family members feel guilty, as if they somehow caused their child's impairment. Staff members frequently hear comments such as "I should have read to him more," "I am so busy. I know I don't spend enough time with her," or "My mother says I shouldn't have gone back to work so soon."

Staff members educate family members about using indirect language facilitation techniques at home to boost their child's language development. Often, family members turn this into an affirmation of their feelings that in some way their child's language is delayed because of something they did "wrong." It is a challenge to explain that although the use of indirect language facilitation techniques will help a child's language acquisition, one cannot assume that a lack of these techniques *caused* the child's language delay.

Supporting Advocacy Efforts

There is evidence that adults (including, but not limited to, teachers) make unfounded assumptions that may reflect negatively on the child after listening to children with speech and language impairments, and to a lesser extent, children with only speech impairments (Rice, Hadley, & Alexander, 1993). It follows that parents not only have to cope with their own emotions, but also have to defend their children and themselves to extended family members and other adults, including teachers, who may bring negative models of causality to the children's speech and language limitations. Adults may assume that these children have lower intelligence, are socially immature, will have less chance of academic success, come from low-income homes, and have parents with little education (Rice et al., 1993). It is, therefore, very important for professionals to assist parents in their response to the initial diagnosis, to help them get beyond blaming to focus their energies on advocacy for their child and themselves. Educating family members about the nature of speech and language impairments and giving interested parents specific suggestions for facilitating language use, through personal communication or a weekly newsletter, may help some families through this time.

Enhancing Language Acquisition

In LAP's language-focused curriculum (LFC), family participation in each child's language intervention program and synchrony between the child's home and the preschool are emphasized. Many of the formal interactions with families at LAP address children's language development and focus on generalizing language skills between the school and home environments. Although LAP encourages all families to become involved in their children's language learning, these skills are emphasized with the families of children with speech and language impairments. The goals of these formal interactions with families are outlined in Table 1 and are described in greater detail below.

Acquaint Family Members with the Typical Stages of Language Development

Some families do not have much contact with preschool-age children other than their own. Seeing their child immersed in a classroom with children using language skills at a more advanced level can come as a shock to some parents. LAP staff members ease this transition by reminding family members of the child's strengths, giving family members a brochure outlining typical language development, alerting parents to areas of weakness in language development before the child enters the classroom, and introducing parents to others who have previously made the same transition.

Some parents struggle with conflicting advice from professionals encouraging enrollment in early intervention programs such as LAP and from grandparents or other respected relatives who cannot understand all the fuss and believe that the child will "grow out of it." Inviting grandparents and other relatives to conferences, to end-of-the-semester programs, and to the observation room has helped in these situations.

Observation Room LAP's observation room is open to family members at any time class is in session. It is a favorite meeting place at pick-up time. The room encourages classroom observation and informal support among parents who are waiting to pick up their children. The family services coordinator and other staff members watch for parents in the observation room and make themselves available to explain the program, point out child progress, answer questions, listen to concerns, and compare notes about the child's behavior in the classroom and at home.

In the observation room, there is a notebook for parents to write down observations about their child's language. This is another way for staff members to learn about the child's progress at home and it is helpful for parents to track their child's progress as well as that of children in

similar situations. Although this type of public sharing is not for everyone, those who use the notebook have appreciated its insights over time.

The observation room also contains brochures about LAP, toys for brothers and sisters to play with while they wait for their parents, and a basket of photographs of children in the classroom for family members to sift through and choose to take home. The observation room is not simply a storage room for the classroom!

Resources for Parents A Resources for Parents shelf in the classroom contains written materials at a variety of reading levels and videotapes for parents about child development, parenting issues, and speech-language development. Although these resources are few in number, they have been helpful to recommend to families who are concerned with a specific aspect of development or discipline. LAP staff members have found that parents frequently indicate an interest in written materials and videotapes on child development and parenting, yet most tend not to browse through the materials themselves. Family members seem to prefer the recommendation of a book chapter when the appropriate occasion arises. For example, one father was particularly interested in fostering his daughter's artistic and creative development and asked for specific reading material on this subject. Another mother appreciated a section of a book on time out as a followup to a conversation over her frustration with the discipline techniques she was using at home.

Classroom Volunteers Family members are encouraged to come to the classroom to share a hobby or talk about their job. The children have played inside a moving van that one father drove for a living and watched a demonstration from a mother who was a beautician. One mother who did not work outside of her home fascinated the children by demonstrating how to give a baby a bath with a doll and a baby bathtub. Perhaps the most successful family participation activities have involved family members who play musical instruments. A father from China played modern Chinese music on an electronic keyboard, and a mother who speaks almost no English entertained the children for 30 minutes by teaching them a song in Korean and playing their favorite songs on the violin.

Family members are recruited to help on special occasions such as field trips or Halloween parades, to bring a treat or party favors for class parties, or to bring ingredients for a cooking or art project. LAP has a "Visitor Day" about once a semester when a friend or relative may spend the last half hour in the classroom playing and being introduced to the others. This is a popular day among brothers and sisters.

Help Family Members Recognize Their Child's Progress in Speech-Language Development

Some families whose children receive speech-language therapy at LAP feel strongly that their child should be "cured" by the time he or she reaches kindergarten. Although some children who attended LAP no longer needed speech-language therapy after age 5 or 6 (see Chapter 11), others still benefit from these services. Staff members share progress, even small steps, on a regular basis with family members through informal conversations at pick-up time, notes, telephone calls, and during conferences. From the observation room, the family services coordinator or director may point out children's progress in language use during dramatic play or when interacting with other children. Family members share success stories through informal conversations with staff members or by writing anecdotes in the notebook placed in the observation room specifically for that purpose.

Help Family Members Understand Their Role in Their Child's Speech-Language Development

As previously mentioned, many family members feel guilty about their child's speech and language impairment. LAP staff members assure family members that their child's speech and language impairment is not their fault. At the same time, family members are helped to understand that they can actively facilitate their child's language skills.

Increase Family Members' Use of Modeling, Repetition, Expansions, and Recasting When Interacting with Their Child

Indirect language facilitation techniques, parallel to those used in the classroom, are introduced to parents. These include modeling, repetition, expansions, and recasting. These techniques are described in detail in Chapter 4 of this volume. The family services coordinator uses a commercially available videotape, *Oh, Say What They See: An Introduction to Indirect Language Stimulation* (Freedman & Lathuen, 1984) to demonstrate these interactive techniques to parents. Parents may observe the classroom at any time to see these techniques in use by the classroom staff. While parents are observing, the family services coordinator or another staff member is available to explain the techniques and ways to transfer the skills to home settings. Ongoing suggestions for using indirect language facilitation techniques are given during conferences and parent night programs, and in the weekly newsletter, *LAPlines*.

LAPlines   *LAPlines* is a weekly newsletter for parents that describes activities for the upcoming week. Brief day-by-day descriptions of curricular activities allow parents to use the newsletter to talk to their children about what they will do at school. Parents also use the descriptions to talk to their child about school activities once the child returns home. Some parents use the newsletter as an aid to decipher an unintelligible comment about something that happened at school.

LAPlines includes an "Ideas for Home" column, which lists activities for parents to do with their children in the course of their normal, daily routine. These activities enhance language and other areas of development.

During the fall semester, the "About LAP: Focus on . . ." column features one portion of the LAP schedule. The column outlines the goals of the featured activity and explains how the activity facilitates language and child development.

General announcements, words for a "Song of the Week," reminders about parent meetings, children's birthdays, or recipes for healthy snacks are often included. When using written communication to make announcements, it is important to remember that not all adults are functionally literate. The family services coordinator gives verbal reminders to family members who do not read the newsletter for this information.

Increase Family Members' Awareness of the Manner in Which They Verbally Interact with Their Child

Family members are asked to think about the ways they interact with their child and to share concerns and progress with staff members. Areas of concern may be addressed by an IEP goal, but more often by encouraging family members to use indirect language techniques with their child. For example, children who are pressured to talk often do the opposite—they refuse to talk. Problem solving with parents to develop ways to apply indirect language techniques to specific situations often results in less pressure on the child and often, more talking.

Increase Family Members' Verbal Interactions with Their Children Throughout the Day by Encouraging Them to Follow Their Child's Interests and to Rely on Daily Routines

Staff members encourage family members to use indirect language facilitation techniques in their daily interactions with their children to increase the quality of these interactions. It is important to remember that family life with young children may be stressful. Children in single-parent families or families with two parents who work outside the home may have only 4 waking hours at home on a typical day, and much of that time is taken up by meal preparation, bathtime, and other household routines. LAP staff members encourage family members to use the indirect language facilitation techniques in the course of these household routines. Specific ideas are given for incorporating these techniques and increasing general verbal interactions while giving a bath, traveling in the car, grocery shopping, and during other routine times.

Family members of children who are learning English as a second language are encouraged to continue speaking the child's native language at home. This will help the child become proficient in both languages.

Family members of all children who attend LAP are strongly encouraged to talk to and read to their children on a regular basis. Specific suggestions for adapting reading styles to children who are beginning to pick out words or for children with very short attention spans are given as appropriate.

Instructional Activities at Home   As discussed previously, families are encouraged to use indirect language facilitation techniques at home. Parents of children with speech and language impairments are invited to view the videotape mentioned above, *Oh, Say What They See* (Freedman & Lathuen, 1984), which uses a combination of animation and footage of parent–child interactions to explain receptive and expressive language and indirect language facilitation techniques. The family services coordinator takes the videotape to the family's home if the family has a VCR, or the family may view the videotape at LAP. Viewing the videotape with a staff member allows the parent to ask questions and the staff member to tailor techniques described in the videotape to the individual circumstances of the child in question.

When a family member expresses an interest, LAP staff members work with him or her to develop specific activities for an individual child to complete at home. The development of these activities takes into consideration time constraints of busy family members and the energy level of the child. The following example illustrates the development of a home program for a LAP child.

During a conference, Georgia mentioned that she would sometimes read to her three children and point out letters in the story. When her son Ray didn't know the letters, his older brother Jack would make fun of him. His younger sister often knew the letters when Ray didn't, and this frustrated Ray. He soon refused to try.

Preacademic skills, self-confidence, and motivation were among Ray's weaknesses. His mother was interested in helping him, but was unsure how. She did not have much energy for extra activities because the job of raising three children fell on her shoulders. Lack of extra money to buy books or fancy educational toys and Georgia's 10th grade educational level were also factors to consider when recommending activities to work on at home.

Based on this information, Ray's speech-language pathologist, Jessica, designed simple at-home activities that expanded on Georgia's previous attempts, helped her solve some of the problems resulting from the interaction between the three children, and encouraged positive feedback to increase Ray's self-concept. She sent home about two activities at a time. Jessica made photocopies of simple activities from kindergarten readiness books and made connect-the-dot puzzles that related to the weekly theme of LAP. Jessica wrote clear notes about the vocabulary words and grammar Ray was working on at LAP. (Example: Today Ray pretended he was a firefighter. He *squirted* water on the fire.)

Jessica problem solved with Georgia to find a time in the day when Georgia could work with Ray undisturbed by his older brother Jack. It became their special time to work on something together.

Each day Jessica asked Ray about his work and checked with his mother about Ray's home activities. She encouraged Georgia to keep up the activities and helped her to recognize Ray's progress. Georgia would sometimes tell Jessica—in front of Ray—how hard he had worked on his activities, giving him positive feedback.

When asked how she felt about the at-home activities, Georgia said she felt it was worth the time spent. Ray enjoyed the activities and was more willing to try to write his name. Eventually these activities evolved into a time Ray, his mother, and his younger sister could work together, with Ray showing his younger sister how to do some of the activities.

Decrease Family Members' Use of Commands and Yes/No Questions When Verbally Interacting with Their Child

Indirect language techniques encourage family members to avoid unhelpful conversational routines, especially ones in which a well-meaning adult unintentionally showers a child with commands and questions, resulting in a child who is increasingly withdrawn or unresponsive. The videotape mentioned above does an excellent job of increasing parents' awareness of these interaction patterns and staff members give gentle reminders and model facilitory techniques when observing these interactions between parents and children.

Providing Child- and Program-Oriented Activities

Although the emphasis at LAP is on language acquisition, other developmental skills are not forgotten. Formal support activities also provide family members with information about child behavior in the classroom and with classmates; therapy and educational planning, including individualized education programs; and information about speech-language impairments, developmental sequences, and childhood health concerns (e.g., asthma, chickenpox). Some of LAP's formal support activities, which address language acquisition and other areas of development, are described below.

Group Get-Togethers

Some formal supports take the form of group get-togethers. Group events provide the opportunity for parents to meet with each other and LAP staff members. Occurring two to three times a semester, these group get-togethers are scheduled at various times during the day and on different days of the week so busy parents will have a greater chance of attending at least one or two of the events.

Recognizing that informal communication and social support are important to parents of young children, the group events are designed to allow time for socializing. This facilitates informal parent-to-parent contact, allowing parents to share their stories with other parents who have been in similar situations. The support generated through these shared experiences cannot be duplicated by professionals (Santelli, Turnbull, Lerner, & Marquis, 1993). The family services coordinator may encourage, for example, one mother to share the story of her son's successful transition into the program with a father who is concerned about his son's own transition. Family members appreciate the chance to talk with other parents whose children are experiencing the same life changes—transition to kindergarten, discontinuation of speech-language intervention, beginning language kindergarten in elementary school, adapting to a new culture, or adjusting to the birth of a new brother or sister.

To encourage attendance at group events, LAP offers a tangible gift or prize to either the children or parents in attendance. The children break a piñata filled with mostly toys and some candy at the family picnic. Gifts, such as an outline of their child's body that has been colored by their child or a calendar featuring their child's artwork, are often given to parents at the end-of-the-semester party. Professionals tend to dismiss the use of tangible gifts to increase family participation in early intervention programming, but mothers endorse such gifts (Saylor, Elksnin, Farah, & Pope, 1990). Both mothers and professionals in the Saylor et al. study encouraged the use of logistical support such as transportation, babysitting, meals, and medical and social support services to maximize family participation in early intervention. LAP family picnics and end-of-the-semester parties include a potluck meal, and babysitting is provided during parent night for families unable to attend without this service. These three group get-togethers sponsored by LAP on a regular basis are described in more detail below.

Parent Night   Once a semester, LAP holds a 1-hour parent meeting on a weeknight. On a typical parent night, 50% of LAP families were represented. Of these families, 73% were families relatively new to the program and 27% were families who were familiar with LAP. Reasons given for not attending have included working at night, conflicting meetings, taking a night class, or staying home with a sick child.

The meetings feature a videotape made by a staff member showing each child in typical LAP activities. The director talks for a few minutes on a topic such as LAP's philosophy, literacy in the classroom, or facilitating language acquisition at home and in the classroom. The talk and videotape portion of parent night does not exceed 20 minutes. The rest of the hour is spent in informal conversation among families and staff members over coffee, punch, and cookies. Verbal feedback from parents on parent night has included comments such as, "We talked about it all the way home" and "I understand why my daughter enjoys it here."

Family Picnic   Each spring, LAP rents a shelter in a local park on a Saturday for the annual family picnic. It is a popular event. In the spring of 1992, 75% of families from the morning class and 87% of families from the afternoon class were represented. Because the picnic is held in a public place—a neutral location—instead of the school, LAP families meet the families of staff members who are not under the pressure of being hosts. Everyone brings potluck food and LAP provides a piñata stuffed with small toys and candy for the children. The picnic officially lasts 1½–2 hours, but some families choose to spend the entire afternoon in the park watching their children play in the playground, hiking on the nearby trails, or chatting with other parents.

End-of-the-Semester Party   Each LAP semester closes with the end-of-the-semester party. Attendance is consistently high, with 60–80 people, including parents, extended family members, friends, and staff members. There is rarely more than one family who is not represented by a family member. In this case, a staff member is assigned to the child whose family was unable to attend, so the child will not feel left out. The party takes place during LAP hours and features songs and drama by the children. Each child has a speaking part in a story or nursery rhyme with lead roles usually going to the children with speech and language impairments. The focus is on fun, and stage fright and outbursts of giggles are par for the course. Following the short program is a social time with one or two tables of potluck fare and punch.

Videotapes

Both commercial and classroom videotapes are effective means of providing families with information in group settings. LAP uses videotapes to inform parents about children's school activities, children's interactions with teachers and peers, and intervention techniques to use at home. Videotapes provide a visual picture of a verbal explanation, which is especially important for families new to the United States and for family members who find reading difficult. Videotapes also permit repeated play-back of important points and give family members an understanding of classroom activities or their child's behavior when they are not present. On an individual basis, videotapes permit a detailed examination of their child that would not be possible otherwise (McConkey, 1985). Videotapes created at LAP are copied for interested families who provide a blank tape. This gives families an ongoing video record of their child's development and increases their understanding of the LAP program.

Family Conferences

Conferences scheduled to formalize individualized education programs and discuss progress on goals are regularly scheduled at the beginning and end of each semester for families of children with speech and language impairments. Conferences regarding child progress are offered mid-semester to family members of all other children enrolled in LAP. These conferences are scheduled with the convenience of the parents in mind and the parents help set the agenda. Discussion usually centers around the child's developmental progress, his or her behavior in the classroom and at home, feedback on the program to LAP staff, and options for future placement.

Actively listening to family members' stories and concerns is one method of family support preferred by parents (Summers et al., 1990). The importance of opportunities for parents to share successes and concerns with staff members cannot be overstated. Family stories are often shared during conferences. One parent told the family services coordinator, "I look forward to my child's IEP because you don't rush through it. We sit and talk about my child." Early intervention programs must begin to recognize the importance of time spent with family members. Staff members must be allowed the flexibility, time, and administrative support necessary to listen to families. Family stories give service providers important information about the child at home, family routines, and family successes and concerns through the informal interactions that are preferred by families (Summers et al., 1990).

Formulating an IEP

The IEP conference for children with speech and language impairments is the culmination of a process that begins when the child's parent first contacts LAP for an evaluation. Once a child with a speech and/or language impairment enters LAP, staff members spend the first 2 weeks of the semester establishing a rapport with family members and getting to know the child. During this time, the family services coordinator talks with parents, explaining the IEP process and asking family members, "What do you want your child to get out of LAP this year?" The child's speech-language pathologist and other staff members observe the child in the classroom and conduct a language sample. Family members are encouraged to observe the LAP classroom and discuss with the family services coordinator similarities or differences in the child's behavior at LAP and at home.

After the director has analyzed the language sample and the family services coordinator has conveyed family preferences to other members of the IEP team, a conference is scheduled at the convenience of all team members (including family members). Conferences usually take place at LAP during working hours with an occasional conference scheduled in the child's home or during weekend or evening hours. Staff members have noted that most families do not relish the idea of a troop of professionals—no matter how well meaning—descending upon their home, but they do appreciate the offer of a home conference under special circumstances, such as a family member's illness or lack of transportation.

Family members vary widely in the extent of their involvement in the development of their child's IEP. Although LAP staff members believe family input is important, they realize that family members may be under stress from outside influences, and they realize that demanding that a parent attend a conference will only create tension between family and staff members. As one recently divorced mother told the family services coordinator:

I just started a second job and my ex-husband works the midnight shift. There's no way we can get our schedules to meet. I just don't have time. I work two jobs and have to sleep sometime. Call my ex. He only sees our son on weekends. He can deal with this and let me know what's going on.

In this situation, a conference was scheduled with the child's father and, after telephone conversations with the child's mother regarding transition out of LAP, arrangements were made for him to be included in the language kindergarten class the following year. Experience has shown that a family who is unable to participate in their child's IEP one semester often will be able to do so the next. Pressures resulting from a job,

---

CONFERENCE TIME!

Child's name: _____

Date and time: _____

Location: _____

The IEP is the individualized education program, which tells us what goals we will be working on for your child. Besides you, Betty, Julie, your child's lead teacher, _____, and your child's clinician, _____, will be at the conference. If you would like anyone else to attend, such as a friend, relative, or another professional, please let Julie know.

During the conference, we will fill out a form listing your child's strengths (things he or she does well) and weaknesses (things to work on). This form will also include some long- and short-term goals. These goals are based on your conversations with Julie and other staff members about your goals for your child this year in LAP, as well as classroom observations, recommendations from past conferences, and sometimes a language sample. These goals are written out before the conference to save time and are often changed, deleted, or expanded on during the conference.

Long-term goals are general changes you would like to see, such as improving vocabulary or social skills. Short-term goals are specific things to work on during the next semester, such as increasing use of the pronouns *he* and *she* or increasing the amount of time playing with other children in the classroom

Before the conference you may want to think about things your child does well. These strengths might include understanding what others say to him or her or playing with other children. Also think about areas to work on. These might be speaking louder or learning the words to stand up to an older brother or sister who won't let him or her have a turn. It may also be helpful to write down questions that you would like to ask or information you would like to share.

If you have any questions about your child's IEP conference, please ask!

Figure 2. An example of a reminder to parents concerning their child's upcoming IEP conference.

personal, or financial crisis (rather than disinterest) are often the reason for this temporary lack of involvement.

Typical IEP Conference Procedures

Parents are given a written reminder about their child's IEP conference and a verbal description of a typical conference about 2–3 days before the meeting. Figure 2 is an example of this reminder. The reminder encourages families' active participation in the development of their child's IEP by explaining the conference in written form and suggesting things to consider before the conference. Some family members have felt awkward bringing written notes to the conference (sometimes hiding them in the palm of their hand or under the table), so the conference reminder also suggests writing down questions or information to share. This has helped put parents at ease with their written notes.

The lead teacher coordinates the IEP conference with a typical agenda, which includes breaking the ice, brainstorming about strengths and weaknesses, determining goals, discussing concerns, and reviewing each team member's responsibility for followup. To break the ice, team members exchange positive anecdotes and make "small talk." The lead teacher introduces team members and explains the conference agenda. Family members are given the chance to begin listing strengths and weaknesses (or "things you would like your child to work on"). Because parents have been warned that they will be asked to contribute to this discussion, they are usually prepared to do just that. If team members notice that a family member is uncomfortable or at a loss for words, a staff member will generally begin the discussion. Interspersed with this discussion are anecdotes from home and the classroom that provide a more complete picture of the child's skills. The conversation generally proceeds from a discussion of the child's weaknesses into the results of the language sample and analysis. Test scores may be mentioned at the IEP conference, depending on the interest of family members, but they are not stressed. LAP staff members regard test scores as only one component of a child's evaluation and have found that presentation of test scores, especially at the beginning of a conference, tends to change the atmosphere of the conference, stifling discussion.

At this point, the team looks at the child's weaknesses and suggests long-term goals. Following the long-term goals and the child's weaknesses, short-term goals are suggested. Family members are asked, "Is there anything else you would like us to work on?" Sometimes, a family member feels strongly about a specific speech goal—one that would enable the child to pronounce her brother's name, for example. Other times, a family member decides to add a self-help goal that will be worked on both at home and at school.

After the goals are completed, family members are asked if they have any other concerns. To generate further discussion, the family services coordinator might note, "You mentioned to me that you were worried about . . . ." The team often brainstorms ways for family members to cope with challenging behaviors at home and in public or discusses upcoming transitions. Once all concerns have been addressed, the team reviews each member's responsibility for followup of the conference and the family services coordinator gives family members a written copy of their rights according to legislation. After the conference, the student in speech-language pathology who has been the primary therapist for the child gives a copy of the IEP to the parents and the family services coordinator files the conference notes, making a list of followup activities as a reminder. As the semester progresses, goals are continually reevaluated according to classroom observation and parent input.

At the end of the semester, the IEP team meets again to discuss the child's progress. The student in speech-language pathology coordinates this meeting, which focuses on the child's progress toward goals and results of language testing, and lays the groundwork for the child's program for the following semester. Figure 3 is an example of the conference reminder sheet for the end-of-the-semester conference.

SERVICE COORDINATION ACTIVITIES

Many of LAP's family services focus on coordination of services for the child and the child's family. Service coordination is provided informally and formally through one-to-one interactions, group meetings, *LAPlines*, and parent conferences. These service coordination activities are particularly important during LAP's initial contact with parents and the enroll-

CONFERENCE TIME!

Child's name: _____
Date and time: _____
Location: _____

We are looking forward to the end-of-the-semester conference for your child. Besides you, Betty, Julie, your child's lead teacher, _____, and your child's clinician, _____, will attend. If you would like anyone else to attend, such as a friend, relative, or another professional, please let Julie know.

  We will talk about your child's progress on his or her goals, the results of our language testing, and things to continue working on. Please remember that the language tests we will discuss measure your child's skills on the day he or she was tested. If he or she was tired or just not in the mood to leave the classroom "to play," the test results will be affected. Observations from the classroom and from home are just as important.

    You might want to think about how your child is doing at home. Have you noticed any difference in the way he or she talks? Have brothers, sisters, other relatives, or friends noticed a difference? We can also discuss concerns you might have about your child's behavior and answer any questions you have about the LAP program.

Figure 3.   An example of a reminder to parents about their child's upcoming end-of-the-semester conference.

ment process and during the transition process from LAP to other programs.

On a regular basis, the family services coordinator makes referrals to outside agencies such as community child care centers, social services, or mental health services. Staff members also coordinate services with other agencies such as Head Start or the public school system when appropriate. Outreach to the community through staff member participation in professional child advocacy organizations at the local level increases awareness of the program in the community and among other service agencies. LAP T-shirt sales to children, students, family members, and staff members also increase community awareness as well as instill a sense of pride in being a "Lapper." Information about the regular or special education systems in the public schools, parental rights, and child advocacy is given as the occasion arises, usually through personal communication. Family members frequently request information and referrals to child care and babysitters in the community. To answer this need, LAP distributes copies of the child care and preschool guide developed by the county child care association. Family members are also referred to other LAP parents who use family child care and babysitters in the community for word-of-mouth referrals.

TRANSITION OUT OF LAP

Family members of LAP children typically begin to ask questions about their child's readiness for kindergarten when the child turns 4 years old. During a fall conference preceding the child's kindergarten year, the family services coordinator asks family members where they anticipate their child attending school at age 5. This opens the floor for discussion about the kindergarten transition, yet does not flag the transition as one that will necessarily be stressful—especially for the children with speech and language impairments. Some parents would like to discuss the transition at this point, but most prefer to wait until the spring semester.

LAP is designed as a 2-year preschool program, with rare exceptions made if the parents and staff members believe the child would continue to grow to his or her maximum potential with a third year of programming. There is a trend among parents and professionals to wait an extra year before sending a child to kindergarten, especially among boys with summer birthdays. LAP encourages all parents to attend kindergarten round-up and base their decision on their child's developmental readiness and their instincts, not on the child's birth date alone. The family services coordinator and lead teacher discuss options for children with speech and language impairments and eligibility requirements for special programs with the child's parents. In the local school district, these options include waiting an extra year before attending kindergarten, regular kindergarten with or without speech-language intervention, language kindergarten followed by a year of regular kindergarten, double-programming of language and regular kindergarten, or private school with or without speech-language services. Each option has advantages, disadvantages, and eligibility requirements that must be considered. The director writes a report for the school district for each child with a speech and/or language impairment and makes an initial recommendation for services based on the family's preference and the child's level of development. At the end-of-the-semester conference, the parent has received information from the school district following kindergarten round-up and a recommendation from the director. The family services coordinator ensures that the family realize the ultimate decision about placement is theirs, with consideration of eligibility restrictions. She also ensures that their questions are answered so they are comfortable with their decision-making role.

LAP staff members coordinate with the local school district through visits to observe other programs, numerous telephone calls, and even showing potential teachers video clips of children in the classroom to ensure that the most appropriate placement is made and that all parties are comfortable with the decision. Families are encouraged to contact their child's future school and teachers and to visit the classroom if possible.

CONCLUDING REMARKS

At LAP, children are seen in the context of their families and their ecological environments. This is derived from the normative aspect of LAP's concentrated normative model. This emphasis encourages parents to be better informed and provides families with opportunities to give feedback in order to synchronize home and classroom activities and goals. Informal and formal family supports evolve from the relationship between the family unit and staff members. This relationship is influenced by individual traits and circumstances of both family members and staff members. Formal supports set the stage for family services at LAP and allow staff members to provide the informal supports that make the difference in a quality family-focused program. To conclude, it is important to reiterate the following guidelines that direct LAP's family support program:

- Family supports are optional, with the family determining the extent of their involvement.
- Staff members are open to suggestions and requests from parents.
- Family strengths and needs are taken into consideration.
- Use of indirect language facilitation techniques is encouraged at home in the course of families' daily routines.

Collaborating with families and providing individualized family support enhances the children's experiences in the classroom and results in the best possible system of services for the child and his or her family.

REFERENCES

Andrews, J.R., & Andrews, M.A. (1990). *Family-based treatment in communicative disorders: A systemic approach.* Sandwich, IL: Janelle Publications.

Bronfenbrenner, U. (1986). Ecology of the family as a context for human development: Research perspectives. *Developmental Psychology, 22*(6), 723–742.

Deal, A. (1991, Winter). Utilizing social support in early intervention. *Family Enablement Messenger,* p. 2.

Donahue-Kilburg, G. (1992). *Family-centered early intervention for communication disorders.* Rockville, MD: Aspen Publishers, Inc.

Dunst, C.J., Trivette, C., & Deal, A. (1988). *Enabling and empowering families: Principles and guidelines for practice.* Cambridge, MA: Brookline Books.

Freedman, L., & Lathuen, R. [Producers]. (1984). *Oh, say what they see: An introduction to indirect language stimulation* [Videotape]. Portland, OR: Educational Productions.

Hanson, M.J. (1981). A model for early intervention with culturally diverse single and multiparent families. *Teaching Early Childhood Special Education, 1*(3), 37–44.

Galinsky, E. (1988). Parents and teacher-caregivers: Sources of tension, sources of support. *Young Children, 43*(3), 4–12.

Kontos, S., Raikes, H., & Woods, A. (1983). Early childhood staff attitudes toward their parent clientele. *Child Care Quarterly, 12*(1), 45–58.

Kontos, S., & Wells, W. (1986). Attitudes of caregivers and the daycare experiences of families. *Early Childhood Research Quarterly, 1,* 47–67.

Lynch, E.W., & Hanson, M.J. (Eds.). (1992). *Developing cross-cultural competence: A guide for working with young children and their families.* Baltimore: Paul H. Brookes Publishing Co.

Mahoney, G., O'Sullivan, P., & Dennebaum, J. (1990). Maternal perceptions of early intervention services: A scale for assessing family-focused intervention. *Teaching Early Childhood Special Education, 10*(1), 1–15.

McConkey, R. (1985). *Working with parents: A practical guide for teachers and therapists.* Cambridge, MA: Brookline Books.

Rice, M.L., Hadley, P.A., & Alexander, A.L. (1993). Social biases toward children with speech and language impairments: A correlative causal model of language limitations. *Applied Psycholinguistics, 14*(4), 445–471.

Santelli, B., Turnbull, A.P., Lerner, E., & Marquis, J. (1993). Parent to Parent Programs: A unique form of mutual support for families of persons with disabilities. In G.H.S. Singer, & L.E. Powers, (Eds.), *Families, disability, and empowerment: Active coping skills and strategies for family interventions* (pp. 27–57). Baltimore: Paul H. Brookes Publishing Co.

Saylor, C.F., Elksnin, N., Farah, B.A., & Pope, J.A. (1990). Depends on who you ask: What maximizes participation of families in early intervention programs. *Journal of Pediatric Psychology, 15*(4), 557–569.

Schrader, M. (1989). *Parent articles: Enhance parent involvement in language learning.* Tuscon, AZ: Communication Skill Builders.

Summers, J.A., Dell'Oliver, C., Turnbull, A.P., Benson, H.A., Santelli, E., Campbell, M., & Siegel-Causey, E. (1990). Examining the individualized family service plan process: What are family and practitioner preferences? *Teaching Early Childhood Special Education, 10*(1), 78–99.

Turnbull, A.P., & Turnbull, H.R. (1990). *Families, professionals, and exceptionality: A special partnership.* Columbus, OH: Charles E. Merrill.

Webster, E.J., & Ward, L.M. (1993). *Working with parents of young children with disabilities.* San Diego: Singular Publishing Group

~9~

Language Outcomes of the Language-Focused Curriculum

Mabel L. Rice and Pamela A. Hadley

A little girl named Kim enters the classroom. It might be just another Monday morning for her, but this morning was different for her mother, Tanya. Tanya has a parent conference with her daughter's clinician, the LAP director, and the family services coordinator. Tanya knows the conference routine—after all, this is the end of Kim's second full year in LAP. Nevertheless, Tanya seems a bit apprehensive. Kim is eligible to start kindergarten in the fall, but her mother wonders if she is ready. Kim's older brother has had trouble in school and Tanya doesn't want Kim to have the same kinds of problems.

Tanya remembers what her daughter's communication skills were like when she first brought Kim to LAP. Kim didn't talk very much, and when she did, she was extremely hard to understand. During the initial evaluation, Tanya mentioned that Kim understood most things that people said to her. This description proved to be accurate. The initial testing revealed that Kim understood the meanings of words and could follow spoken directions as well as most children her age. However, Kim's abilities to produce individual sounds in words and combine words into sentences were very limited.

During the 2 years that Kim attended LAP, her expressive language skills improved dramatically. Even though Kim still doesn't pronounce all of her sounds correctly, her family and friends always know what she is talking about now. She can carry on a conversation with her grandmother over the telephone and she can even persuade her older brother to let her watch her favorite afternoon television program instead of his. Although her mother knows Kim has come a long way, Tanya wonders whether her daughter has made enough progress to handle the increased language demands of kindergarten.

As the conference begins, the clinician reviews Kim's progress on her semester goals and then the director reviews the results of Kim's final testing. Kim has scored in the average range on all of the standardized tests of language development that have been administered. This means that her oral language skills are what is expected for the typical 5½-year-old child. Now it is time to discuss the upcoming transition to kindergarten. Tanya begins asking questions: "But do you think Kim can handle kindergarten? Is she going to be like her brother and have trouble learning to read?"

The staff address each of her concerns, reminding Tanya that Kim's ability to understand language has always been her strength. They talk about Kim's knowledge of the names and sounds of individual letters and the sight words Kim already knows how to read. Yet, at the same time, they acknowledge the fact that some children with a history of oral language problems experience difficulty learning to read later in school. Tanya leaves the conference feeling more confident about Kim's readiness for kindergarten.

Kim's story presents the desired outcome at the end of her experience in the Language Acquisition Preschool (LAP). Kim made clinically significant gains in her speech and language during her enrollment. Evidence of such outcomes is necessary in order to establish that the language-focused curriculum (LFC) (and associated concentrated normative model [CNM]) does in fact lead to changes in children's speech and language skills. Nevertheless, such individual cases, although certainly very encouraging, do not provide sufficient evidence of a program's effectiveness. Perhaps Kim was just ready to learn at the time she entered the program, so the program's effectiveness was a coincidence with her gains, such that she would have improved her speech and language without participation in the program. Or perhaps she, at the same time as her enrollment in the program, began other kinds of experiences outside of LAP that would have led to change. In the first of these possibilities, speech and language change might be attributable to maturation relatively independent of changes in her environment; in the second, such change might be attributable to other environmental adjustments, independent of enrollment in LAP. Either way, change might be falsely attributable to enrollment in the LFC.

These possibilities are among the reasons that it is difficult to evaluate the effectiveness of language intervention programs. The nature of young children's speech and language development is such that change over time is to be expected. What is needed, then, is a demonstration that the change over time exceeds the expected change attributable to maturation. It is also important to know if these changes are likely to be the result of participation in a specialized program.

Because we were interested in the outcome effectiveness of the LFC, we collected systematic evaluation data on the children's speech and language status at the time of enrollment in LAP, at regular intervals during their enrollment, and at the time they left the program. In order to control for possible maturational effects, we used measures that provide an estimate of expected developmental change. In order to control for possible environmental effects outside of the classroom, we looked for replication across children. If children from different home situations who enrolled at different periods of time demonstrated similar effects, we had reason to think that the program was probably responsible for change instead of other coincidental changes in a specific child's environment.

Other studies suggest that preschool children with speech and language impairments are not likely to resolve their early problems without help of some kind. Followup studies report that 50%–80% of these children continue to demonstrate persistent difficulties with oral and written language throughout the school-age years, depending on the individual characteristics of the children followed (cf. Aram & Hall, 1989). Other studies suggest that, for children who are "late talkers," with early expressive language delay, about 50% do not reach the normative range of performance by 4–5 years of age (Paul & Alforde, 1993; Thal, Tobias, & Morrison, 1991). Thus, a clinically significant change, without intervention, is probably not to be expected, especially for children with limited comprehension of language as well as limited language use. But actual empirical documentation of the outcomes for children enrolled in a particular preschool intervention program is sparse. For classroom-based programs with an LFC, there are no available reports that we know of.

What we report in this chapter is what we have learned from the outcome data we collected. The example of Kim, in this chapter's opening vignette, serves to highlight that one of the major findings is that certain individual characteristics of the children are likely to influence the outcomes observed. In Kim's case, one factor is that her oral language problems were identified relatively early. As a result of early identification, she began receiving language intervention services at age 3 and received services for 2 full years prior to kindergarten entry. Early identification and early enrollment in intervention are important positive predictors of outcome. Another factor is that Kim's receptive language abilities were age-appropriate at the time she was enrolled. This provided a solid foundation for increasing her expressive language abilities. This is also an important asset for language growth in the LFC.

In this chapter, we report on the language outcomes for 65 children who were enrolled in the Language Acquisition Preschool for an extended period of intervention. Thus, our consideration of the *program* outcomes are based on the *individual* outcomes for 65 children. We begin first by considering what is involved in demonstrating that children have made "clinically significant progress" (i.e., progress beyond that expected by maturational momentum alone). Second, we examine the language outcomes made by the children who received all of their speech and language services in this LFC/LRE setting. We then explore three factors that may have mediated the extent to which individual children benefited from the intervention services, including severity or the children's initial profile of language impairment as well as the age at which they were enrolled and the length of their enrollment. We conclude that the LFC and the associated CNM of language enrichment offer an appropriate and highly effective model for providing services to young children with specific language impairment (SLI).

IS LAP'S MODEL OF LANGUAGE INTERVENTION EFFECTIVE?

How do we know when children have benefited from language intervention services? The question appears simple, but the way to an answer is
laden with a number of challenging clinical and scientific issues (cf.
Olswang, Thompson, Warren, & Minghetti, 1990). The question can be
partitioned into two related questions: Have the children made gains on
some outcome measure of language development? Do these gains exceed
the rate of learning we would expect if the children were not receiving
services (i.e., as a function of general development alone)?

An ideal way, perhaps, to answer these questions would be to have
two equivalent groups, alike in all relevant respects except that one
group received the intervention in question and the other group did not.
Then a test of the two groups' performance could reveal whether or not
the children receiving intervention performed better than those not receiving intervention. Such a control group was not available for our evaluation of the LFC model. (In fact, because of all the practical problems
involved, such control groups are seldom available for evaluations of language intervention.) An alternative is to examine gains on standardized
measures of language development after a period of intervention. When
used on an annual basis, gains on standard scores may indicate that an
intervention program has accelerated the children's rate of learning effectively. (There is, however, a warning to be issued here; frequent readmin-
istration of standardized tests is *not* recommended, in that if tests are
given too frequently, outcomes may be invalidated because of the children's familiarity with items, recall of earlier performance, or other such
spurious effects on performance.)

For children with a history of language-learning difficulties, improved performance on standardized measures of language development
represents an impressive achievement. At age 3, when many children
with SLI enter preschool language intervention programs, they demonstrate a slower rate of language learning relative to peers. Importantly, if
this slower rate persists, the gap between the standard scores of children
with SLI and their typical peers will continue to widen. Thus, for children with SLI to make clinically significant language gains, they must
demonstrate an accelerated period of language growth relative to peers
who are progressing at a typical rate of development.

Interestingly, standard score gains are not often reported in large-
scale intervention studies. More commonly, investigators report increases in raw scores, or the actual number of correct items on a given
measure (e.g., Cole & Dale, 1986; Dale & Cole, 1988; Friedman & Friedman, 1980; Lee, Koenigsknect, & Mulhern, 1975). However, this does
not provide us with a clear indication of intervention effectiveness relative to the normative expectations for language development. To understand this difference, it is important to review the relationship between
these two types of scores. A *standard score* is based upon how different a
child's *raw score* is from what is expected for a group of children of the
same age. The average score for the group and the variability from one
child to another in the group both contribute to an estimate of the child's

standard score. To obtain a higher standard score after a period of intervention, a child must increase his or her raw score above and beyond the average increases made by the peer group. In essence, increases in standard score performance reflect an *accelerated rate* of language learning relative to the peer group.

Figures 1 and 2 illustrate this point by plotting the relations between age with raw scores and standard scores, respectively, on the Peabody Picture Vocabulary Test–Revised (PPVT–R) (Dunn & Dunn, 1981). We first examine the increase in raw scores required to maintain the peer group's average standard score of 100. Consider Abby, a child with typically developing language abilities. To maintain a steady *standard score* of 100, Abby increased her *raw score* by 31 points between the ages of 3½ and 5½ years. Although her knowledge of vocabulary increased (as measured by the change in her *raw score*, illustrated in Figure 1), her rate of learning matched the average increase demonstrated by her age group (as measured by the consistent *standard score*, illustrated in Figure 2). Now let us turn to three children who were identified as having SLI at 3½ years of age. Over the same 2-year period, Billy continued to learn words slowly, more slowly than was expected for children his age (see Figure 1). As can be seen in Figure 2, the gap between Billy's and Abby's standard scores increased. Carl began to learn words at the *same rate* as Abby, yet because of his slow start, his abilities still remained considerably below hers 2 years later. Meanwhile, by age 5, Dennis demonstrated age-appropriate receptive vocabulary abilities (i.e., a standard score ≥ 85). In order to catch up, Dennis had to increase and maintain a rate of word learning above the rate of his age peer group. This is illustrated in Figure 1 by the sharply rising line for Dennis, as compared to that for Abby.

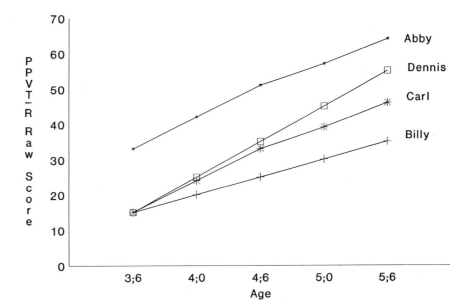

Figure 1.   Raw scores on the Peabody Picture Vocabulary Test–Revised (PPVT–R). One child (Abby) has average receptive vocabulary skills, and three children (Billy, Carl, and Dennis) were initially diagnosed with specific language impairments.

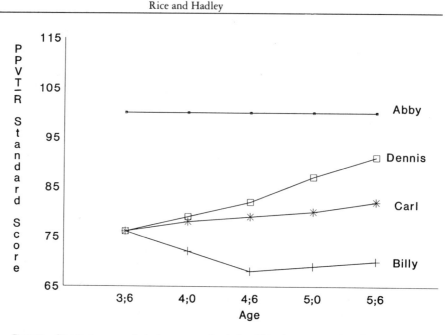

Figure 2.   Standard score equivalents corresponding to the children's raw scores from Figure 1.

The point of this comparison is that standard score gains demonstrate that an increased rate of learning has occurred, an increase that exceeds normative expectations. Furthermore, it is more difficult to demonstrate that learning has exceeded normative expectations (i.e., increases in standard scores) than to demonstrate that learning has occurred (i.e., increases in raw scores). Thus, even when children have maintained a relatively constant standard score over time, it demonstrates that they have matched the typical rate of learning. From our perspective, this too can be interpreted as a generally positive outcome in that the children are not falling further behind. Recall the difference between Carl's and Billy's progress over time, where Carl maintained a steady acceleration in word learning over time, but Billy did not and fell further behind relative to his age peers.

LANGUAGE OUTCOMES OF THE LAP CHILDREN

We are able to report on the language outcomes of 65 children enrolled in LAP over a 6-year time period. Originally, 36 children with SLI were enrolled. The remaining 29 children were enrolled as typically developing language models and therefore provide an interesting comparison group for our purposes here. We will not report formally on the children who were learning English as a second language (ESL) in this chapter (see Chapter 6). All 65 children met the formal enrollment criteria for their respective groups outlined in Chapter 1 and were enrolled for at least 2 consecutive semesters.

The language outcome data are based upon four standardized measures of language development drawn from the battery used to determine initial enrollment in LAP (see Chapter 1 for additional details). The four

measures focus on different aspects of language development. The PPVT–R (Dunn & Dunn, 1981) is a specific measure of children's single-word receptive vocabulary knowledge. In contrast, the Reynell Developmental Language Scales–U.S. Edition (Reynell & Gruber, 1990) assesses more general language abilities. The receptive scale encompasses children's comprehension of single words, simple sentences, and the ability to follow simple and complex oral directions. The expressive scale requires children to label objects and pictures and describe the sequence of events in a logical order. Finally, a mean length of utterance (MLU) is obtained from a 100-utterance spontaneous language sample. An MLU provides a general measure of the complexity of the children's sentence structures. MLUs were converted to standard score equivalents using the normative data provided in Miller (1981).

For most children, initial evaluations occurred during the summer months, and these measures were then readministered to all children during April of each year. This allowed for comparison of language gains over time. Approximately 52% of the children were enrolled for a 10-month period, and the remaining 48% were enrolled for approximately 22 months.

General Language Gains

We begin first by asking the most basic question. Did the children enrolled in LAP make gains on the standardized measures of language development? And more specifically for the children in the SLI group, did the rate of learning continue at a slower pace than that expected for typical preschoolers (as in the case of Billy)? Or, did the rate of learning increase to match that of typical peers (as in the case of Carl)? Or, did the rate of learning accelerate relative to typical peers, thereby narrowing the gap between typically developing children's abilities and the abilities of children with SLI (as in the case of Dennis)?

On average, children in both the typically developing and SLI groups made gains across all measures of interest. The typically developing children increased their average performance between preschool entry and exit by approximately 5–8½ standard score points across the set of language measures (see Table 1). The average performance of the typically developing group shifted from average standard scores (i.e., 96–102) to scores slightly above average (i.e., 105–107). However, the children with SLI, *as a group*, scored below average on all four language measures at preschool entry (i.e., all scores < 83). At preschool exit, the group with SLI also increased its performance on all measures, ranging from an approximate 8½-point increase for MLU to more than 11 points on the PPVT–R. More importantly, as a group, the children had moved into an average range of performance on three of the four measures (see Table 1). In general then, this group of children with SLI had accelerated its rate of learning dramatically, performing most like Dennis in Figure 2. However, on an individual basis, this characterization certainly did not hold for all of the children with SLI. We turn now to a number of general characteristics that may have systematically mediated the differences between the dramatic and more conservative language gains observed for individual children.

Initial Profile of Language Impairment

Many factors may contribute to the long-term language outcomes for children with a history of early communication problems. However, the nature and severity of initial communication difficulties have been repeatedly shown to influence the persistence of later language problems (Aram & Hall, 1989). In other words, children who only experience difficulty in pronouncing individual speech sounds are less likely to demon-

Table 1.   Language gains for the typically developing group of children and the group of children with SLI

| | | Standard scores | | |
Measure	n	Entry	Exit	Average gain
Typically developing group	29			
PPVT–R		100.52	107.48	6.97
Reynell–Receptive		101.55	106.59	5.03
Reynell–Expressive		96.03	104.62	8.59
MLU standard score		NA	NA	
Group with SLI	36			
PPVT–R		83.47	94.81	11.33
Reynell–Receptive		78.53	88.25	9.72
Reynell–Expressive		71.61	82.39	10.78
MLU standard score		76.56	85.39	8.83

strate later communication problems than children who have primary language problems, such as difficulty understanding and/or formulating sentences (Hall & Tomblin, 1978; King, Jones, & Lasky, 1982). Among children with primary language impairments, those with good comprehension skills demonstrate better language and educational outcomes than those with problems in both language comprehension *and* production (Bishop & Edmundson, 1987; Rissman, Curtiss, & Tallal, cited in Bashir & Scavuzzo, 1992). Given the evidence from these followup studies, we were interested in how the children's profile of language impairment influenced the kinds of language gains observed.

Each child's initial profile of language impairment was determined from his or her performance on the intake battery. All children demonstrated expressive language limitations as indicated by below-average performance on the expressive language measures. However, children demonstrated different combinations of strengths in receptive language and speech sound production as measured by the Goldman-Fristoe Test of Articulation (GFTA) (Goldman & Fristoe, 1986). Three general profiles were apparent from the various combinations of speech and language strengths and weaknesses. Children identified as fitting Profile A demonstrated age-appropriate receptive language skills but had clinically significant speech and expressive language limitations. These children can be characterized in a general way as having expressive-only limitations (henceforth, E). Children identified as fitting Profile B demonstrated age-appropriate speech sound production but had limitations in both receptive and expressive language. These children can be generally characterized as having language-only limitations (henceforth, L). The third profile, Profile C, was applied to children with below-average abilities in all three areas. Their limitations could be described as global (henceforth, G). A total of 18 children (or 50%) fit this latter description. These children could be characterized as having the most severe involvement, although certainly there was variability within this group itself. The remaining children were equally divided among Profiles E and L with nine children in each.

How then might the initial profile of language impairment have mediated the language gains observed? Interestingly, the most dramatic language gains, those that shifted a group's performance by approximately one standard deviation unit (i.e., approximately 15 standard score points) varied according to the different profiles (see Table 2). It was not the case that the children with the most severe involvement made the most dramatic gains simply because they had the most ground to cover. Rather, the children in Profile E, those with good receptive language abilities, made dramatic gains on the expressive language measures, but made gains similar to the typically developing group on the receptive measures. In fact, as a group, these children demonstrated age-appropriate language abilities across all language measures at the time of preschool exit (i.e., all standard scores ≥ 87). In contrast, the children in Profile L demonstrated dramatic gains on the two receptive measures, while maintaining steady performance on the expressive measures. (Note that the average MLU for this group was within the typical range at preschool

Table 2. Language gains for SLI profiles

Measure	n	Standard scores		
		Entry	Exit	Average gain
Profile E	9			
PPVT–R		100.78	109.11	8.33
Reynell–Receptive		100.22	108.44	8.22
Reynell–Expressive		76.44	94.44	18.00
MLU standard score		73.00	86.95	13.95
Profile L	9			
PPVT–R		78.67	92.89	14.22
Reynell–Receptive		69.78	89.44	19.66
Reynell–Expressive		78.44	79.44	1.00
MLU standard score		89.20	92.65	3.45
Profile G	18			
PPVT–R		77.22	88.61	11.39
Reynell–Receptive		72.06	77.56	5.50
Reynell–Expressive		65.78	77.83	12.05
MLU standard score		72.55	80.95	8.40

entry.) The average standard scores on the two receptive measures had moved from significantly below average to within the average range, while the general measure of expressive language abilities remained significantly below average. This may suggest that for those children with both receptive *and* expressive language limitations, longer periods of intervention may be necessary before dramatic gains in expressive language will be evident. Finally, the children in Profile G demonstrated substantive gains, between 5 and 12 standard score points, across the set of measures. Therefore, even the children with the most severe language-learning problems were able to accelerate their rate of learning above normative expectations. As a group, they demonstrated sufficient gains in their comprehension of single words to score within the typical range on the PPVT–R. At the same time, their general language abilities remained significantly below age expectations. Their gains may be characterized as more general, across-the-board gains, rather than as a "specialization" in either comprehension or production.

As a final indication that longer-term language outcomes are partly a function of initial communication status, we examined the number of children continuing to receive speech and language intervention services during the school-age years. (See also Chapter 11 for additional followup details.) Of the 36 children with SLI described in this chapter, 26 have been followed into the early elementary grades. As might be expected, 79% (11/14) of the children initially classified in Profile G continued to receive speech and language intervention in kindergarten and throughout the early elementary grades. Five of the nine children (56%) initially classified in Profile E continued with their speech and language services during kindergarten. However, two of these children "graduated" from services by second grade, bringing the current percentage of children in Profile E still receiving services to 33%. Finally, followup information is available for only three of the nine children initially characterized in Profile L. Only one of these children received services during kindergarten, with services discontinued the following year.

Summary of Gains Among Children with Language Impairments

In this sample of children with SLI, the differences in the children's initial profile of language impairment were related to two aspects of the language outcomes observed. First, initial communication status appeared to influence the type of gains observed (i.e., whether the language gains were of a general nature or were more specific to either language comprehension or production). Second, children classified in Profile G, those with the most global impairment at preschool entry, were more likely to require intervention services following the transition to school. It is important to highlight the fact that *some children in each profile* made clinically significant gains and were functioning at age-appropriate levels on all (or most) of the standardized measures of language development during their final semester of LAP enrollment. This suggests that factors other than the initial severity of the language impairment influenced their positive outcomes. We now turn to an examination of two such factors: age at initial enrollment and length of intervention services prior to kindergarten.

Age at Initial Enrollment and Length of Treatment

To examine the relationships among age at initial enrollment, length of intervention services, and language outcomes, all children were organized into three different treatment conditions, defined in terms of child age at time of enrollment and intervention duration prior to kindergarten (see Table 3). Children in the first condition were enrolled between the ages of 29 and 43 months and attended LAP for 2 semesters only (i.e., 1-year Younger). Children in the second condition were also enrolled for 2 semesters, but were 44 months of age or older at the time of initial enrollment (i.e., 1-year Older). These children were eligible for kindergarten immediately following their period of LAP enrollment. The final condition consisted of children enrolled between the ages of 34 and 53 months (i.e., 2-years Younger). These children were enrolled in LAP for a period of 4–6 semesters. Again, the language gains demonstrated by the children in the typically developing group are provided here merely for purposes of comparison, with our primary attention directed toward the gains of the children with SLI.

Table 3. Children by language group and treatment condition

Treatment condition		Typically developing group		Group with SLI	
		n	*M* age	*n*	*M* age
1	1-year Younger (3½–4½)	10	37.3	9	37.4
2	1-year Older (4½–5½)	7	52.9	8	50.9
3	2-years Younger (3½–5½)	12	40.8	19	39.1

The distribution of children across the three treatment conditions allowed us to ask two additional questions: 1) given approximately 9 months of language intervention, do 1-year Younger and 1-year Older children with SLI make equivalent language gains? and 2) does a longer period of language intervention result in better language outcomes for children enrolled at approximately the same age? Although intuitively it would seem that the combination of an early start and long-term services would be most optimal, the different situations under which the children were enrolled and retained in the LAP program allowed us to examine these questions more systematically.

To examine the effects of age, we compared the performance of the 1-year Younger and 1-year Older children with SLI (Condition 1 versus Condition 2). In general, the Older group demonstrated greater standard score gains on the receptive measures than the Younger group (see Table 4). However, once individual differences in the children's abilities at preschool entry were taken into consideration, the apparent gains for the Older group did not prove to be statistically significant.

Similarly, the performance of the children with SLI enrolled for only 2 semesters was compared to the performance of those enrolled for 4–6 semesters (Condition 1 versus Condition 3). This comparison examined the influence of length of enrollment on language outcomes. The standard score gains of the children enrolled for approximately 2 years were clearly superior to those of children enrolled for only 2 semesters (see Table 5). Importantly, the length of enrollment appeared to play a more prominent role in facilitating general receptive and expressive language development, as compared to vocabulary knowledge. The standard score gains on two Reynell measures and for MLU were two to four times greater when children benefited from an additional year of intervention. Despite the apparent differences between the measures, significant differences as a function of length of enrollment were not apparent once children's initial entry scores were factored into the equation.

Although the observed language gains did not differ statistically as a function of age or length of enrollment, some valuable clinical suggestions can be drawn from these data, particularly with regard to the value of 2 continuous years of preschool intervention. When intervention was restricted to 2 academic semesters, equivalent to approximately 9 months, dramatic gains were evident only for older children on single-word and general measures of language comprehension. Two semesters did not appear to provide sufficient support for fostering expressive language skills. It appeared that the children set as their first task learning to comprehend the rich concentration of language flooding the classroom environment, and once saturated, only then began to focus on language production. Therefore, to observe dramatic gains in expressive language, 2 years of intervention were required, unless children started off initially with age-appropriate receptive skills (i.e., Profile E).

The notion that novice language users require an incubation period is certainly not new, as discussed at length with regard to children learning English as a second language (see Chapters 1, 2, 3, and 6). These findings suggest that periods in which children with SLI participate rela-

Table 4. Preschool entry and exit scores by age of initial enrollment

Group	Condition	n	PPVT–R		Reynell–Receptive		Reynell–Expressive		MLU-SS	
			Entry	Exit	Entry	Exit	Entry	Exit	Entry	Exit
Typically developing	1 (1-year Younger)	10	96.7	104.9	101.9	105.8	93.3	103.6	NA	NA
	2 (1-year Older)	7	100.3	106.3	105.1	104.0	98.4	106.1	NA	NA
SLI	1 (1-year Younger)	9	79.0	85.2	73.3	77.1	70.0	76.6	77.4	81.1
	2 (1-year Older)	8	76.0	96.8	76.6	89.1	71.9	78.3	80.4	86.4

Table 5. Standard score equivalents for preschool entry and exit by length of enrollment

Group	Condition	n	PPVT–R		Reynell–Receptive		Reynell–Expressive		MLU-SS	
			Entry	Exit	Entry	Exit	Entry	Exit	Entry	Exit
Typically developing	1 (1-year Younger)	10	96.7	104.9	101.9	105.8	93.3	103.6	NA	NA
	3 (2-year Younger)	12	103.8	110.3	99.2	108.8	96.9	104.6	NA	NA
SLI	1 (1-year Younger)	9	79.0	85.2	73.3	77.1	70.0	76.6	77.4	81.1
	3 (2-year Younger)	19	88.7	98.5	81.8	93.2	72.3	86.9	74.7	87.1

tively passively or do not demonstrate evidence of obvious gains in expressive language should not be interpreted as a lack of progress. Rather, these periods may represent a time in which children are making great strides in their language comprehension, the necessary foundation for facilitating future gains in language production.

In summary, all of the children with SLI improved their communication abilities during the course of their enrollment in this LFC program regardless of the severity of their initial communication status, regardless of the age at which services were initiated, and regardless of the length of time that they were enrolled. Importantly, the children either matched or exceeded the expected normative rate of language learning across at least three of the four outcome measures obtained. Concurrently, the extent to which the individual children benefited depended primarily on their initial communication status and the length of their enrollment in LAP. These data provide strong evidence that children with SLI, as well as those developing language typically, benefited from the educational services provided in an LFC, based on a concentrated normative model of language intervention.

CONCLUDING REMARKS

As noted in earlier chapters, there is a call for classroom-based preschool language intervention, motivated by theoretical reasons and clinical reality. The data presented in this chapter suggest that such models are indeed empirically sound as well. All of the children with SLI in this setting matched or exceeded the rate of learning demonstrated by typically developing peers, although some benefited more than others. This individual variability in outcome, however, is not as likely to be related to the intervention program as much as to the intrinsic characteristics of the children themselves. In short, there is reason to think that enrollment in the program is likely to lead to gains that exceed the amount expected to be achieved by maturational momentum alone, and that such gains are not attributable to some chance occurrences with outside, unrelated changes in the environment.

We cannot address whether children enrolled in this particular program achieved greater language outcomes than would be observed in alternative service delivery models. However, we suspect that in addition to demonstrating gains in fundamental aspects of language comprehension and production in the areas of vocabulary and word and sentence structure, the concentrated normative model also supports children's *use* of language with peers as well as with adults in a naturalistic setting (see Chapter 7). Moreover, because classroom-based models of intervention reduce the distance between clinical and natural settings, they are more likely to result in the increased use of newly acquired words and structures outside of the intervention context itself (cf. Wilcox, Kouri, & Caswell, 1991). There remains much work to be done in documenting the effectiveness of LFC models of language intervention, particularly in identifying the factors that mediate the observed outcomes. For the moment, we offer the basic conclusion that the concentrated normative model provides an appropriate and highly effective model of service delivery for young children with communication disorders.

REFERENCES

Aram, D.M., & Hall, N.E. (1989). Longitudinal follow-up of children with preschool communication disorders: Treatment implications. *School Psychology, 18,* 487–501.

Bashir, A.S., & Scavuzzo, A. (1992). Children with language disorders: Natural history and academic success. *Journal of Learning Disabilities, 25,* 53–65.

Bishop, D.V.M., & Edmundson, A. (1987). Language-impaired 4-year-olds: Distinguishing transient from persistent impairment. *Journal of Speech and Hearing Disorders, 52,* 156–173.

Cole, K.N., & Dale, P.S. (1986). Direct language instruction and interactive language instruction with language delayed preschool children: A comparison study. *Journal of Speech and Hearing Research, 29,* 206–217.

Dale, P.S., & Cole, K.N. (1988). Comparison of academic and cognitive programs for young handicapped children. *Exceptional Children, 54,* 439–447.

Dunn, L.M., & Dunn, L.M. (1981). *Peabody Picture Vocabulary Test–Revised (PPVT–R).* Circle Pines, MN: American Guidance Service.

Friedman, P., & Friedman, K.A. (1980). Accounting for individual differences when comparing the effectiveness of remedial language teaching methods. *Applied Psycholinguistics, 1,* 151–170.

Goldman, R., & Fristoe, M. (1986). *Goldman-Fristoe Test of Articulation (GFTA).* Circle Pines, MN: American Guidance Service.

Hall, P.K., & Tomblin, J.B. (1978). A follow-up study of children with articulation and language disorders. *Journal of Speech and Hearing Disorders, 43,* 227–241.

King, R.R., Jones, C., & Lasky, E. (1982). In retrospect: A fifteen-year follow-up report of speech-language-disordered children. *Language, Speech, and Hearing Services in Schools, 13,* 24–32.

Lee, L., Koenigsknect, R., & Mulhern, S. (1975). *Interactive language development teaching.* Evanston, IL: Northwestern University Press.

Miller, J.F. (1981). *Assessing language production in children: Experimental procedures.* Needham Heights, MA: Allyn & Bacon.

Olswang, L.B., Thompson, C.K., Warren, S.F., & Minghetti, N.J. (1990). *Treatment efficacy research in communication disorders.* Rockville, MD: American Speech-Language-Hearing Foundation.

Paul, R., & Alforde, S. (1993) Grammatical morpheme acquisition in 4-year-olds with normal, impaired, and late-developing language. *Journal of Speech and Hearing Research, 36,* 1271–1275.

Reynell, J.K., & Gruber, C.P. (1990). *Reynell Developmental Language Scales–U.S. Edition.* Los Angeles: Western Psychological Services.

Thal, D., Tobias, S., & Morrison, D. (1991). Language gesture in late talkers: A one-year follow-up. *Journal of Speech and Hearing Disorders, 48,* 18–24.

Wilcox, M.J., Kouri, T.A., & Caswell, S.B. (1991). Early language intervention: A comparison of classroom and individual treatment. *American Journal of Speech-Language Pathology, 1*(1), 49–62.

~10~

Speech Outcomes of the Language-Focused Curriculum

Kim A. Wilcox and Sherrill R. Morris

It is time for Pamela's final parent conference. Pamela is almost 5 years old. She has been enrolled in LAP for 2 years and will be attending a regular kindergarten classroom in the fall. When she entered the program, Pamela's speech was essentially unintelligible. Only her parents and her brother could understand what she said. At that time, she produced few consonants and almost never put consonant sounds on the ends of words.

About midway through the parent conference, Jean, Pamela's mother, reminds the staff of an event that occurred approximately 1 year earlier. On that day, Pamela and Jean were at a local convenience store. Jean had given Pamela some money for a candy bar and had then gone off to pick up a gallon of milk. Unbeknownst to Jean, Pamela's candy bar of choice was located above the adult-size counter and out of Pamela's reach. As Jean was returning from the milk cooler, Pamela was telling the clerk, "I want a Three Musketeers, please" to which the clerk simply handed her the candy bar. At that moment, Jean and Pamela looked at each other and they both smiled, for they both realized what had just happened. Pamela's simple sentence had been understood by the stranger—something that had never happened before.

One year later, Pamela's speech is easily understood by nearly everyone she meets. She completes all of her words and correctly produces most of her sounds. Although Pamela has some remaining phonological errors, exit testing has confirmed that she is performing well within the normal range.

Events such as Pamela's candy bar purchase serve as important markers of phonological progress. However, Pamela's success in the convenience store was actually the culmination of many months of small adjustments, or improvements, in her phonological system. Unfortunately, children with intelligibility problems may be understood in one situation but not in another. In fact, in the months after her success in the convenience store, Pamela still experienced frustration at not being understood. Different listeners, more complex messages, fewer contextual cues, and other variables conspired to make some of Pamela's speech unintelligible.

How then, when faced with a succession of relatively small changes in a very large sound system, do we assess phonological development accurately and reliably? Just as in most areas of development, the method of choice is to observe a set of target behaviors in a fixed, or at least well-described, environment. Given that "normal" or "typical" performance must be defined relative to that of others, we also need information about the performance of a group of predefined peers attempting the same task(s). In Chapter 5 of this volume, we saw how articulation therapy has traditionally been organized in terms of the phonemes of the language. Similarly, most articulatory, or phonological, assessment has also relied on the phonemic system for its basic organizational structure.

This chapter describes the phonological progress achieved by children enrolled in the Language Acquisition Preschool (LAP). Much of that progress is defined in terms of traditional articulation testing. Thus, we begin the chapter with a description of the variables affecting articulation testing and then review standardized test results for a group of LAP children.

PHONOLOGICAL ASSESSMENT

The phonological system dictates which sounds are acceptable in a language, how those sounds are produced, and in what ways they can be combined. Although there is an unlimited number of allophones in any language, each language (or dialect) has a well-defined set of phonemes that serve to contrast linguistic meanings. In English, there are 42 such phonemes. The widespread agreement on what constitutes a phoneme, their relatively limited number, and their linguistic centrality have made phonemes ideal targets for articulatory testing for many years. Because all allophones relate to a particular phoneme (or group of phonemes) either directly or indirectly, the systematic observation of a child's production of each of the phonemes is generally seen as an organized sample of his or her entire phonological system.

As a result, articulation testing typically begins by asking a child to produce each of the phonemes of the language (cf. Bernthal & Bankson, 1988). Although it is impossible to assess all of the allophones of even one phoneme, most articulation tests suggest eliciting at least two to three samples of each sound. Usually these are organized by word position, so that, for example, a child is asked to produce a word with /p/ at the beginning, a word with /p/ at the end, and perhaps a word with /p/

somewhere in the middle. Many articulation tests include a sampling of all 42 phonemes, but most tests focus only on the consonant sounds. This emphasis is due to the preponderance of consonant versus vowel errors in misarticulated speech.

The child's production of each item on the test is individually judged for accuracy relative to the standard adult form of the sound. In most cases, the total number of correct versus the number of incorrect productions is then compared with normative data collected from a large sample of children. In this way, a determination can be made regarding the age-appropriateness of a particular child's speech. So, for example, Art, a 4-year-old child, might incorrectly produce 10 of 75 consonants on a given articulation test. Within the original normative sample for that test, 10 errors was the best score achieved by any 4-year-old child. Art's raw score of 10 translates to a very high standard score and to a score near the 99th percentile. Both this standard score and percentile score indicate that Art is performing at a level beyond that of most of his age peers. However, a raw score of 10 for an older child might mean that he or she is at a level comparable to, or even below that of, his or her age peers.

Most articulation tests have a format similar to that described above. However, variations from this basic format also exist. Notable among these are numerous analysis protocols for describing phonological processes, or incorrect, but regularly occurring, patterns in children's speech (cf. Hodson & Paden, 1986; Shriberg & Kwiatkowski, 1980; Weiner, 1979). These phonological analysis protocols are used in therapy planning and organization as well as for making judgments regarding the age-appropriateness of a given child's speech. However, the utility of process analyses for assessing relative performance has been limited by the lack of consensus concerning the preferred set of processes to be used and because the number of identifiable and interpretable patterns decreases sharply with age. As a result, most decisions about phonological age-appropriateness are based, at least in part, on articulation tests like those described above.

As with most types of developmental assessments, there are a host of variables that affect the results obtained from articulation tests. These variables include the choice of phonemes tested, the words or sentences used to elicit the phonemes, the scoring system, the specific demographics of the normative group of children, and the comparability of the normative group of children to any given test subject. Many of these variables have been critically discussed elsewhere (Bankson & Bernthal, 1981; Noll, 1970) and so are not addressed here. There are, however, two assumptions underlying articulation testing that bear directly on this discussion.

The first assumption is that a corpus of items selected on the basis of their phonemic relationship is appropriate for differentiating performance among children. As a result, most articulation tests are composed of a set of equally distributed phonemic exemplars. However, standard practice in test construction dictates that test items be selected based on their ability to differentiate levels of performance across individuals.

Among the infinite number of allophones and allophonic combinations in the language, it seems likely that a better set of test items exists for purposes of differentiating performance than the phonemic inventories currently in use. Exactly which items might constitute that set is, at present, unknown. The point, however, is that the authors of few, if any, articulation tests have selected test items based on their ability to discriminate among levels of competence.[1] Nonetheless, the results of these articulation tests are widely used in making decisions about the developmental status of individual children.

The second key assumption underlying articulation testing is that all children eventually reach a comparable state of mastery of the phonological system. However, as noted in Chapter 2, researchers and clinicians now realize that many children do not "outgrow" their early language difficulties; instead, they have residual difficulties even into adulthood. Just as with semantics and syntax, it is unlikely that all children achieve the same level of phonological competence (Wilcox, Catts, Larrivee, & Morris, in preparation). Instead, some children will grow up to be more phonologically facile than others. For example, we know that some adults are more adept than others at creating and appreciating puns and other types of sound games. Similarly, some adults are less likely to become "tongue-tied," even when in situations of considerable speaking stress. The formulation of most articulation tests, however, ignores this typical distribution of abilities and assumes that at some point during the early elementary years, all children will reach a similar level of phonological adeptness. At that point, all children should also correctly produce all of the items on a particular articulation test.

Taken together, these two assumptions have serious consequences for comparisons of performance across individual children and for the interpretability of longitudinal articulation performance data. Moreover, this impact is particularly troublesome for interpretations of group effects and, in turn, assessments of program effectiveness.

Nonetheless, the same criteria for program effectiveness that were outlined in Chapter 9 for language outcomes are also appropriate for speech outcomes. In order to confirm that the children with speech impairments have actually improved phonologically, their raw scores on standardized tests should increase at a rate greater than that of their age peers. Next, we review the standardized articulation test data for children who attended LAP.

SPEECH OUTCOMES OF LAP CHILDREN

The data reported here are derived from the same assessment protocol described in Chapter 9 and are drawn from 57 of the 65 children included in the study outlined in that chapter. The eight children who are not reported on here include four typically developing children and four children with SLI for whom exit measures of articulation were not avail-

---

[1]One notable exception is the predictive screening test of articulation developed by Van Riper and Erickson (1969).

able.[2] Thus, these data represent 32 children with SLI who were originally enrolled in LAP and 25 children with typical language skills at entry. In most cases, the initial evaluations occurred during the summer months, and the testing was readministered to all children in April of subsequent years.

The primary assessment instrument was the Goldman-Fristoe Test of Articulation (GFTA) (Goldman & Fristoe, 1986). This test includes 61 consonant items, composed of one occurrence of 23 different phonemes, in each of their allowable word positions (word-initial, word-medial, and word-final), plus 12 consonant clusters (e.g., /bl/, /st/, /skw/). Raw scores are calculated as the number of items produced in error out of a possible total of 73. Raw scores are then converted to percentile ranks.

General Speech Gains

As in the other language areas, there was a general growth in articulation skills for all children while enrolled in LAP (see Table 1). This is confirmed by the decrease in the mean number of errors on the GFTA for both groups, decreasing 43% (14.1–8.2) for the typically developing children and 42% (40.5–23.7) for children with speech and/or language im-

Table 1.   Group means and standard deviations for Goldman-Fristoe Test of Articulation scores

Group	n	Number of errors			Percentile score		
		Entry	Exit	Difference	Entry	Exit	Difference
Typically developing children	25	14.1 (11.4)	8.2 (9.4)	5.9	61.3 (30.2)	59.0 (31.7)	(2.3)
Children with specific language impairment	32	40.5 (12.7)	23.7 (11.1)	16.8	11.3 (18.7)	18.2 (21.3)	6.9

pairments. Although these changes in group raw scores were substantial, they translated into only minimal changes in percentile scores. More specifically, the typically developing children, as a group, increased their phonological skills at a rate roughly equal to that expected for their age, while the children with SLI evidenced a developmental increase slightly greater than that expected for their age.

Initial Profile of Speech and Language Impairment

Using the same categorization system described by Rice and Hadley (see Chapter 9), the 32 children with SLI were organized according to their individual language profiles at the time of their initial enrollment in the program. Children in Profile L (consisting of children having language-only limitations) were those with clinically significant limitations in both receptive and expressive language, but with typical speech sound production skills; children in Profile E (consisting of children having expressive-only limitations) exhibited difficulties in speech and expressive language but had typical receptive language skills; and children in Profile G (consisting of children with global limitations) showed significant limitations in all three areas.

Within this organizational system, we would expect to see a different pattern of performance on the GFTA for children in Profile L from those in Profiles E and G. This is because the children in Profile L entered LAP with essentially typical scores on the articulation test. Indeed, Table 2 shows the striking comparability of entry and exit scores for the children in Profiles E and G, while the mean scores for those children characterized in Profile L are more like those of the typically developing children. Given this similarity of performance, the data from children

Table 2.   Group means and standard deviations for Goldman-Fristoe Test of Articulation scores

Group	n	Number of errors			Percentile		
		Entry	Exit	Difference	Entry	Exit	Difference
Typically developing	25	14.1 (11.4)	8.2 (9.4)	5.9	61.3 (30.2)	59.0 (31.7)	(2.3)
Profile L	6	23.0 (6.7)	15.3 (12.1)	7.7	45.2 (20.8)	45.3 (36.1)	.1
Profile E	8	43.4 (16.2)	25.4 (14.5)	18.0	4.6 (4.1)	11.5 (11.1)	6.9
Profile G	18	45.1 (6.1)	25.8 (8.0)	19.3	3.1 (2.8)	12.1 (8.5)	9.0

characterized as exhibiting Profiles E and G are considered together in the remaining discussion.

Age at Initial Enrollment and Length of Treatment

Table 3 presents the GFTA scores for the typically developing children and children with SLI (Profiles E and G), categorized by age at program entry (Younger: 29–43 months versus Older: 44 months or older) and length of enrollment in the program (1 year versus 2 years). Although all of the groups made substantial gains in the total number of errors observed, the children in Profiles E and G showed consistently greater percentile score increases than the typically developing children. As with the language measures in Chapter 9, when enrollment in LAP was limited to 1 year, it was the older children who made the larger gains in percentile score. Also analogous to Chapter 9, the children in Profiles E and G who were enrolled in the program for 2 years showed the largest gains of all of the groups.

A Note on Interpretation

The two assumptions introduced earlier in this chapter need to be reconsidered in reference to interpretation of test results. Let us begin with the assumption that most children reach a comparable level of mastery of the phonological system. This assumption leads to the significant ceiling effects seen in most articulation tests. In other words, there is a developmental point at which most children get all, or most, of the items on a test correct. Although this may provide confirmation of an individual child's relative mastery of the production of a set of specific allophones, it seriously limits the power of the test to discriminate among children, or to measure changes in performance across time. The following example illustrates that point. For girls age 4 years, 9 months–4 years, 11 months, raw scores of 30, 31, 32, or 33 errors on the GFTA all yield the

Table 3. Entry and exit scores for Goldman-Fristoe Test of Articulation by age at initial enrollment

Group	n	Number of errors			Percentile		
		Entry	Exit	Difference	Entry	Exit	Difference
Typically developing children							
1-year Younger	7	21.0	14.9	6.1	49.3	51.6	2.3
		(14.4)	(13.7)		(35.9)	(40.2)	
1-year Older	8	9.0	6.4	2.6	65.1	61.9	(3.2)
		(12.3)	(7.2)		(35.4)	(33.6)	
2-years Younger	10	13.3	5.1	8.2	66.7	61.9	(4.8)
		(5.4)	(4.7)		(21.0)	(25.6)	
Children with SLI							
1-year Younger	6	47.7	31.8	15.9	3.8	9.3	5.5
		(5.8)	(4.4)		(3.7)	(5.3)	
1-year Older	4	38.5	22.0	16.5	3.3	11.3	8.0
		(13.6)	(7.3)		(3.3)	(6.6)	
2-years Younger	16	44.9	24.3	20.6	3.5	13.0	9.5
		(10.2)	(11.5)		(3.3)	(10.9)	

same percentile score (see Table 4). In other words, for children performing near the bottom of their age group, mastery of three additional test items may yield no change in percentile ranking. At these same ages, however, a child performing near the top of the group may gain as many as 28 percentile points by mastering the same number of test items.

The second assumption, that phonemic inventories are appropriate markers of articulatory development, results in test items with varying degrees of discrimination. In fact, some test items may seldom, if ever, be produced incorrectly, even by the least able speaker. These items offer little information when assessing a child's relative status or when measuring changes in his or her performance across time. In the example from Table 4, the three allophones mastered by the child with low ability might be particularly helpful in describing her phonological status because of their roles in the phonological system, their relationships to each other, or their importance to the child's particular speech pattern. Conversely, the three allophones mastered by the child with high ability may be of relatively little consequence to her or to her sound system. Nevertheless, it is the child who is performing at the 71st percentile who will show a large improvement in her standardized score with additional correctly articulated phonemes, while the other child will show none.

It is not surprising, then, that the observed improvements of more than 40% in GFTA raw scores by the LAP children produced different patterns of percentile change for the typically developing children and the children with SLI. Furthermore, the very nature of articulation tests may conspire against children with SLI in terms of their ability to show substantial gains in percentile scores. As a result, the approximately 8 percentile point increase seen in the children in Profiles G and E may represent significant phonological growth on the part of these children.

Table 4.   Sample normative data for females, ages 4 years, 9 months–4 years, 11 months, for the Goldman-Fristoe Test of Articulation

Number of errors	Percentile score
0	99th
1	89th
2	79th
3	71st
•	•
•	•
•	•
30	3rd
31	3rd
32	3rd
33	3rd

CONCLUDING REMARKS

In sum, these group data show progress for all children enrolled in LAP. The children with speech impairments made sizable gains in percentile scores, while those with typical speech production skills, on average, maintained a nearly constant percentile score during their enrollment in the program. Furthermore, the children with speech impairments who were enrolled in the preschool for 2 years made the greatest percentile increases. Although not presented here, individual data confirm that all of the children enrolled in LAP made phonological progress while enrolled. Some children's (especially some children in the typically developing group) percentile rankings slipped, but there were no cases in which raw scores failed to improve between the entry and exit testing. Furthermore, the slight decrease seen in some percentile scores is considered to be as likely due to test variables as it is to child variables.

In order to document the efficacy of the language-focused curriculum, this chapter has focused on standardized test scores. By their very nature, such scores are easily summarized and compared across children. The chapter has not included data of the type represented in the opening vignette, nor has it included data taken from other informal measures of speech production. Such nonstandardized measures are extremely useful and may in fact provide a more accurate picture of many children's speech. However, such measures do not lend themselves to comparisons across children. Thus, even though they did not receive equal attention here, all indicators of therapeutic progress, including gains in other language areas, are important to the assessment of an individual child's communicative success.

The summary finding of group gains in articulation test scores is significant, considering the widespread skepticism regarding the feasibility of implementing phonological remediation in a classroom setting. It is important to remember that all of the articulatory training received by these children was completed within the structure of the preschool day, and most of the work was embedded in regular curricular activities. As a result, these group effects, combined with the high attainment rates of individualized education program (IEP) phonology goals, indicate that the language-focused curriculum facilitated the implementation of individualized therapy for all of the targeted children.

Although these data are far from definitive, they nonetheless provide important evidence in support of the LFC and its utility in phonological remediation. Furthermore, when viewed with the data presented in Chapter 9, these results support the applicability of the concentrated normative model to all aspects of intervention for speech and language impairments.

REFERENCES

Bankson, N., & Bernthal, J. (1981). Assessment of articulation. In L. Lass, J. Northern, D. Yoder, & L. McReynolds (Eds.), *Speech, language, hearing.* Philadelphia: W.B. Saunders.

Bernthal, J.E., & Bankson, N.W. (Eds.). (1988). *Articulation and phonological disorders*. Englewood Cliffs, NJ: Prentice Hall.

Goldman, R., & Fristoe, M. (1986). *Goldman-Fristoe Test of Articulation (GFTA)*. Circle Pines, MN: American Guidance Service.

Hodson, B., & Paden, E. (1986). *Targeting intelligible speech* (rev. ed.). Danville, IL: Interstate Press.

Noll, J.D. (1970). *Articulatory assessment* (American Speech and Hearing Association Report No. 5). Washington, DC: American Speech and Hearing Association.

Shriberg, L., & Kwiatkowski, S. (1980). *Natural process analysis*. New York: John Wiley & Sons.

Van Riper, C., & Erickson, R. (1969). A predictive screening test of articulation. *Journal of Speech and Hearing Disorders, 34*, 214–219.

Weiner, F. (1979). *Phonological process analysis*. Baltimore: University Park Press.

Wilcox, K., Catts, H., Larrivee, L., & Morris, S. (in preparation). *The normal distribution of phonological abilities: Implications for assessment and intervention*.

~11~

Life After LAP

Julie F. Sergeant

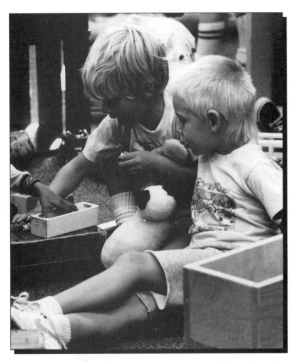

"I gave his teacher the papers and reports from LAP personally because I didn't want them to get lost," said Sam's mother, Kelly. Sam is in his first semester of kindergarten. "The teacher says she has to repeat directions to him. He had a terrible time settling into the routine. The teacher knows he is smart and says he talks just fine. She complains, 'I *know* he can hear me.' It is his behavior that she is worried about."

"The way Sam understands what others are saying is still hard for him," the family services coordinator reminded Kelly. "His receptive language, or how well he understands what you say, was just borderline for what we would expect for kids his age. The area that was hardest for him was following complex directions. If you tell him 'Put all your papers in your desk,' he does fine. But understanding 'Put all the math papers in your desk and get out your spelling book' is difficult for him."

"I remember the director saying that following directions at group time was hard for him," said Kelly.

The family services coordinator continued, "We recommended monitoring his ability to follow directions. The audiologist included some suggestions for his classroom teacher—like getting his attention and facing him when giving directions."

Kelly sounded frustrated, "I don't think she buys the intermittent hearing loss, which the audiologist put in her report. At LAP, everyone was Sam's advocate. Now no one is except me."

"Why don't you try talking to the speech-language therapist at his school?" suggested the family services coordinator. "If you give her a copy of the papers and tell her what you told me, she should understand the problem. She could explain to the teacher how language problems might be affecting Sam's classroom behavior or she might recommend more speech-language therapy for him."

"That's a good idea. I know who she is and I can talk to her," Kelly replied, sounding positive.

"If you want anything else from us, let me know. The director could talk to someone from the school or write a letter explaining Sam's history in more detail. She or I might be able to come to a conference if that would be helpful."

This chapter focuses on the progress of children with speech and language impairments through the elementary and special education systems. The number of children receiving special services, the types of services received, and their progression through the educational system give a picture of children's experiences once they have left the Language Acquisition Preschool (LAP). Anecdotes from family members help describe their transitions, and four case studies illustrate the diversity of their experiences. The data presented here, combined with the anecdotes and case studies, attest to the need for long-term advocacy for children with speech and language impairments and their families.

ELEMENTARY SCHOOL FOR CHILDREN
WITH SPEECH AND LANGUAGE IMPAIRMENTS

Special Services

In general, 50%–80% of children with a history of speech and language impairments *and* a typical nonverbal IQ have shown language problems as much as 20 years after their initial diagnoses (Aram & Hall, 1989). Reviewers have concluded that a language impairment is a persistent reality that will affect other language-dependent areas (e.g., social, behavioral, academic).

Rice, Hadley, and Alexander (1993) investigated the social consequences of speech and language impairments in kindergarten children. They found that teachers and other adults tend to assume that children with speech and language impairments have cognitive and social limitations and are lacking social maturity and school readiness skills. This assumption has repercussions for both academic and social success. Other research has shown a relationship between speech and language impairments and reading disabilities. In a study of first and second graders, many children with speech and language impairments were found to be lagging behind their peers in reading achievement (Catts, 1992). In this study, word-processing skills were linked to phonological-processing skills, and reading comprehension was linked to language ability. However, approximately 50% of the children with speech and language impairments in the same study scored within normal limits on reading achievement tests. Still other research describes the speech and language skills of students with the label of behavior disorder (Ruhl, Hughes, & Camarata, 1992).

In a study that examined children's transitions across and out of special education programs, children with speech and language impairments were the most transient group, with 78% experiencing a program change in a 3-year period (Halgren & Clarizio, 1993). Of six special education categories, students classified as having mild speech and language impairments most frequently terminated services in this 3-year period, while students classified as having severe speech and language impairments were more likely to be moved into more intensive services.

Grade Retention

Retention in an academic grade level emerges as an issue in the early elementary years of children with speech and language impairments. In a longitudinal study examining the relationship between reading disabilities and speech and language impairments, Catts (1992) noted that 23 of 56 children with speech and language impairments either repeated kindergarten or attended a developmental first grade (D-1) following their kindergarten year. Children enrolled in D-1 typically attend first grade the following year. This intervening year of instruction is thought by some to be beneficial because it provides an additional year for maturation.

These high retention rates appear in spite of research that retention, including placement in prefirst or prekindergarten classes, is not beneficial to children over the long term (Doyle, 1989; Smith & Shepard, 1987). In a study on grade retention, Mcleskey and Grizzle (1992) found that, in Indiana, 58% of children with a learning disability were retained before being diagnosed as having a learning disability. These results suggest that retention is being used as a remedial measure, although parental choice may have been a factor in some cases. It is possible that school districts and/or parents are giving children with speech and language impairments a year to "mature," hoping that their language skills will catch up to those of their peers.

Other authors have attempted to explain the reasoning behind the retention of children in the face of contradictory research evidence. Five issues that influence retention in the elementary grades are discussed by Smith and Shepard (1987):

1. Teachers' perceptions of the relative progress made by students affect retention rates. Teachers observe immediate progress by the children who have been retained, yet they fail to compare the performance of these children with that of their peers who were promoted to the next grade. Early elementary teachers do not follow the progress of retained children into later years.

2. Philosophical views of child development affect school retention rates. Schools that tended to retain children had teachers with *nativist* views. These teachers believe that linguistic or cultural stimulation or experiences at home will not facilitate a child's developmental readiness for school. Alternatively, schools with low retention rates were dominated by teachers with *remediationist* viewpoints. These teachers believe that individual work with children who are not "ready" for first grade and altering of instructional strategies to coincide with individual learning styles will increase school readiness skills.

3. In many schools, kindergarten curricula have become what was once considered first-grade material. Schools with linear, literacy-focused curricula expect mastery of colors, shapes, words, and numbers upon entry into first grade, and they expect children to work independently at their desks for extended time periods. These schools are

likely to retain children or make referrals for special education placement. In other schools, there are different expectations for the kindergarten year. Children may be expected to know their addresses, distinguish letters from numbers, and have developed good work habits prior to first grade. These schools will tolerate and promote slow readers who are motivated and progressing in other areas.

4. Parental pressure affects decisions for high-speed curriculum packages and may influence school entrance and retention policies. Some parents have admitted delaying children's entry into kindergarten a year to give their children a competitive edge.

5. Bureaucratic decisions regarding the use of standardized testing and the amount of flexibility allowed within curriculum guidelines are linked to retention rates. Teachers who must use standardized test scores to respond to demands for accountability will want to ensure that children enter their classrooms fully prepared. Principals who set strict promotion standards and discourage creativity with the curriculum tend to work in schools with high retention rates and with high numbers of children who follow an atypical educational progression.

Evidence also indicates that it is not educational professionals who are advancing this trend toward retention, but groups such as state legislatures, state boards of education, and local school boards (Doyle, 1989). These groups are less familiar than educational professionals with educational research findings. When this fact is added to the complexity of the five issues outlined above, an understanding of the reasons behind the high rate of retention and atypical educational progression of children with speech and language impairments begins to emerge.

ELEMENTARY SCHOOL EXPERIENCES OF CHILDREN WHO HAD ATTENDED LAP

To better understand how the experiences of LAP children correspond to the results reported in the literature, family members were interviewed twice a year after their children left the preschool program. These conversations with family members served several purposes:

- To track children's educational progress and learn about the special services they were receiving after they left LAP
- To learn about the elementary and special education programs that former LAP children were attending
- To better understand the transition process and the types of support that families receive during the transitions
- To provide continuing support to families during the transition process

Over a 4-year period, followup interviews were conducted with family members of 29 children with speech and language impairments and 18 children whose language skills were developing typically. Parents of children with speech and language impairments were interviewed continually over the 4-year period. Parents of children with typically devel-

oping language skills were interviewed through kindergarten and first grade only. Information about the special services received by these children and their progression through elementary schools in 11 school districts is summarized in Tables 1, 2, and 3.

Speech-Language Therapy

Of the children who received speech-language therapy in LAP as preschoolers, 66% received speech-language pathology (SLP) services during at least 1 year of elementary school. Of the kindergartners, 64% required speech therapy; this number dropped to 55% in first grade. Al-

Table 1.   Services received by children with speech and language impairments

Services received	Number of children	Percentage
Speech-language pathology services	19	66
Other special services	10	34
Occupational therapy/perceptual-motor therapy	3	10
Chapter 1: reading	2	7
Chapter 1: math	2	7
Counseling services/behavior disorder[a]	3	10
Special tutoring[b]	3	10
No special services[c]	9	31

Note: The data provided in this table are longitudinal, compiled over a 4-year period. The total number of children followed was 29; percentages are based on this total.

[a]One child received counseling for attention-deficit/hyperactivity disorder; one child participated in group therapy for children who have been sexually abused; and one child received services for a behavior disorder.

[b]Special afterschool program sponsored by the school district.

[c]One child attended developmental first grade.

Table 2.   Educational progression for entry transitions into kindergarten and first grade

	Number of children		Percentage	
Educational progression	Speech and language impairments	Typical development	Speech and language impairments	Typical development
Total number of children	29	18	100	100
Typical progression	18	17	62	94
Atypical progression	11	1	38	6
Retained	3	0	10	0
Chose alternate sequence	3	1	10	6
Delayed kindergarten	5	0	17	0

though the percentages increased for the second through fourth graders, the small sample sizes of these groups make these trends difficult to interpret. As the children in the sample progressed through these higher grades, these percentages changed. Neither of the two children in the fifth-grade sample received speech or language therapy.

Other Special Services

Of the children with speech and language impairments who received services as preschoolers, 34% received other types of special services in elementary school. These services included occupational or perceptual-motor therapy, Chapter 1 services for reading or math, special tutoring, or some type of counseling. Of the children whose language skills were

Table 3.   Cross-sectional data on services received and educational progression

Grade[a]	Speech	Other services	No special services	Atypical progression	Total
Preschool[b]	60% (3)	40% (2)	40% (2)	100% (5)	
Kindergarten					
Speech and language impairments	64% (21)	21% (7)	30% (10)	15% (5)	(33)
Typical development	0	6% (1)	94% (17)	0	(18)
Grade 1					
Speech and language impairments	55% (11)	25% (5)	40% (8)	5% (1)	(20)
Typical development	0	23% (3)	77% (10)	8% (1)	(13)
Grade 2					
Speech and language impairments	67% (10)	27% (4)	33% (5)	0	(15)
Grade 3					
Speech and language impairments	70% (7)	10% (1)	30% (3)	0	(10)
Grade 4					
Speech and language impairments	50% (2)	0	50% (2)	0	(4)
Grade 5					
Speech and language impairments	0	0	100% (2)	0	(2)

[a]Children repeating a grade are counted twice.
[b]Delayed kindergarten enrollment by 1 year.

developing typically, one (6%) received special services in kindergarten and three (23%) received special services in first grade.

Educational Progression

Of the children with speech and language impairments, 62% followed a typical progression through school. They began kindergarten the year they turned 5 by September 1 and advanced one grade per year thereafter. Of the children with speech and language impairments, 38% deviated from the typical progression. These children either repeated a year of programming; delayed kindergarten enrollment a year; or followed a 2-year alternative program sequence, such as language kindergarten/ kindergarten or developmental first grade/first grade. The deviations from expected school progression occurred during the kindergarten or first-grade transitions. Of the children with speech and language impairments as preschoolers, 10% were retained in kindergarten or first grade. This may be compared to an approximate retention rate of .7% for kindergarten and first grade in the local school district (M. Merrill, personal communication, January 18, 1994). One typically developing child (6%) in the LAP followup experienced an atypical progression, attending a developmental first-grade class.

Case Studies

The four case studies in this chapter are provided to introduce some of the children who attended LAP. The case studies illustrate the diversity of educational experiences and transitions that LAP children and their families have encountered.

Karen

Karen, now in third grade, is the oldest of three daughters. Her father owns a small business and travels frequently. Her mother keeps the books for the business and is the primary caregiver for Karen and her sisters. Karen attended LAP for 3 semesters and 2 summers. While enrolled in LAP, Karen's language goals focused on expressive language skills and articulation. She also received perceptual-motor therapy as a preschooler.

After LAP, Karen attended a "language kindergarten" class, which placed a special emphasis on enhancing language skills. She left the public school system to attend kindergarten and first grade in a private, church-affiliated school, thus repeating kindergarten. Karen's transition to kindergarten at her private school was smooth, but first grade was a little more difficult. Karen's younger sister, Ellen, missed Karen when she was gone all day. It was somewhat difficult for Karen to adjust to the full-day routine of first grade, but by October, she had decided she liked going all day like "one of the big kids."

In first grade, Karen did well in almost all subject areas. One of her favorite activities was science experiments. Her teacher believed Karen should put more effort into her schoolwork, as Karen tended to hurry through assignments. Karen enjoyed having class with the older children in the combined grade model of her private school. She often eavesdropped on the other grades. She would come home and say to her mother, "You know what the second graders did today?"

While Karen attended private school, she received SLP services and occupational therapy through the school district. Her mother was happy with the coordination between the private school and the school district and between the school therapists and her. She would take Karen to the neighborhood school for therapy on an itinerant basis. The speech-language pathologist and the occupational therapist arranged their schedules to accommodate Karen's private school schedule and called Karen's mother at home if they were sick or unable to meet on a given day. Karen's mother really appreciated these efforts.

During the fall of her first-grade year, Karen began grumbling about going to speech-language therapy when no one else at her school had to go. By the following spring, she began asking how much longer she needed to go to therapy. She felt it was unfair that the spring breaks of her private school and the public school system were at different times. In spite of the complaints, her mother noted that Karen liked both of her therapists and talked positively about her therapy after she went.

Karen returned to the public school system for second grade. It was a bit of an adjustment from a class of 9 children to a class of 25. She was used to a lot of individual attention from the teacher. This change prompted her to learn more independent study skills. In second grade, Karen declared that she hated speech-language therapy. Karen's mother reported that Karen was working on /r/. "It's just hard work and she doesn't like to do it!", she said.

In third grade, Karen's mother describes her daughter as a day-dreamer. Karen is still receiving SLP services and does not like leaving class for therapy. She is afraid she will miss something.

Margaret

Margaret is in fifth grade this year. As a preschooler, she attended LAP for 4 semesters and 3 summer sessions. The 10th of 12 children, Margaret has a younger brother and younger sister who also received speech-language therapy at LAP.

In kindergarten, Margaret received individual SLP services, for which she left the classroom to meet with the speech-language pathologist. Her mother mentioned that communication between LAP personnel and the public school staff eliminated the need for duplicate testing, which made the transition to kindergarten especially smooth for Margaret and her family. Throughout kindergarten, Margaret told her mother that she didn't like her SLP services. She felt "different" when she had to leave her classroom to receive individual therapy.

In first grade, the speech-language pathologist recommended that Margaret no longer needed SLP services. In second grade, Margaret received individual SLP services three times a week. During this year, however, her SLP began to conduct Margaret's therapy in a small group with some of her classmates. This change made a difference in Margaret's attitude. Margaret seemed to like therapy better when receiving these services in a small group.

During the first semester of third grade, Margaret received SLP services two times a week in a group setting. In the spring semester, the decision was made that Margaret no longer needed services. The speech-language pathologist met occasionally with the group during the spring semester to wean them away from services.

Education is a priority in Margaret's family. Margaret's mother maintains ongoing contact with her children's teachers and has appreciated the steps the school and individual teachers and speech-language pathologists have taken to facilitate school–home communication. She regards Margaret's school transitions as typical. She found it especially helpful that the speech-language pathologist and Margaret's teachers cooperated well, working together to coordinate Margaret's services. She feels that the positive school experiences of Margaret's older brothers and sisters helped Margaret with her school transitions. Neither Margaret nor her younger sister, who also received SLP services, encountered bias by their classroom teachers because of their speech and language impairments. She believes this is because the older brothers and sisters "broke the ground" and established a reputation as being competent students.

Margaret's mother was pleased with the way the speech-language pathologist handled Margaret's transition out of SLP services and appreciated the "graduation" gift that Margaret received. She believes this way of handling the transition was good for Margaret's self-esteem. Margaret is proud that she will no longer need SLP services—she feels that she has mastered her goals and accomplished something important.

Jacob

Jacob is the oldest of three children and is in third grade this year. He has a younger brother who also received speech-language therapy at LAP and a younger sister with typically developing language skills who attended LAP. Making ends meet is difficult for Jacob's family. Jacob's father's job has many physical demands that do not leave him with much energy for day-to-day household routines. Childraising has fallen almost entirely to Jacob's mother. She follows her children's educational progress closely because she wants to ensure that they will complete high school, something she did not have the chance to do.

While enrolled in LAP, Jacob received targeted SLP therapy for both expressive and receptive language. He was enrolled continuously for 1½ semesters and 1 summer session.

When he was 5, Jacob attended both kindergarten and a language kindergarten class. He repeated the kindergarten/language kindergarten combination the following year. Although some parents have found double programming of kindergarten/language kindergarten to be tiring for children, Jacob's mother said she would not have changed her decision about his placement. She believes both the staff and transition procedures at his public school were helpful to her during the time she was making the decision to have Jacob repeat kindergarten. She agreed with the teachers that he just was not ready for first grade.

The following year, Jacob was nervous about attending first grade, but his mother felt he was ready both educationally and emotionally. Jacob adjusted well. First grade sparked his motivation; he enjoyed the work. By April, Jacob loved school and his mother described him as "thirsty for knowledge." At the end of his first-grade year, she felt she had done the right thing in holding him back for an extra year in kindergarten.

In both years of kindergarten, Jacob received SLP services in his language kindergarten class. In first grade, Jacob began receiving individual speech-language therapy and Chapter 1 math services. Jacob's mother was pleased with these services, stating that he enjoyed the one-to-one attention and his attitude toward math was more positive than before he began receiving Chapter 1 services. It was important to Jacob's mother that his teacher, the speech-language pathologist, and the Chapter 1 teacher communicated with each other. It was also important to her that the school district provided free book lending and transportation to and from school.

In second grade, Jacob began to have problems with reading. He graduated from the Chapter 1 services for math, but began receiving Chapter 1 services for reading. He also received SLP services and went to special tutoring sessions after school. In spite of the difficulty with reading, he surprised his teachers with his persistence. If he was wrong, he would try again. He just would not quit.

Jacob is good at making friends. From the first day of second grade, he had three or four friends. But that wasn't enough—he wanted to be friends with the whole class!

Jacob's mother was ill and had surgery during his second-grade year. During this time, his teacher, the counselor, and the principal were very supportive. One day, for example, Jacob decided to stay home, refusing to get out of the car. The principal intervened and gave him two choices—either stay in her office for the day or go to class, but he couldn't go home with his mother. The day after his mother's surgery, he was allowed to stay home to visit her in the hospital. After that, there were no more problems about attending school.

Jacob is in third grade now. The year got off to a rocky start. He began with a 3-1 reader but was not comfortable with it. He said he didn't want to go to school, protesting that it was too hard. The teacher let him use a 2-2 reader, which helped. Writing is also difficult for Jacob, but he is doing well in other areas. This year he is receiving SLP services, Chapter 1 services for reading, and afterschool tutoring.

Terry

Terry is the oldest of three boys and is in second grade this year. One of his younger brothers has special needs that require medical attention and special procedures at home. While Terry was enrolled in LAP, his father was a student at the university. His father graduated and began to job hunt in the middle of the 1980s recession. Terry's family has moved several times for employment reasons, and Terry's transitions between school districts have crossed state lines.

When Terry first began to attend LAP, his mother was concerned about his speech and his attention span. He attended LAP for 4 semesters, taking off summers. His therapy focused on expressive language, articulation, and social interaction skills. Throughout his enrollment, Terry's short attention span and sometimes aggressive behavior toward his brother and his classmates concerned his parents and LAP staff members. However, as his expressive language skills improved, his social interactions improved and his aggressive actions became less frequent.

The summer that Terry turned 5 was a difficult one for his family. This was the time period during which his father graduated and began to search for a job. The family moved in with Terry's grandparents in a rural midwestern community while his father continued to look for a job in his field.

Terry's parents agonized over decisions regarding his upcoming school year. Ideally, they would have liked to place Terry in a 5-day-a-week structured preschool, thus delaying kindergarten a year. However, in the rural area where they were living, few service options were available. They considered an excellent kindergarten program in a nearby community, but housing was not available in that district. They finally chose a kindergarten near his grandparents' house over a preschool that met only 2 days a week.

Terry's transition into kindergarten was difficult. Terry's parents did not have all the information they needed to send him to school. What they did know, they discovered by word of mouth. Terry's mother had been told she would receive a letter telling her what Terry would need for school. She did receive a letter regarding the first day of classes from his teacher, but supplies were not mentioned. On the day before school started, Terry's parents learned that he did need school supplies. It was difficult to locate everything Terry needed on a Sunday in a small, rural community, and what they did locate was different and not of the same quality as the other children's school supplies. This made Terry feel left out on his first day.

Terry was enrolled in a "rowdy" kindergarten class with 24 kids. His mother helped to call all of the other parents to encourage them to complain to the school district, which then divided the class. Terry was placed in the afternoon class and had to adjust to missing his afternoon nap. He didn't like the schoolwork. His teacher said he did well, but his mother felt his work was hurried and sloppy.

Terry received individual speech-language therapy in kindergarten. His mother was able to observe his therapy sessions and the therapist sent work home with him, which pleased her. Terry also began to receive what his mother understood to be Chapter 1 math services. The school screened all of the children and Terry's mother was notified by mail that her son's results were "borderline" and he would be receiving services. Terry liked leaving his classroom for the services he received. His parents were not sure why he received these services or what they were working on, but his mother felt that the special attention was good for him. The Chapter 1 teacher was not helpful or communicative until Terry's mother sought out information about the program. Until his mother initiated this contact, the Chapter 1 teacher assumed that she did not need or want to know about the programming. Terry's mother eventually talked to other parents who had pulled their children out of Chapter 1 services because they were working on reading and not math. She began to suspect that Terry was pulled out of the classroom for Chapter 1 services because his classroom teacher did not understand his abilities fully or did not want him in her class all day.

In the spring of his kindergarten year, Terry's father got a job in another state. At first, Terry was nervous about riding the bus and making friends in his new school, but although he was occasionally sad because he missed his old friends, he adjusted. His mother was happy with the amount of contact she had with Terry's new school. The teacher sent notes and work home everyday. Once a week Terry's mother received a letter telling her what was happening at school and once a month she received a calendar with ideas to do at home. These ideas included things like naming three Easter symbols or practicing letter writing. It was easy for Terry's mother to find time to do these things with him. Terry adapted well to the schoolwork in his new school.

Due to varying state guidelines for eligibility for speech services, the number of Terry's age-appropriate misarticulations decreased overnight from nine to only two. Although Terry did not technically qualify for speech-language services in his new state, the local district honored Terry's out-of-state individualized education program and provided SLP services for 6 months. Terry said his new therapist was "mean" and she admitted to his mother that she is very strict. Terry received therapy with a group of children and seemed to like that. Terry's teacher came to a meeting his mother had with the speech-language pathologist, which was helpful.

Terry gained confidence and learned that he is competent. He used to assume he couldn't do things, and therefore, often did not try. His previous school district had recommended that Terry repeat kindergarten, but the teacher in his new school did not even recommend prefirst grade. She felt he would be ready for first grade with the rest of his class the following year.

Terry's story continues. His parents bought a house, which meant Terry attended first grade in a different school from his kindergarten year. He was placed in a high-risk first-grade class. He had several problems during his first-grade year. He was lost in the school bus system for 1½ hours the first day of school. He had problems listening to his teacher, and his mother wondered if he might be bored. He did not complete much of his schoolwork. He would come home crying and complain to his mother that the other kids didn't like him. By April, Terry's mother was very frustrated. In 1 week, she received three notes home from the school, Terry was sent to the office twice, and she received a telephone call from his teacher, all concerning his classroom behavior. Terry's parents requested a full evaluation for attention-deficit/hyperactivity disorder (AD/HD) and wondered if family counseling would be helpful. He was evaluated by a psychiatrist and diagnosed as having AD/HD. The evaluation also indicated that he is gifted.

Terry's father again changed jobs the summer following Terry's first-grade year, this time to a large, urban area. The family put a bid on a house and prepared to move the August before Terry's second-grade year. At the last minute, the deal with the house fell through. Because the family was moving to an unfamiliar area and did not have prospects for housing when school began, Terry began second grade while staying with his grandparents. This returned him to the rural midwestern community of his kindergarten year. The family plans to reunite and have Terry change schools once they have a permanent place to live.

Terry's story illustrates the complex relationship that exists between children's education and their home lives. Many families do not have control over job changes, within or between places of employment. Moves, especially those that cross state lines, can result in drastic changes in children's educational programming and even diagnoses. In Terry's case, his parents and extended family members were important sources of support through his multiple transitions. They are his best advocates.

Common Themes

During the years in which followup interviews have been conducted with LAP parents, some issues have emerged. These issues involve speech-language services; communication between school and home; communication between professionals; decisions regarding educational progression; and parental input, especially in IEP conferences.

Speech-Language Services

As illustrated in the case studies above, many children are not happy with individual therapy services for which they must leave the classroom. They are afraid they might miss something or that they will be stigmatized as "different." Some children have indicated that they prefer receiving SLP services with a small group of classmates when the alternative is individual therapy away from the classroom. As more and more schools are becoming fully inclusive, therapy services are beginning to be offered in the classroom setting. It has been interesting to hear feedback from families during these program transitions. One mother mentioned:

She used to get pull-out speech. Then they tried in-class only. Now they are doing both. I prefer both, and my daughter doesn't care either way.

Another mother described her daughter's reaction to her first semester of receiving services in the classroom:

This year, she is getting speech, but it is not pull-out. One teacher is a resource room teacher for speech, Chapter 1, and everything else. It is all done in the classroom. Jill doesn't like doing speech therapy in the classroom. In her mind, the other kids know more about her speech problems. Even though the teachers do not try to single her out, it draws attention to her. They are still working out the bugs in the system.

I am optimistic they will work this out—but I guess I did like pull-out better. She got more one-to-one attention, 20 minutes four times a week. Now, it is not as individualized. Now other kids are in her class with more severe problems. The teachers have to deal with them first.

Jill's mother is willing to give the new system a chance, but she has some concerns. She believes that her daughter's fears about being stigmatized by the other children are more Jill's perception than reality. However, she is afraid that Jill's special needs may get lost in the shuffle because they are not as prominent as those of other children in the class. Clearly, further research is needed to track children's adjustment and parent satisfaction with new service models.

Frustration at the lack of information from the speech-language pathologists is a common theme when parents are asked about their child's speech therapy. One mother had assumed that her daughter would no longer need SLP services because she had received paperwork indicating this plan at the end of the previous school year. She was therefore surprised to hear her daughter talking about her speech work at school. Another parent complained:

I don't get any information from my daughter's speech teacher. I have no idea what they are working on. The therapist had not read her file, which recommended daily speech services. My daughter is now, after I intervened, receiving therapy four times a week—two times individually and two times with other kids from her class.

Other parents, such as Margaret's mother, are happy with the amount of contact with their child's speech-language therapist. Some parents may feel reluctant to call the school to request more information from the speech-language pathologist. When asked if they have attempted to contact the speech-language pathologist for more information, some parents have indicated that they do not want to create waves or bother a busy professional. These parents are not asking for daily reports. They would be happy with a monthly note sent home describing current and future activities and progress.

Communication Between School and Home

Just as parents feel communication with their child's speech-language pathologist is important, they also want communication with their child's classroom teacher. In our area, many schools are facilitating school–home communication with a folder system. Schoolwork is saved and sent home each week on the same day. Some schools have a special folder for this purpose, which must be signed by the parent; some classrooms include a weekly newsletter describing past and future activities. Parents' responses to these folders have been overwhelmingly positive.

His sister's teacher sends home a note every Monday, saying specifically what she will be studying that week. I like that.

I like getting the week's work at one time. It helps me see her progression through the week. When things come home daily, they get lost in the shuffle.

I check her school folder once a week. A parent has to sign the folder. One—it teaches responsibility, and two—the parents see the work. I like the system—once I worked through "Don't wake Mom up at 7:30 in the morning to sign your folder on the way out the door to school."

Linking the speech-language pathologists with this folder system would be one way to communicate with parents. Speech-language pathologists could give classroom teachers a weekly or monthly note to send home in the child's folder. This would also facilitate communication between the speech-language pathologists and classroom teachers.

Communication Between Professionals

Early in the course of the followup interviews, it became clear that parents believed that school records were not being adequately transferred between educational settings. LAP staff members began to give an extra copy of educational records to parents to deliver by hand to whomever they chose at their child's new school. This has helped ensure that the records are delivered to someone chosen by the parent, instead of becoming lost somewhere in an administrative file.

Many of the difficulties encountered in children's transitions could have been avoided if the teachers had read the child's file before the beginning of the school year. Some teachers may purposely not read children's files to avoid "self-fulfilling prophecies" and to get to know the children first. Some files, however, contain important information. One mother who experienced a negative transition into her son's second year of first grade commented:

His new teacher was not aware he needed to sit close to the blackboard. She was not aware that he was repeating first grade until I visited the school and informed her.

The vignette that opens this chapter mentions a teacher who read the child's file yet refused to believe information in it and follow suggestions in a report from an audiologist. Professionals may find it helpful to make a telephone call to service providers in future service settings to answer questions and ensure that important information is received.

Decisions Regarding Educational Progression

Comments from parents confirm the suspected causes of high retention rates discussed earlier. When asked if they are happy they made the decision to retain their child, all of the parents who made a decision to retain or otherwise hold their children back have responded affirmatively. Some families are more enthusiastic than others:

He is in second grade but is reading at a third-grade level. He gets straight As. He's doing great. He only missed one spelling word all year. He's got a lot of friends. He's a very popular little boy.

This child appears to be doing well academically, perhaps at the top of his class, after attending a year of developmental first grade. However, the case study of Jacob, who repeated his kindergarten year, portrays a little boy who progressed well in first grade but is now struggling with reading and writing skills in third grade.

The children in our followup study whose kindergarten entry was delayed are now succeeding in their kindergarten year. As parents reflect on the progress of their individual children, they report that they are satisfied with their decision to delay kindergarten:

The decision to wait a year to send him to kindergarten was worth it. There is an in-
credible improvement in his drawing. The attention span for his age is probably low,
but since he is one of the older kids now, he fits in with the younger ones.

Although some parents believe that retention or delay of kindergarten is the best decision, their children may disagree. One mother had
to cope with the reaction of her son when he realized he needed to wait
another year before going to kindergarten. She has been happy with her
decision:

Justin was mad when he first realized his friends were going to kindergarten and he
wasn't. I am elated at his progress this year. He is more self-confident—a leader.

While these anecdotes suggest that grade retention may benefit children, it is important to remember that parents' evaluations of their own
decisions are not unbiased. It is also unclear what the long-term effects
of retention will be in terms of later academic success. Researchers need
to examine and compare the academic progress of children with speech
and language impairments who have been retained and similar children
who have not.

Parental Input

Federal legislation has given family members the right to be the decision
makers regarding their child's special services. In actuality, this occurs in
many ways. Most families have been pleased with their involvement in
their children's programming. One mother explained:

We had been monitoring his behavior and working with a behavioral consultant. This
year, I called to say it was time to do something more about this. Once I called, the
process started quickly.

It is important to recognize the influence that speech-language
pathologists, classroom teachers, and school administrators have on educational decisions made by parents. Before parents make a decision, they
will usually ask for a professional's opinion, and a professional's opinion
is difficult to contradict. A mother of a child attending LAP told the family services coordinator about a decision she was facing regarding her oldest son. After the first quarter of his first-grade year, her son's teacher
ended the parent–teacher conference with the question, "Have you ever
considered holding him back a year?" In the second quarter, the question
turned into a full-fledged recommendation. Just before the semester
break, the mother tearfully told the coordinator that "She [the teacher]
had just about made her decision. She would probably retain him." It is
interesting to note that this recommendation seems to have come from
his classroom teacher and not the IEP team.

It is obvious that some professionals will go out of their way to accommodate a family's schedule. Most of the parents have said that the
school personnel coordinated with their schedules when arranging conferences. One mother in another school district had a different story:

I was notified 2 weeks in advance when the meeting would take place. No one made
any attempt to work around my schedule or to reschedule it when I couldn't attend.
They just sent me a copy of his IEP. I signed it and sent it back.

Most of the families interviewed believed that school personnel really listened to what they had to say. As one parent commented:

The things I suggested, they were willing to respond to, listen, or try—depending on the situation.

Asking parents for input on children's goals, giving relevant advice, following up on conversations, and providing options when asked were all things done by professionals that made parents feel their opinions were valued.

CONCLUDING REMARKS

Certain issues are significant to elementary-age children who received SLP services as preschoolers. These children are more likely to be singled out for special academic arrangements and are less likely to stay with their peers and follow the typical educational progression. It is difficult to pinpoint the role of speech-language competencies in these academic decisions. It is likely to be a relatively complex interaction among social consequences of speech and language impairments, especially with peers; teacher judgments and expectations; relationships of speech and language to reading and other academic subjects; parents' reactions to their child's disability; and recommendations from school staff members.

Parents are often concerned with the amount of communication that exists with their children's speech-language pathologists and classroom teachers. They would generally like more information, especially from the speech-language pathologists, yet are reluctant to initiate contact with the school. Parents are also concerned with their child's attitude toward his or her SLP services. Many children seem to feel that receiving therapy singles them out as "different." This occurs across service models.

Although preschool intervention can prepare a child and his or her family for elementary school and the special education system, long-term advocacy for children with speech and language impairments is necessary. As a followup to this chapter's opening vignette, Sam's mother, Kelly, eventually located an advocate in Sam's new school. She followed the family services coordinator's advice and spoke with the school's speech-language pathologist. The therapist agreed with Kelly that there may be more to this situation than a "behavior problem." She plans to speak with Sam's teacher and reevaluate his speech and language skills, providing services if necessary. Early intervention programs should help families locate advocates in new service settings. These advocates should be aware of parents' concerns and other issues relevant to elementary-age children who have received SLP services. These steps will facilitate transitions and help ensure a positive educational experience for young children with speech-language impairments and their families.

REFERENCES

Aram, D., & Hall, N. (1989). Longitudinal follow-up of children with preschool communication disorders: Treatment implications. *School Psychology Review, 18*, 487–501.

Catts, H.W. (1992). *The relationship between speech-language impairments and reading disabilities.* Paper submitted for publication.

Doyle, R.P. (1989). The resistance of conventional wisdom to research evidence: The case of retention in grade. *Phi Delta Kappan, 71*, 215–220.

Halgren, D.W., & Clarizio, H.F. (1993). Categorical and programming changes in special education services. *Exceptional Children, 59*(6), 547–555.

Mcleskey, J., & Grizzle, K.L. (1992). Grade retention rates among students with learning disabilities. *Exceptional Children, 58*(6), 548–554.

Rice, M.L., Hadley, P.A., & Alexander, A.L. (1993). Social biases toward children with speech and language impairments: A correlative causal model of language limitations. *Applied Psycholinguistics, 14*(4), 445–471.

Ruhl, K.L., Hughes, C.A., & Camarata, S.M. (1992). Analysis of the expressive and receptive language characteristics of emotionally handicapped students served in public school settings. *Journal of Childhood Communication Disorders, 14*(2), 165–176.

Smith, M.L., & Shepard, L.A. (1987). What doesn't work: Explaining policies of retention in the early grades. *Phi Delta Kappan, 69*, 129–134.

ᵔ12ᵕ

The Language-Focused Curriculum in Other Settings

Betty H. Bunce, Ruth V. Watkins,
Julia Eyer, Terri Torres,
Susie Ray, and Janet Ellsworth

A doctor's office has been set up in the dramatic play area. Children are pretending to be doctors, nurses, patients, or the mommies and daddies of patients (dolls). "Next," says a 4-year-old girl wearing a nurse's hat and holding a clipboard. A 5-year-old boy with Down syndrome who has been sitting in the "waiting room" moves forward. The girl points to the child in a wheelchair who is wearing a stethoscope. She says to the first child, "The doctor will see you now." The child in the wheelchair uses a stethoscope and listens to the other child's heart beat and says, "You sick." He then proceeds to give the "sick child" a pretend injection. A teacher expands on what the "doctor" has said by saying,"Tommy, the doctor says you *are* sick."

In another classroom, a hair salon activity has been set up. Several children are putting curlers in one doll's hair, others are combing a doll's hair, and still others are pretending to wash several dolls' hair. A nonverbal child is near the hairdryer, which is hooked up to a switch that is operable by this child. Other children approach with their dolls and request, "Turn the hairdryer on (or off), Sam." Sam responds to their requests and enjoys being part of the dramatic play activity. With his communication board, Sam is also able to make requests of the other children.

These two scenarios are from preschool programs in the midwest that have adapted the language-focused curriculum (LFC) developed at the Language Acquisition Preschool (LAP). A major feature of this curriculum is the provision of speech and language intervention in a classroom setting using a concentrated normative model (CNM). This chapter describes four such programs, labeled A, B, C, and D.[1] Two of these programs, like LAP, are located at university settings and involve training of practitioners as well as providing direct services to children with speech and language impairments. The other two programs are affiliated with, or are part of, their local public school system. These programs provide direct services to a range of young children with special needs, including children with developmental delays in speech and language, cognitive skills, and/or motor skills.

The four preschool programs were in existence prior to their adaptation of the LFC model. For each program, the adoption of the LFC model occurred in a different way and under a unique set of circumstances. One of the programs, Program A, had a staff member who trained at the University of Kansas in LAP and later became the director of Program A. Two of the programs, Programs B and D, had staff members who first observed LAP and then attended inservice sessions provided by the first author of this chapter. Two staff members from Program C attended a Kansas Speech-Language-Hearing Association conference (Bunce, 1991), where the LAP model was presented. Followup, on-site inservice sessions were provided to all staff members involved in Programs B, C, and D. In some cases, personnel from other programs also attended the inservice sessions.

Following the inservice sessions, staff members from the various programs continued to have contact with LAP personnel by telephone or written communication. Additional site visits to the programs were also made to help solve problems in implementing and adapting the LAP procedures to the other classrooms. The 10 principles developed as guidelines for LAP (see Table 1) are also adhered to by these preschool programs; each program is described in this chapter. The two university-based programs are described first, followed by the two programs associated with public schools. Each description addresses the following topics: 1) setting, 2) population served, 3) staff members involved, 4) program implementation of the CNM, and 5) adaptations of procedures used in LAP.

The population served is a topic that has become an issue when adapting the LFC model in other settings. The LFC and associated CNM are designed for a least restrictive environment (LRE). The presumption that accompanies this design is that a mixture of children with varying communicative abilities is a vital component of the LAP model. If chil-

---

[1]*Program A* refers to the Preschool Language Development Program located at the Callier Center, University of Texas–Dallas, when Dr. Ruth V. Watkins was the director. *Program B* refers to a language preschool located at the University of Oklahoma's Speech-Language-Hearing Clinic, when Dr. Julia Eyer was the director. *Program C* refers to the Early Education Center located in Hutchinson, Kansas. Terri Torres and Susie Ray are two of the speech-language pathologists responsible for adapting the LAP program for use at the center. *Program D* refers to the Jenks Enriched Early Education Program (JEEEP) located in Jenks, Oklahoma. Janet Ellsworth was instrumental in developing the program.

Table 1. Operational guidelines for the concentrated normative model

1.	Language intervention is best provided in a meaningful social context.
2.	Language facilitation occurs throughout the entire curriculum.
3.	The language curriculum is rooted in content themes.
4.	Language intervention begins with the child.
5.	Verbal interaction is encouraged.
6.	Passive language learning and overt responses are encouraged.
7.	Children's utterances are accorded functional value.
8.	Valuable teaching occasions can arise in child-to-child interactions.
9.	Parents are valuable partners in language intervention programming.
10.	Routine parent evaluations are an integral part of the program.

dren with speech and language impairments are attending a classroom composed only of children with similar limitations, there are fewer opportunities for communicative interactions and the richness of the language offered by the children without impairments is lost. For various, often financial, reasons, a LRE with equal distribution of children with and without impairments is difficult to achieve. This is perhaps especially the case in university-based programs, as we know of several with this configuration. Nevertheless, the programs described in this chapter have been able to include typically developing children in the classroom and have found the mixture of children advantageous for all. Peer interaction allows practice in real situations where there is negotiation for toys, friendships, and play activities. Interactions with adults may not provide the same kinds of language practice nor do they usually achieve the same results.

PROGRAM A: UNIVERSITY-BASED SERVICE AND TRAINING PROGRAM

Program A is a university-based service and training program for children with speech and language impairments. It is also a training institution for graduate students in speech-language pathology. This program integrates three central objectives: 1) service delivery to children with language impairments, 2) graduate student clinical training, and 3) research activities addressing the nature and treatment of language impairments. Although Program A maintains the theoretical perspectives that are fundamental to LAP and builds on the LAP curriculum and general orientation, several adaptations have been implemented to meet the unique needs of this setting. These adaptations center around four major areas: 1) the population served, 2) the central role of graduate student clinicians in staffing the classroom, 3) the language enrichment strategies emphasized, and 4) the methods of program evaluation implemented. Each of these adaptations is discussed below.

Population Served

The enrollment of Program A differs from the LAP classroom in two key ways. First, the majority of the children participating in Program A have language impairments; in a typical semester, 10–12 children with language-learning difficulties are enrolled and 1 or 2 children with typically developing language skills participate as models. Second, the children enrolled in Program A exhibit a range of linguistic and social strengths and weaknesses. In this way, Program A serves children with a continuum of language impairments, including children with cognitive disabilities requiring intermittent to limited support and children with difficulties in social interactive skills. The unifying characteristic of all participants, however, is an impairment in understanding and/or using language to participate fully in the important contexts of their everyday lives.

Program Implementation and Adaptations

In general, the basic LAP curriculum, daily schedule, and activities have been successfully extended to match the needs and interests of the children enrolled in Program A. Minor adjustments in daily schedule have been beneficial, specifically reducing the emphasis on structured teacher-directed activities, such as circle and group times, and, in turn, devoting a greater proportion of each day to child-directed components, such as center activities. These minor adaptations have generally taken the form of reducing the time spent in particular activities, rather than eliminating them from the classroom day.

Role of Graduate Students

An additional difference between LAP and Program A is the role assumed by speech-language pathology graduate students. Whereas LAP involves three or four student clinicians per semester, Program A typically includes five. These graduate students form the foundation of Program A, working in conjunction with the lead teacher. Each graduate student clinician is typically assigned two to three children with language impairments; the student clinician's role includes identifying appropriate semester goals for that child, serving as the liaison between the program and the child's family, and monitoring the implementation of language facilitation strategies and intervention outcomes. Thus, the graduate speech-language clinicians in Program A assume considerable responsibility for program implementation and serve a number of central functions. The lead teacher in the classroom also acts as the supervisor for these students.

Two important steps are necessary to ensure that students are prepared for these responsibilities. First, the students who participate in Program A are at the graduate level and have completed introductory training in the field. Second, an intensive 1-week inservice training session is implemented prior to each Program A semester. This inservice session reviews topics such as strategies for identifying appropriate goals, methods of classroom-based language intervention, and techniques for interacting with families.

Language Enrichment Strategies

As a language enrichment classroom, Program A is built on the CNM of language facilitation developed in LAP. Thus, language teaching strategies that enrich the linguistic environment while maintaining the basic character of typical language learning are implemented in the Program A classroom (e.g., focused contrasts, modeling, recasting, expanding, event casting). However, the diversity of the linguistic, cognitive, and social competencies of the children participating in Program A has encouraged the evolution of supplemental language facilitation techniques. Two such techniques are: 1) procedures for promoting child–child interactions in the classroom, and 2) methods of using book-reading activities for teaching language.

Promoting Child–Child Interactions   Informal and formal observations of the Program A classroom revealed that a large proportion of the utterances produced by all of the children were directed to adult teachers and student clinicians (Watkins, Seymour, & Davis, 1993). This pattern occurred even when the desired communication partner was another child; the general tendency was to use an adult as a filter or mediator for child–child interactions. It is plausible that the relatively high number of adults and the low number of typical language learners in the Program A classroom contributed to this interactive pattern.

Because a primary goal of Program A was to enhance children's ability to communicate efficiently and effectively with the important people in their lives, a systematic procedure for promoting direct child–child exchanges was implemented. The procedure involved three levels of assistance, with the level provided dependent on the linguistic and social competence of the child. At the first level, a general prompt was given. For example, if a child directed a request through an adult, the adult simply redirected it (see Chapter 7 for a discussion of the use of redirects in the LAP classroom). In a situation where a child requested a particular toy presently in use by another child, the adult instructed the child to go to the child with the request (e.g., "Ask Mike for the ball."). At the second level, specific verbal direction was provided (e.g., "Say, 'Mike, it's my turn' "). Finally, at the third level, a specific verbal model and physical assistance were offered; the adult would accompany the child to the conversational partner and model an appropriate request. The child may or may not subsequently imitate the model provided.

Ultimately, the aim of this assistance was to move children toward lower levels of assistance, in the direction of independent functioning. Thus, the notion implicated is much like scaffolding, wherein help is provided as needed and reduced or removed as child competence increases. The process also parallels Vygotsky's zone of proximal development; the assistance provided must be accessible to the child, or within the child's zone of proximal development, if it is to be beneficial. Thus, limited assistance is not beneficial for a child with low verbal and social competencies. For this child, a greater level of help is necessary to promote growth. In contrast, for the child with greater abilities, high levels of aid do not optimize language and social growth, but instead tend to maintain existing abilities.

It is the impression of our staff that implementing these levels of assistance has facilitated the verbal social interactions of children in Program A; however, these observations have not yet been documented empirically. One important note is that specific training and guided instruction were required to assist classroom personnel in understanding and using the procedure. In particular, instruction was directed toward recognizing the level of assistance appropriate for a given child's language and social abilities.

Book Reading for Language Stimulation   As in LAP, a portion of each Program A classroom day has been devoted to book reading. In addition, opportunities for book reading exist during centers and at various transition points during the day. Despite this emphasis on book reading, common in many preschool language intervention programs, few empirical studies have assessed the influence of book-reading activities on the linguistic skills of children with language delays. Two investigations were conducted in Program A to address this issue (Watkins, 1992; Watkins & Davis, in preparation). In the first study, children's use of imitation during seven interactive readings of the same story was assessed. Results revealed that children with language impairments were able to imitate story text across readings, successfully using the language they heard during previous readings to participate in subsequent story sessions. The second study assessed word learning during four readings of a book designed to present new vocabulary. Seventeen target words were modeled during story readings. Results revealed significant gains in ability to produce target words following the four reading sessions. Overall, these findings suggest that children with limited language skills can capitalize on the routinized, predictable language-learning opportunities provided by group book-reading sessions.

These findings led Program A staff to consider ways to increase the role of book reading in the classroom and to make existing book-reading routines more powerful language-learning opportunities. Two modifications were implemented. First, the time allocated for book reading was increased slightly, and additional opportunities for book reading were developed (e.g., circle time, arrival time). Second, particular attention was directed to the style and method of book reading likely to optimize language learning (Watkins, 1992). For example, repetition will enhance learning occasions. Repeating the same books frequently and building familiar routines related to those books, such that the same comments are made about various pictures and story actions from one reading to the next, will enrich language-learning potential. With advance planning and preparation, particular target words and grammatical structures can also be embedded in story text. Furthermore, an interactive book-reading style, in which children's comments are encouraged and expanded, is likely to enhance language development. The adult reader can create opportunities for child input by asking open-ended questions (e.g., "What do you think will happen next?") and pausing expectantly to allow time for the child's contributions. In addition, describing pictures and discussing story characters' actions, rather than directly reading the story text, tends to promote a more active role for the child. Finally, the adult's role in book reading should be adjusted according to child competence. Early in the child's language development, the adult assumes greater responsibility for structuring the book-reading session and for modeling and prompting comments about particular aspects of the story. Later, as the child is able to use new language forms and lexical items to discuss pictures and actions, and as he or she develops skill in telling a story with limited assistance, the adult can relinquish greater responsibility to the child.

These adaptations to the role of book reading in the Program A classroom have been easily integrated within the overall framework provided by the language-focused curriculum and the concentrated normative model of language facilitation. A portion of the Program A inservice training session has been allocated to discussion and practice of strategies for interactive book reading; this training has been particularly beneficial for the graduate student clinicians.

Program Evaluation

Program A has implemented a three-level approach to program evaluation, integrating standardized testing, observational measures, and a social validity questionnaire completed by parents. Although these methods are similar to those used in LAP, some specific differences exist. Selected standardized measures are administered at the beginning of each fall semester (Expressive One-Word Picture Vocabulary Test–Revised [EOWPVT–R] [Gardner, 1990], Goldman-Fristoe Test of Articulation [GFTA] [Goldman & Fristoe, 1969], Peabody Picture Vocabulary Test–Revised [PPVT–R] [Dunn & Dunn, 1981], and Test for Auditory Comprehension of Language–Revised [TACL–R] [Carrow-Woolfolk, 1985]). Language samples are collected each semester, and measures that complement the standardized test protocol are computed (e.g., mean length of utterance, type–token ratio, grammatical morpheme profile). An observational rating scale, which involves observational ratings of language use, content and form, speech abilities, and school survival skills, is completed each semester by the student clinicians in the classroom. Finally, a questionnaire is completed each semester by the families of children enrolled in Program A. This questionnaire assesses parents' perceptions of their children's language and speech skills and asks parents to evaluate their perceptions of the strengths and weaknesses of the Program A classroom.

These measures serve the important function of evaluation of program efficacy, both through statistical evaluation of progress in standardized tests scores and results of observational measures, and perhaps more importantly, family perceptions of changes in their children's communication skills.

PROGRAM B: INNER-CITY, UNIVERSITY-BASED HOSPITAL SETTING

Program B is located in an inner-city, university-based hospital setting. Children with multiple disorders, including those with complex health needs, attend the preschool. This setting is also a training site for graduate students in speech-language pathology to learn to provide effective language intervention in an interdisciplinary preschool setting.

Setting

LAP's language-focused curriculum was applied to an existing language preschool in a university training program at a major academic medical center. There were two preschool classrooms located side by side in the university's speech and hearing clinic. Some daily activities were conducted within the confines of a particular classroom, while at other times the door between the two classrooms was opened for free flow of children and adults. During center time each day the door was open, and at least two centers were available in each classroom. The two groups were also frequently combined for music, group learning, or other activities that fit the range of ages and skills of the children. Over time, video and audio systems were installed for the remote recording of children from the adjacent observation room and playground equipment was acquired for the building courtyard.

Children were assigned to one of the two classrooms, based on their level of language functioning and on cognitive and motor considerations (Johnston & Johnston, 1984). Generally, one class contained 2- and 3-year-old children with simple language targets while the other included 4- and 5-year-old children with complex language objectives.

Staff Members

The core preschool staff consisted of an early childhood educator, who served as the lead teacher in the younger classroom; a speech-language pathologist, who served as the lead teacher in the more advanced classroom; and a preschool coordinator, who supervised the graduate students and administrative tasks. Two to four graduate students in speech-language pathology were assigned to each classroom each semester.

Consultants included a physical therapist, a clinical psychologist, and an audiologist. Other members of the interdisciplinary team included a variety of physicians (e.g., pediatricians, ophthalmologists, neurologists) who consulted on a particular child usually for a short period of time; the public health nurse, who conducted the vision testing; and a number of social workers, who participated primarily in cases involving foster care.

Finally and most importantly, members of the child's family were considered critical participants of the interdisciplinary team. In the inner-city environment, the preschool presented a range of family situations. A few of the children lived in traditional family constellations with a biological mother, father, and siblings in one household. Much more common, however, were children who lived with a mother or with grandparents. In a few cases, the children had no consistent residence but spent short periods of time in a number of households within their extended families.

Population Served

Each of the 2 classrooms contained 10 children. Of the children in each class, three were children with typical language who had been recruited from acquaintances of the staff and from the area Head Start programs.

Seven of the children in each class had language impairments. Eligibility for participation as a child with a language impairment required that the child's primary educational disability be a speech-language impairment. This criterion excluded children with cognitive, emotional, or hearing impairments. As with LAP, other preschool programs were available in the community to assist children with these impairments.

Participation in the language preschool was not restricted to inner-city children with language impairments or children with language impairments and complex health needs. However, because of the preschool's location in an inner-city medical center, children from the inner city and/or children with complex health needs made up nearly the entire classroom.

In addition to common medical conditions such as chronic otitis media, many of the children had experienced premature birth. With gestational ages as young as 24 weeks, these preschoolers collectively presented a number of medical conditions resulting from their prematurity. These conditions included bronchopulmonary dysplasia, asthma, motor delays, delayed physical growth, and language delays. Typically, these children entered the language preschool between the ages of 2 and 4 years with virtually no verbal communication. Some of the children with more severe conditions continued to require hospitalization several times per year during the course of their participation in the language preschool. The high concentration of children of premature birth and the resulting motor delays prompted inclusion of a physical therapist in the classrooms once a week.

A second health concern was physical neglect and/or abuse. Children in these cases were typically in foster care but often experienced long-term medical consequences of abuse (e.g., the effect of fetal alcohol syndrome or acquired aphasia secondary to stroke). However, in each child's case, the primary educational disability was determined to be language impairment as opposed to cognitive or emotional disability. Children who had been abused or neglected typically entered the language preschool with only nonverbal communication skills, even when they were as old as 3½ years at the time of entry. Each of these children required ongoing, long-term assessment from the interdisciplinary team while they participated in the language preschool.

Other children with language impairments who were enrolled in the preschool were more typical of the clinical classification of specific language impairment (SLI). Developmental histories of these children were sometimes suggestive of factors contributing to the language difficulties, but no specific etiologies were available. These children tended to enter the preschool between the ages of 2 and 4 with a small single-word vocabulary and no multiword combinations.

A noticeable exception to the inner-city and/or complex health needs components of the population served by Program B was the enrollment of four hearing children of deaf parents, from three different households. These children and one Nigerian child represented the preschool's counterpart to LAP's children who were learning English as a second language.

Program Implementation and Adaptations

The basic format and curriculum design in the preschool were borrowed directly from the LFC and CNM of the LAP program. Language teaching took the form of focused contrasts, modeling, and expanding utterances with the desired targets in the context of familiar routines, dramatic play, and supported exposure to novel experiences. Also, like the LFC of LAP, the curriculum was geared to the interests and skills of the children and was designed by the staff and graduate students in a weekly meeting.

Classroom

The actual content of the weekly curricula was somewhat different from the LAP version of a LFC because of differences in the children in the two programs. First, because of the generally lower age and language levels of many of the children, specific routines were modified to produce opportunities for language target elicitation. For example, in LAP, snack-time food and drink were provided to each child automatically as he or she returned from outside play with seconds on food and drink provided upon the child's request (i.e., child asks peer or adult for more juice or crackers, and the pitcher or plate is then passed with the child assisted as needed). In this adaptation of the CNM, basic requesting was a target for many of the children so multiple opportunities to request cups, drinks, napkins, cookies, and so forth were provided from the beginning of snacktime.

Second, the life experiences of the children enrolled in this preschool were different from those of most children in LAP. These differences were due to both socioeconomic status and personal medical histories. Sensitivity to the differences was especially important in the design of dramatic play themes. For example, in middle-class society most children see their physician in his or her office, know the physician's name and perhaps the name of the nurse, and receive their medical care from essentially the same person over most of their childhood. This was not the case for the children in Preschool B. Their life experiences involved medical care at large, public facilities, seeing many different physicians and nurses in the same visit, and multiple episodes of hospitalization for some children. Thus, different roles and reactions would be appropriate in portraying a visit to the doctor in dramatic play. Other contexts for consideration included the use of personal versus public transportation, the availability of telephone communication, and early literacy experiences.

From a classroom management standpoint, some procedures had to be established to solve problems not encountered in LAP. In such cases the staff attempted to employ the principles of language learning articulated in the CNM. For example, the children's intense excitement about participation in dramatic play resulted in near-riot conditions as 20 children attempted to participate in a center designed for four or five children. The outcome was fighting over props, knocking over structures, and little appropriate language. Although the staff encouraged children to try other centers first, take turns in roles, and negotiate the sharing of props, the activity was not allowing an atmosphere conducive to language facilitation. Following the principle of encouraging peer interaction, a new classroom routine was established. Necklaces made of yarn with a laminated colored square pendant were introduced as the ticket to participation in a particular center. The color of the square represented the center to which it permitted access, and any child participating in a center was required to wear the appropriate necklace during that activity. The number of necklaces of a particular color could be varied to fit the exact activity planned for the day (e.g., ironing leaves between pieces of wax paper might be appropriate for only two children at a time), but the children still selected their own course of action with a few restrictions. No child was denied access to a center for the entire center time. Negotiations between children were encouraged and modeled frequently, and significant direction by the adults was necessary only in the first few days. Within a week, even the youngest children understood that they would eventually get a turn at their desired activity, and disappointment at not being first every time was diminished. The quality of dramatic play and participation in other centers improved remarkably, and peer negotiation increased even among the younger children.

Parent Participation

Some procedures for parent interaction were borrowed directly from the LAP program. Weekly classroom newsletters gave parents an opportunity to assist their child in anticipating or remembering a particular activity for parent–child conversations. This communication was particularly beneficial in cases where the parent was seldom seen for face-to-face conversation with the staff. The newsletters also served as a demonstration of the power of written language for the children. In waiting to be picked up after preschool, some of the children were observed to "read" the newsletters to each other by inventing information they thought might be written there.

A second procedure for parent interaction borrowed from LAP was the parent program and open house at the end of the semester. The programs consisted of songs and nursery rhymes performed by the group. Invitations and snacks were created by the children, and the children's artwork decorated the walls. An amazing number of mothers, fathers, and grandparents attended the programs, providing a first-time encounter with the staff in many cases.

In an effort to expand interactions with parents, the staff members initiated parent dialogue notebooks that described specific accomplishments and responses of the child not available in the newsletter. The notebooks were sent home with the child at least once a week, and the parents were invited to respond with their observations and concerns. Care was taken to keep the tone casual, including visible revisions of the text written by the staff. It was hoped that in this manner the parents would be less intimidated by the activity. The success of this exchange varied widely across families. Some children never returned the notebooks; others returned them without additional entries. There were some families, however, who responded by providing examples of generalization, who raised questions, and who documented language skills not observed in the classroom. Sometimes these responses were difficult to understand, but clarification was requested in writing, by telephone, and in person where warranted. In all cases where the notebooks were returned, additional teacher messages were logged within 1 week. In cases where the notebooks were not returned, loose-leaf messages including an invitation to respond were sent home on a weekly basis. The teacher-generated messages were always read to the child in an effort to demonstrate the use of written communication as well as to reinforce the accomplishment described. The notebooks and loose-leaf messages became status symbols among the children, suggesting to the staff their importance in documenting achievement to the child as well as the parent.

Additional demonstrations of achievement employed the video mode. Language samples taken at the start of each semester and during participation in daily activities throughout the semester were recorded and compiled on a single tape to demonstrate progress. For some children these tapes covered 3 years of intervention progress. The videotapes were shown to the parents in conferences, and copies were provided to both the parents and to the public school speech-language pathologist when the child graduated from the preschool. The videotapes were also extremely useful to the graduate student clinicians upon entering the language classroom as an example of the child's progress to date.

Official parent conferences were scheduled early and late in each semester, and official individualized education program (IEP) meetings were held at least once per year. Parents' attendance at these meetings was typically inconsistent in the early stages of enrollment. Once significant gains were observed, however, many parents appeared to be eager to discuss their child's progress. Often at this point, the staff members began to see several family members attend the parent conferences, where previously none were available to meet. Some families were unable to attend parent conferences regardless of when they were held or how much progress had been observed. In these cases, telephone and written communication had to substitute for the meeting. The preschool staff would mail the reports, progress graphs, and examples to the parents prior to the scheduled telephone conversation. In this manner, the parents and staff members could refer to specific pieces of data with the documentation in full view.

IEP Conferences

IEP conferences seemed especially intimidating to the parents, possibly because of the large number of professionals present and the extensive number of documents to be signed. In an effort to create more comfort with the paperwork and to facilitate a transition into the local public schools, the IEP documents of the child's local district were used throughout their language preschool enrollment.

Student Training

Because the primary objective of the preschool was the training of speech-language pathology students to provide group language intervention, many of the responsibilities and documentation procedures were modified from the LFC model to address the students' needs. Throughout the course of the semester, the graduate students were involved in implementing language facilitation techniques, data collection, and group planning. Over the course of the semester, however, the students gradually accepted more of the teachers' responsibilities such as preparing the specific materials and newsletters, writing in parent journals, and leading group activities.

Extensive planning and documentation were found to be most helpful in teaching the student clinicians to address language skills in a group setting. Like LAP, the use of language sampling at the beginning and end of each semester for each child was helpful in determining the child's productive abilities. However, syntactic and morphological analyses alone were inappropriate for some children due to their low language levels upon entry. As an alternative, Lahey's (1988) Content/Form/Use Analysis was adopted throughout the preschool.

The teaching required of the students was conducted in the context of group activities rather than individual pull-out therapy. Student clinicians needed to learn to maintain the activity and to employ language facilitation techniques appropriate for specific language targets for a number of children simultaneously. This approach obligated students and staff members to know the objectives of all children in the class. Each classroom contained seven children with language intervention objectives. Each of the seven children had between 5 and 10 objectives at any particular time, creating a significant memory load for the adults to highlight particular targets with the appropriate children. Poster-size lists of the objectives for each child were hung in both classrooms and could also be viewed from the observation room. In this way, an adult engaging a particular child in conversation could glance at the chart to assist in recall of specific objectives to model in the exchange. Also, adults from the opposite classroom could have access to such information for times when the children were combined. This strategy of posting specific objectives for the children is also used by LAP staff members.

A class language profile was constructed for each classroom by incorporating a shorthand version of each child's semester objectives on one sheet of paper. Class profiles allowed the clinicians to see similarities and differences among the language objectives for the various children. Facilitation of targets could be accomplished more efficiently when the adults could recognize which children were working on the same general targets. These profiles had to be updated frequently as children met various objectives, but they allowed the students and the staff to plan opportunities to highlight each objective for each child every day.

Data collection was also conducted in group activities, although only one or two children per classroom were targeted on any given day. Over the course of a week, data were collected for each child. A rotation among the lead teacher and the two graduate students assigned to a particular class found one assigned as the activity director; one as the assistant who especially handled individual crises, clean-up, and set-up of the next materials needed; and one person to collect data. In cases where only two adults were available, the assistant and recorder responsibilities were combined. At the end of each session, the data recorder incorporated the day's results into line graphs for each objective in the student's folder. This graphic representation was helpful in determining lack of progress on a particular objective, insufficient quantities of data, and when it was time to move to a higher level of responding.

The students demonstrated an increased ability to perceive significant improvement (or lack thereof) in the language skills of the children over time when data were collected and recorded in this manner. Other problems, such as lack of progress or insufficient quantities of appropriate contexts, were also perceived by using the graphs and were then addressed in the weekly planning session if necessary.

PROGRAM C: PRIVATE AND PUBLIC SCHOOL COLLABORATION

Program C provides direct services to 300 children from birth to 5 years of age in a large early childhood center. The center is an interagency organization serving six school districts. Approximately 100 children with special needs attend the center-based program. These children exhibit a range of disabling conditions. Another 50–60 children who are developing typically come to the center for preschool experience. Other children receive home-based programming. The center follows the same annual schedule as the local public schools.

Setting

In Program C, seven classrooms make up three classroom groups. Children come to the center for five half-day sessions per week, attending either a morning or afternoon class. The preschoolers who need services in one or more areas (i.e., fine or gross motor, cognitive, speech-language, social, self-help) attend heterogeneous classes.

Staff Members

The core staff members for the center-based program include five Early Childhood Handicapped (ECH) certified teachers who are assisted by eight paraprofessionals, two speech-language pathologists (SLPs) who are assisted by one speech paraprofessional, one physical therapist (PT), one occupational therapist (OT), and one motor paraprofessional. Program C has additional staff members who are responsible for the home-based programming and administration.

Population Served

Approximately one third of the children enrolled in Program C are typically developing. The other children have speech, language, cognitive, and/or motor impairments ranging from mild to severe. Some have multiple disabilities. The children are integrated so that each class contains four children who are typically developing and five to eight children with disabilities.

Program Implementation and Adaptations

Prior to 1990, Program C provided special services to the children wit disabilities using a pull-out therapy model. Children left their classrooms and received the designated therapy (e.g., speech, physical) in another room. In addition, the classrooms were not completely integrated. For example, two classrooms contained only children with disabilities, generally those with the more severe delays. The other classrooms included a few typically developing children in their classes of children with special needs; however, each child's age determined the class to which he or she was assigned (e.g., 3-year-old or 4-year-old class).

Classrooms

For the 1990–1991 school year, all classrooms were inclusive. Consideration was made when assigning children to classes so that a variety of ages and learning abilities were represented in each classroom. Some therapy was also implemented in the classroom. Staff training focused on how classroom staff members could employ techniques throughout the day that would enhance speech and language, motor, and cognitive development. In order to provide opportunities for classroom staff members to practice their new skills, one area during free-play time was designated as the "language center." The two speech-language pathologists planned activities for the language center. Once each week, the SLPs attended the language center, either to train the staff or to monitor the progress of the teachers and paraprofessionals. Usually the language centers consisted of props for dramatic play. For example, the "camping" center had a tent, sleeping bags, a cook stove, backpacks, binoculars, and so forth. Because these centers were originally created as the backdrop for staff members' practice, the centers were initially set up to stay in each classroom for a 3-week period. However, it was quickly discovered that the children lost interest in these centers within a week, and so it became necessary to shorten the life span of each center. In addition to the language center, there was also an activity set up in the classroom that was led by either the OT or the PT, in which he or she modeled appropriate teaching methods for the observing staff members so that motor development techniques could also be ongoing throughout the day. This was the initial attempt at becoming more interdisciplinary and at providing therapy in the classroom.

Following an inservice session, the LFC model was implemented in the fall of 1991. With this model, a centers approach was incorporated into the preschool curriculum. The LAP planning guides provided a basic format for the lesson plans, including the weekly plan, the daily plans, and the skills to be facilitated in each developmental area. However, the planning guides were redesigned so that several centers could be planned on each sheet, as well as other events during the day such as snacktime, storytime, and motor group. This single sheet of information could then be copied and sent home to parents as their weekly guide to the activities at the school. The daily plans provided space to write specific skills to be addressed in the language, cognitive, social, and motor areas. Much like

LFC, a theme was adopted for each week, and, to the extent possible, the activities for the week reflected the theme.

Planning

During the initial year of implementation of the LFC, therapists and teachers of Program C learned to generate specific skill emphases in all areas, not just their own areas of expertise. The paraprofessionals also were expected to gain competency in designing activities and choosing appropriate teaching methods. Each of the three planning teams brings its own preferences and skill specialties to the planning sessions, so the three groups operate in different ways. Over the period of a year, each team's planning style has evolved into a smoothly operating unit that meets the needs of its members and also accomplishes the goals of weekly planning. Some teams choose to post blank weekly planning sheets for a whole month in a conspicuous place in the classroom so that everyone can jot down ideas for themes, centers, art activities, and so forth. Then, when it is time for planning, many of the basic ideas are already planned. Other teams prefer to do all the brainstorming for theme and activity ideas during the weekly planning sessions.

One of the great benefits of team planning is that the sessions lead to cross-training of the staff members in a variety of developmental areas. Speech-language pathologists learn about motor skills, teachers learn about language skills, paraprofessionals understand classroom goals more fully, motor therapists learn about social skills, and so forth. However, these benefits were not seen at Program C until the teams had learned to work together cooperatively and share ideas openly. This process of mutual cooperation had to be nurtured and guided throughout the year. It was very difficult for some staff members to give up their traditional "turf" and allow others to share ideas, and for some it was terrifying to let others see what it was they had been doing in their therapy rooms. However, with the goal of providing the most developmentally appropriate practices and least restrictive environment for students, the staff members persevered until team planning became a smoothly functioning aspect of the program. When new staff members are hired, inservice sessions are held to acquaint them with classroom curricula and intervention procedures using the CNM.

Centers

As the different teams began to implement the planned activities, the individuality of the three teams became apparent. The number of centers varied from three to five, and the placement and management of the centers were different in each room. In some instances, the group size varied, necessitating more or fewer centers; and at other times, it was teacher preference that determined the number of centers. The dramatic play area is always present as a center. Other possible centers include a book/quiet area, a manipulative area, a block area, an art area, a science area, a computer area, and/or a motor (gross motor) area. Sometime centers rotate in and out of the schedule over a period of weeks. The dramatic play area is important enough to always be included because the

majority of the students have speech and language delays. However, the dramatic play activities were modified so that all children could take part. For example, some children used augmentative and alternative communication (AAC) devices in order to participate, other children needed to be physically assisted through the role playing because of their physical disabilities, and others needed guidance because of their inability to fully grasp the meaning of the roles. Modeling is a technique that can work well in dramatic play and is a very important component of language teaching in every activitiy throughout the day.

Intervention Procedures

Because of the number of children served by each speech-language pathologist (approximately 60 children) and because of the use of teacher paraprofessionals in all of the classrooms, we have concentrated on using general techniques in our centers rather than ones focusing on specific IEP objectives. Techniques that we have stressed include modeling, expanding, asking open-ended questions, and using positive correction. It can be overwhelming to one staff person in charge of 5–20 children passing through a center to remember specific speech-language, social, cognitive, and motor objectives for each child. Therefore, we have concentrated on developing general skills among our staff members with the intention that the therapists will implement their specific objectives with each child as they have the opportunity during center time or at other appropriate times throughout the day.

Attendance of Typically Developing Children

Another vitally important component of the program is the attendance of the typically developing children who are enrolled in each of the classrooms. Many times they give the "spark" to the activity that is missing with the children who have developmental delays, and they are the best models for a range of activities, from talking to toileting. It is heart-warming to see a typically developing preschooler tap a child with a hearing impairment on the shoulder and sign to him "come play" and to watch the faces of both children light up as understanding touches them. No adult could do as well.

IEP Objectives

As a means of implementing specific IEP objectives with individual children, our therapists have utilized a number of approaches. Motor therapists conduct at least one whole-class motor group each week with an emphasis on specific skills. Speech-language pathologists also present a classroom language activity each week targeting specific objectives. In both groups, the typically developing "model" children help by demonstrating and participating in the activities. Small group sessions with certain target children may also be conducted, with the focus on acquisition of specific skills. Unlike LAP, some children are also seen individually for therapy. These children usually have severe motor delays or severe articulation delays. Finally, therapists may be present in a particular classroom at any time (usually during center time) that it is possible to work with a child on developing particular skills.

Monitoring Progress

Tracking the progress of the children is difficult. The teachers and therapists of Program C have had to modify their data-keeping systems because no longer is all the therapy adult directed. By following the child's lead and focusing on the child's interest, the adult does not have control over specific therapy stimuli and/or responses in the same manner as in individual therapy sessions. Therefore, a variety of techniques has been used to document progress. Some of these techniques include taking field notes on specific behaviors, charting classroom observations, and utilizing various types of probe items. (Probe items might involve the production of a specific structure such as past tense or a specific sound such as/k/.) In addition, 12-week progress reports are written, and the children are evaluated annually using standardized testing instruments.

The benefits of the implementation of the LFC model have been numerous for both the staff members and the children at Program C. The implementation has helped in the use of developmentally appropriate practices and has encouraged all staff members to recognize language-learning opportunities in every daily activitiy. It has provided a framework for including the important objectives of the whole program at the center.

PROGRAM D: A PUBLIC SCHOOL PROGRAM

Program D is located in a suburban public school district and serves approximately 100 children from 2 to 5 years of age. These children include those enrolled in at-risk programs (Chapter 1 and Head Start) as well as children with varied disabilities, which range from mild to severe. Program D is housed in a single building with several classrooms on each side of a large hallway. A large playground with adaptive playground equipment adjoins the building.

Population Served

There are 2 half-day sessions for 3- and 4-year-old children with special needs that meet Monday through Thursday for 2½ hours per day. Also attending these classes are several typically developing children. There are also 2 half-day sessions of Chapter 1 classes for 4-year-olds and 1 half-day Head Start class also meeting Monday through Thursday. In addition, the local Parents as Teachers program is located in the building. Services are provided in this program to children with speech, language, cognitive, and/or motor impairments.

Staff Members

Staff members include early childhood educators, speech-language pathologists, special educators, occupational and physical therapists, a consultant for children with visual and orthopedic impairments, and several paraprofessionals. The lead teachers vary for each class. For example, the lead teacher for the Head Start program is an early childhood educator while the lead teacher for another classroom is a speech-language pathologist. A teacher with early childhood special education certification is the lead teacher for the classrooms including children with severe and multiple disabilities. All classrooms have speech-language pathologists, occupational therapists, and physical therapists who provide intervention in the classroom.

Program Implementation and Adaptations

The main adaptations of the LAP program by Program D are dictated by the inclusion of children with a range of disabilities. Some of the adaptations are similar to those made by staff members in Program C. These include additional planning necessary to include other interventions in the classroom such as occupational therapy and the need for adapting props and other materials to allow the use of AAC devices. For example, a tape recorder can be adapted for use by a child with motor difficulties by pasting tongue depressors on the operating levers. The tongue depressors make it easier for a child to find and push the correct lever. A variety of switches can be designed for a child with limited motor movement so that child can turn equipment on and off. In planning an activity, the staff members must also plan for how and where a child can use a device such as an IntroTalker (Prentke Romich Co.). Appropriate programming of an AAC device is important so that the child can interact with the others in a dramatic play or other activity.

Team Planning

There are several types of planning activities that occur— those that occur once each semester, those that occur monthly, and those that occur weekly. Initially, all curriculum planning was done weekly. The program has evolved and now the overall theme planning is done on a semester basis with themes for each week of the semester selected at the beginning of each semester. At the monthly meetings, the monthly newsletter is prepared. Like the LAP program, the newsletter is provided to the parents before the activities are done, rather than after completion. Unlike LAP where the newsletter is distributed weekly, Program D's is a monthly newsletter; therefore, Program D's activities for a whole month are presented instead of activities for only 1 week.

Two types of staff meetings are held each Friday. One includes all staff members and is designed to finalize the next week's activities by preparing materials, creating overall lesson plans, and so forth. The building-wide planning meeting facilitates the implementation of coordinated themes. This meeting also allows for discussion of common problems and decision making regarding which classroom is implementing which dramatic play activity on a particular day. All dramatic play activity props are stored in the staff room in cardboard boxes that are clearly labeled and organized alphabetically. As new props are developed, they are put in the appropriate boxes. The central storage allows access by all classrooms.

The second staff meeting involves individual classroom staff members who meet to adapt the overall plans for their classroom. The staff members also use this time to discuss children's progress and to address issues affecting their particular classroom. Following the staff meetings, the paraprofessionals prepare the materials and the classrooms for the next week. The certified staff members complete evaluations, conduct parent conferences, and make home visits.

Implementation of Activities

Although each classroom has a somewhat different schedule of activities, they each include a center time, circle time for large group sharing (e.g., reading stories, show and tell, calendar concepts), motor activities, and a snacktime. Center activities vary among the classrooms but usually include dramatic play, art, book reading, and fine motor manipulative activities. Unlike LAP, dramatic play activities change every 2 days rather than every day. Even though the dramatic play activities do not change every day, new props and/or roles are added each day. The organization and planning of the dramatic plays across classrooms ensure that each classroom has available the appropriate activities and props when needed.

Approximately twice a semester, the center hall is set up with special activities that follow the theme. For example, for a farm theme, a pretend farmyard was set up, complete with a cow to "milk" (a mock up with white gloves filled with white water so that the children could really "milk" the cow). Different classes were able to "go to the farm" at different times during the week. In addition, monthly language-experience field trips are taken. Examples of trips include visiting a firehouse, a grocery store, a pizza restaurant, and a beauty shop.

Intervention Procedures

Like LAP, all intervention activities are implemented in the classroom setting. The activities include those provided by speech-language pathologists, occupational therapists, physical therapists, and other educators. Similar language-focused intervention techniques that were described in Chapter 4 are used in all of the classrooms. These strategies include focused contrasts, modeling, event casting, open-ended questions, expansions, recasts, redirects, and prompted initiations.

Attendance of Typically Developing Children

A small number of children who are typically developing and who have language skills within typical limits are also enrolled in many of the classrooms. These children may attend a special needs classroom for half of the day and then attend an employee's child care program during the other half of the day. Sometimes children from one classroom are allowed to participate in the center time activities of another classroom. For example, two children may leave the Chapter 1 classroom and cross the hall into one of the special needs classrooms. The two teachers plan the activities to facilitate the children's interactions. Even though the children from the Chapter 1 classroom have reduced language abilities, they still often have more language skills than the children with physical and/or cognitive disabilities. Therefore, the children from the Chapter 1 classroom can act as communicatively adept peers for the children with severe disabilities. Program D is committed to providing opportunities for peer interactions as well as adult interactions.

IEP Objectives and Monitoring of Child Progress

Some of the children enrolled in this program have IEPs. For these children, long- and short-term goals are posted in the classrooms so all staff members are aware of each child's specific objectives. The skill levels and learning of children without official IEPs also are monitored. One way that this is accomplished is through the classroom learning outcomes that are established for each week's curricular units (e.g., pronouns, one-to-one correspondence, shape recognition). Another monitoring tool is a checklist of 4-year-old objectives. Teachers, therapists, and assistant teachers meet on a weekly basis to review and monitor individual IEP and classroom goals.

Parent Participation

Parents are encouraged to participate in their child's program, not only as members of the IEP team, but also as resources for the classroom. Parents are encouraged to observe the classroom, participate on field trips, and share their skills by demonstrating or teaching about their hobbies or vocations. Home visits are made at parents' requests. Parents also serve on an advisory board.

CONCLUDING REMARKS

Programs A, B, C, and D have all made some adaptations of the program used in the Language Acquisition Preschool. However, what is readily apparent is that these different programs have retained the essential qualities of the language-focused curriculum utilizing a concentrated normative model. All of the programs have a commitment to: 1) providing intervention in a classroom setting, 2) having language facilitation throughout the curriculum, 3) utilizing a language curriculum rooted in content themes, 4) having a child-centered approach to intervention, 5) encouraging verbal interaction with both adults and peers, 6) encouraging passive as well as overt responses, 7) recognizing that much learning can take place in child–child interactions, and 8) recognizing the importance of parent participation in a child's intervention programming. The programs have all found ways to include typically developing children as well as children with disabilities in a particular classroom. All of the programs use language facilitation techniques similar to those used in LAP. The environment is constructed so there are many opportunities for language to occur. Specific language intervention strategies include the use of focused contrasts, modeling, event casting, open-ended questions, expansions, recasts, redirects, and prompted initiations. Although some of the details of implementation have been adapted, these programs demonstrate that a variety of children can benefit from a language-focused curriculum.

REFERENCES

Bunce, B.H. (1991, May). *Language intervention within a preschool classroom: The LAP Model.* Workshop presented at the Kansas Speech-Language-Hearing Association Early Childhood Regional Conference, Overland Park, KS.

Carrow-Woolfolk, E. (1985). *Test for Auditory Comprehension of Language–Revised (TACL–R).* Allen, TX: DLM Teaching Resources.

Dunn, L.M., & Dunn, L.M. (1981). *Peabody Picture Vocabulary Test–Revised (PPVT).* Circle Pines, MN: American Guidance Service.

Gardner, M.F. (1990). *Expressive One-Word Picture Vocabulary Test–Revised (EOWPVT–R).* Novato, CA: Academic Therapy Publications.

Goldman, R., & Fristoe, M. (1969). *Goldman-Fristoe Test of Articulation (GFTA).* Circle Pines, MN: American Guidance Service.

Johnston, E., & Johnston, A. (1984). *The Piagetian language nursery: An intensive group language intervention program for preschoolers.* Rockville, MD: Aspen Publishers, Inc.

Lahey, M. (1988). *Language disorders and language development.* New York: Macmillan.

Watkins, R.V. (1992). Read it again please: Bookreading to promote language development. *Tejas, 18,* 3–7.

Watkins, R.V., & Davis, C. (in preparation). *Language learning during bookreading: Evidence from a preschool intervention classroom.*

Watkins, R.V., Seymour, P.J., & Davis, C. (1993, November). *The language of normal learners in a preschool intervention classroom.* Paper presented at the American Speech-Language-Hearing Association Convention, Anaheim, CA.

Index

Page references followed by t or f indicate tables or figures, respectively.